THE QUEST

A LAKOTA LEGEND

CHARLES RICHARD LATONA

The Quest
Copyright © 2022 by Charles Richard Latona. All rights reserved.

All rights reserved. No part of this book may be reproduced or transmitted in any form or by any means, electronic or mechanical, including photocopying, recording, or by any information storage and retrieval system without express written permission from the author, except in the case of brief quotations embodied in critical reviews and certain other noncommercial uses permitted by copyright law.

Published in the United States of America

Brilliant Books Literary
137 Forest Park Lane Thomasville
North Carolina 27360 USA

Contents

BOOK I
THE JOURNEY

Chapter 1 The Gift 9

Chapter 2 The Savages 24

Chapter 3 The Disgraced Ones 36

Chapter 4 The Night Of Fire 45

Chapter 5 The Homecoming 59

BOOK II
THE PATH

Chapter 1 The Fox And The Wolf 81

Chapter 2 The Snake And The Possum 91

Chapter 3 The Angry Man 105

Chapter 4 Counting Coup 120

BOOK III
THE INITIATION

Chapter 1 Stories..137

Chapter 2 Legends 151

Chapter 3 The Sweat Lodge..165

Chapter 4 Dance To The Sun 177

Chapter 5 The Hunt...197

Chapter 6 Morning Star And Thunder Eyes 217

Chapter 7 The Gauntlet 240

BOOK IV
THE WICASA

Chapter 1 The Flaming Eagle 257

Chapter 2 Meadow Lark...271

Chapter 3 Cycles..286

Chapter 4 Tatanka...297

Chapter 5 The Last Combat 309

Chapter 6 The Final Offering 323

Epilogue...337

About The Author 345

This story is dedicated to the memory of
White Wolf and
Flaming Eagle

The tale would never have been told without the
hard work and devotion of my Spirit Helpers,

Judith Kay Roy and
Marilyn Ruth Heide

BOOK I   THE JOURNEY

Chapter 1

THE GIFT

The old man carefully picked up the pipe. It was not the ceremonial pipe, but rather his daily prayer pipe. It was plain and long stemmed, with only a lone eagle feather for decoration. Yes, it was quite different from the hand-painted, highly-decorative, white-clay pipe he kept safely in the Black Hills. He understood the value of the ritual pipe as an important symbol to his people. Just as important, he knew the Grand Father, the Great Spirit who protects and guides the tribe, would hear his prayers just as clearly, even when the smoke and the words were offered up with the more modest pipe.

He passed the pipe leisurely and deliberately over the campfire four times, purifying it for its purpose. From his waistband, one at a time, he removed the four pouches of sacred herbs, carefully laying them on a rock next to the small wooden bowl. Slowly, in turn, he opened each pouch. Taking a large pinch of the moist cacota and rubbing it between his fingers, he watched the crumbling herb descend safely into the waiting wooden bowl. Repeating the process with the dried white sage, he added fresh pomatote, and finished by blending in a small amount of very dry and extremely strong tobacco.

Using a small rock, he crushed and blended the herbs into an integrated mixture. One measure at a time, he packed the combination firmly into the bowl of the pipe. Taking a small, burning stick from the fire, he lit the pipe, releasing the smoke to the four winds of Creation. Moving slowly in a circle, with his head bowed, he offered prayers of gratitude for all the gifts the Great Spirit had bestowed upon His people. Facing the north, he repeated the ageold prayer of the people. "Great Spirit, we need your strength to help keep us strong in good times as well as bad. We rely on you, Great Spirit, as we face life's challenges. Be with us today."

Having paid homage to the north wind, White Wolf turned, gazing into the western sky. Exhaling the ceremonial smoke, he again addressed the Great Spirit. "As the sun sets and darkness covers the earth, we thank you, Great Spirit, for the gifts of today. Unite us together as family, as friends, as Your People."

He remained silent, watching the smoke drifting into the night sky. Turning a half-circle, he stood looking into the sky to the east. To the eastern horizon he prayed, "Let us lift up our hearts in prayer for the Grand Father to see and hear. Lead us, Great Spirit, by the light of your wisdom."

He completed the circle by facing the desert to the south. To the south he sent the remaining prayer to be carried by the sacred smoke to it's ultimate destination. "Great Spirit, loving Grand Father, you give us life when we take food from the earth, our Mother. We thank you for your gifts. Keep us from wasting them, and help us to remember the needs of others."

Even in the dim light of the campfire, signs of a lifetime of harsh winters and hot, dry summers were easily seen etched deeply in his brown skin. Although his face was furrowed with wrinkles, and his long straight hair streaked with grey, his warm, earthen-coloured eyes

The Quest

remained clear and lively. His face and body may have begun showing signs of aging, but, behind his eyes, his spirit was burning brightly.

Having completed this part of his evening ritual, White Wolf sat silently by the fire for a moment, contentedly warming himself. Slowly and deliberately, he drew the smoke of the sacred herbs up through the long stem of the pipe, holding it as he focused on the remaining prayers within the quietness of his mind. "Releasing the smoke, I offer up my prayers, which are transported by the gentle evening breeze. Let me watch the light wind carrying my prayers to You, Wakan Tanka, the Great Spirit of our ancestors." His eyes followed the smoke as it drifted, spreading itself in between the vast distances separating the countless stars. Time and space were truly in harmony. Sighing lightly, he returned to his nightly ritual of devotion to the Grand Father.

In the distance he heard the mournful calling of his green-eyed sister, his spirit guide, his namesake, the white she-wolf, and she was not alone. The clear night sky added to the illusion that the moon was shining more brightly than usual in the transparent desert air. He sat in the reflecting light of the moon, praying for the one who was to follow him. It was the path to which White Wolf had been born, but it was one not always walked with ease.

"It is a hard, dark road leading to the light," he thought. "It will take a brave with special courage to follow this less traveled trail. I shall only teach him just so much, for my time knows its limits. The rest he will learn from the Grand Father."

Taking another long draw of the herbs within the bowl, White Wolf released the smoke and waited. Retreating into the inner space that dwelled concealed within his mind, he remained there in deep meditation. Sometime during the night, his meditations gave way to the waking sleep. All thoughts were gently fading, like smoke from the campfire. His mind retreated more deeply inward, like a great grizzly lumbering into the safety of it's hidden cave. Here he patiently waited to be touched once more by the hand of the Great Spirit.

He did not have a long wait, as his mind quickly filled with the crystalline, blue light. Surrendering himself fully to the experience, he felt his soul expanding outward, attempting to embrace the clarity surrounding him. Like the air and the sky, his spirit and the light were merging into a harmonious oneness, as his image emerged.

Advancing more fully into the light, he heard the shrill call of a great eagle filling the endless sky. Intently, he watched the stars shooting across the vast nothingness, plunging headlong into the earth's atmosphere. Exploding as they collided with the earth's outer protective coat, they created a resounding mixture of fire and thunder. The fire burned with a blinding light as thick, white smoke came pouring out of the flames. Swirling and shimmering, the dense smoke gradually shaped itself into the form of an enormous golden eagle. The great bird stood proudly, engulfed by the reddish-orange robe of dancing flames. In their fury, it appeared the flames were consuming the mighty bird. However, on the contrary, instead of being destroyed, the eagle stepped forth from the inferno, unmarred, except for a burn on the inside of its right wing, which would, no doubt, leave a scar. From the position of its wings, it seemed to be carrying something. White Wolf could not make out exactly what it was, but it was obviously alive.

The bird defiantly stood there, gazing directly into White Wolf's eyes. It was as if the eagle were sounding the depths of the old man's soul, right to the very core itself. Feeling himself ascending into the endless column of blue light, White Wolf's image faded, once again returning to the source from which it had been created.

The medicine man received his vision, and he understood it. The Holy One for whom he was waiting is a flaming eagle. "The Grand Father's message was clear," he thought. "Curiously, the only drawback to witnessing this prophecy is that I do not know anyone who bears this name." However, as always, he accepted the vision, knowing, when the time was correct, the veil of mystery would be withdrawn, thereby clearly exposing the one chosen to follow in the footsteps of a Wicasa.

The Quest

He awakened from his night's slumber as the rays of the sun were warming the valley floor. The campfire had long since extinguished itself. In the faint morning breeze, the cool ashes were lazily swirling, like long-forgotten dreams. He sat with the sun's rays caressing his body, while his mind carefully sifted through the memory of the vision he had seen. Pondering it, he gazed to the north, recognizing it was now time for him to make the necessary preparations for his homeward journey.

After having been gone for several moons, he was anxious to return to the land of his birth. Once more his quest had taken him far from his ancestral mountains. He would have to cross the scorching deserts and endure the harsh windy prairies before reaching the great mountains standing sentinel to the lush green plains of his people since the beginning of time.

Even though he missed the buttes and the big sky of home, he perpetually felt renewed after meditating in the southern deserts. In the north, he heard the Grand Father's voice in the thunder. He could hear His whispers carried on the endless prairie wind; but, here in the desert, the Great Spirit spoke with a hot, flaming breath. His energy was strong and unimpeded, burning its way across the fiery sands. At night His voice echoed endlessly through the rainbow canyon, where the old shaman was camped.

Without the mountain mist acting as a protective veil, the stars here shone more clearly, revealing their true colours. Allowing himself to be lost in the vastness of the never-ending heavens of the desert, his blood surged through his veins with renewed fire. His mind quickly became as quiet as the silent stars themselves. With his vision quest completed, and his supply of healing desert herbs and plants replenished, there was nothing holding him here any longer. It was time for him to return to the rolling valleys and gentle, wide rivers of home.

Returning his attention to the tasks at hand, he picked up the water skin and walked toward the nearby stream. Reaching the bank of the shallow water, he stopped momentarily, enjoying the cheerful song of the brook. This lively music blended with the higher pitch and faster cadence of the miniature waterfalls populating the stream. Flowing more swiftly through the larger rocks and boulders, the stream produced a sound similar to the deafening din of a buffalo herd stampeding across the prairie. His peaceful mind was filled with a calm clarity as he relaxed, becoming at ease with his environment. The soothing sounds of flowing water were always a natural tranquilizer for his spirit. He stood there peacefully for several moments, enjoying his communion with nature.

Without warning, the serenity of the scene was shattered by a clattering that was very much in discord with his present surroundings. White Wolf was hearing the futile struggle with death taking place nearby. It was a sound all too familiar to him. He ventured toward the frantic, desperate, rustling noises upstream. The fearful sounds of water splashing and flesh tearing increased in intensity as he approached. Clearing an outcropping, he saw her. Her soft brown eyes were wildly scanning everything in sight. Her body was quivering as she fought in vain to free herself from the mud and roots ensnaring her. Sharp pieces of bloody bone were protruding through her skin, as her left hind-leg was badly fractured in at least two places. He recognized, as did she, that she was beyond all help…even his.

Wounded as she was, the doe would become easy prey for the wolves that would surely come. By the time the sun was high, they would smell the scent of death in the air. Remembering the howling he heard the previous evening, White Wolf estimated the wolf pack consisted of approximately ten.

"They will take their time coming for her…but, eventually, they will come," he thought aloud. "I have seen them on the attack before. They will begin by slowly and deliberately encircling her, while simultaneously intimidating her with their savage growling and snapping of their sharp, white teeth. Snarling and yelping while

The Quest

faking frontal assaults, they will pretend to withdraw, only to attack anew. They will continue approaching her, tightening the circle as they do. The attacks themselves are merely ploys designed to discover her vulnerabilities.

"After continuously confusing her with their sudden and erratic attacks and withdrawals, the leader of the pack will move in for the kill," mused White Wolf aloud. He had witnessed the pack's ritualistic behavior enough to understand their tactics. "The leader will feign many charges, distracting his prey's attention. The others will continue advancing and withdrawing, until the leader seizes the right moment to make his deadly move. His primary target will be her vulnerable throat. Once he starts ripping at her, the rest of the pack will savagely and mercilessly descend upon her, shredding and tearing her apart while she is still alive. No!" White Wolf exclaimed. "I refuse! This shall not happen to her!"

Speaking to her in a soft, gentle voice, he slowly and steadily decreased the space between them. He spread his arms out wide, his palms turned upward, exposing them to be empty. The closer he approached, the more calm and accepting of her fate she became. Continuing to speak quietly to her in a comforting and soothing tone of voice, he knelt carefully in front of her, cupping her face gently between his brown hands as he looked deep into her eyes. Leisurely stroking the soft, warm fur of her face and neck, he was able to calm her while she resigned herself to her fate.

Looking into her eyes, he whispered to her, "Thank you for the sacrifice which you are about to make. I offer up a prayer of thanks to the Great Spirit for once more having provided for me."

Talking to her in a hushed voice, while gently stroking her silken coat of light brown, he deliberately withdrew his knife from his waistband. Momentarily looking at the deer, he froze. Then, with one quick, sure motion, he plunged the knife swiftly into her heart. She remained mute as her entire body quivered momentarily before she stiffened. Releasing her last breath, the doe went limp, dying in his arms.

Removing her from her ensnarement, he carried her to shore. After offering up a silent prayer, he went about the task of dressing her carcass. The scent of the sage milk was strong and hot to the touch. The warm blood oozed thick and sticky, clinging to his hands and forearms, and the pungent aroma of the sage milk, blending with the smell of the blood, was intoxicating. At the same time, however, he found himself humbled by the entire experience. White Wolf carefully removed her internal organs, one by one, laying them intact on the riverbank. He quickly and expertly went about the skinning process. Her young, blemish-free fur was healthy, and very thick; however, his knife easily cut through it.

After he finished removing the hide, he respectfully laid it on a grassy area near the stream. Gathering up the heart, liver and the other internal organs, he carried them downstream beyond his camp to a place where the water flowed fast, shallow, and clear. Meticulously, one at a time, he washed her internal organs, placing them carefully on a large rock. Usually he would have immediately cleaned the skin for preservation; but, until he had concluded his duties, that task would have to wait.

Picking up her vital organs and carrying them with him, he returned upstream to his camp. Carefully laying them aside, he set about rekindling the campfire, placing dry sagebrush and small twigs on the red and black pieces of smoldering charcoal. The smoke, growing gray and thick, swirled aimlessly in the lazy breeze. Gently blowing on the coals, he watched them glowing brighter and brighter as they burst into small darting flames of red, orange and yellow. He continued feeding the flames with twigs and small dried branches, until he was sure he could safely add larger pieces of wood to the fire without smothering it. He remained attending the campfire until he had built a small, but extremely hot, funeral pyre.

The Quest

Slowly standing, he raised the offering high above his head, speaking to the Great Spirit in a muted voice. "Grand Father, I stand humbly before You. By leading me to her, You have given each of us a precious gift. For her: a swift and painless death. For me: her meat to feed me and her skin to warm me."

After a moment or two he lowered his arms and, as they came to rest chest high, he resumed his invocation. "It is You who gives life to all things of the earth. As You designed, the earth has nourished her, and now she is to do the same for me, as her kind have always done. Oh, Wakan Tanka, I thank you for this day and for this blessing."

When he finished praying, he knelt with his head bowed. He laid his offerings on the pyre, placing them in an area where the flames were burning a deep blue. First came a sharp, searing sound, followed by a hissing noise, as the moist organs initially cooled the heat of the fire. He sat transfixed, watching the grayish-white smoke swirling and dancing upward toward the heavens.

Breathing the scent of the smoke deeply into his lungs and holding it there for a long while, he then quietly breathed it out. Sitting in silence, he waited for the flames to flare up again. Once the fire was again blazing, he covered the offerings with freshly harvested sage, watching as the smoke grew thicker and darker. Following the smoke with his eyes, he watched the four winds soundlessly conveying it into the waiting arms of the Grand Father. White Wolf remained sitting and praying, until the drifting fragrance of his offering dissipated in the warm desert breeze.

The gift of the deer delayed White Wolf's departure by only one day. After he finished offering up the sacrifice, he prepared some of the fresh meat for his evening meal. It was a welcome change from the roots, fish, and small game he had been living on for so long. The process of drying the rest of the deer in strips by the fire and curing the hide took up the remainder of the day, and a good part of the night; however, the results were well worth the time invested. His horse was heavily laden with herbs, cacti, and now the dried strips of meat and the deer hide. Due to the abundance of his cargo, he would have to once more lead his pony the entire way home. The more he transported, the less often he had to make the tedious journey into this dangerous territory. His only objective was to return these rare plants safely to his people. It was a responsibility he gladly shouldered for more than half of his lifetime. Finishing refilling the water skins, he added them to the horse's burden.

His heart was full of hope and anticipation as he once again reviewed his message from the previous night. Although the picture itself was clear, its meaning remained a mystery to him. White Wolf had been receiving images from the Great Spirit his entire life, but seldom did he recognize their true meaning immediately. Eventually, in their own time, his visions always yielded their secrets. It would be the same with the likeness of the great bird within the flames; it was only a matter of time until the truth revealed itself to him.

He added the newly cured deerskin as the very last article of the horse's load. Throwing it on top of the pile, he cinched it into place. His noble pony, as usual, snorted and nodded her willingness to increase her strength to the level needed to carry her cargo. Although it was barely past dawn, the sun was already warming the desert air. By mid-day the sun would be pounding fire on his body. The nights, however, became very cold, very quickly, and it would be good to have easy access to the warmth of the deer hide. Slinging his quiver of arrows and his bow across his back, he rechecked the area, making sure his campfire was completely extinguished. Satisfied that all was in order, he took the first step of his long trek homeward.

Slowly walking, he reminisced about his first venture into the deep southern desert alone. It stood out clearly in his mind, as did his last trip to the searing red sands, four winters ago. All of the other journeys blended together. Specific incidents stood out in his mind, but he maintained very little awareness of their chronological sequence. The order in which they occurred was of less importance than the events themselves. He clearly remembered the return trip

The Quest

home after his first solo pilgrimage, returning in time to witness the night of the flaming tears in his own sky. It was the night Flaming Sky was born to Running Fox and Skipping Bird. His mind often reflected back to his first journey, recalling the trip from winter camp to the southern desert as uneventful. While strolling, his thoughts transcended into experiential recall:

He was exceptionally lucky. Many of the precious plants he came to collect were far more plentiful than usual, thereby taking less time for him to complete the harvesting. There was no need for him to venture very deep into the land of the savages, thus increasing his chances of returning home safely. He was sure he would arrive home in time to watch the flaming sky in his own land, with his own people. He had never witnessed such an awesome event in his lifetime. Oh, yes. He saw flaming stars racing through the night sky from time-to-time. In fact, the number of sightings was always higher in the desert than in the shadow of the Sacred Hills. But the night of the Grand Father's Tears would humble the appearances of those occasional shooting stars. They would appear as a light rain when compared to an erupting deluge in the land of fiery waters.

Excitedly, White Wolf turned, speaking aloud to his only companion, who seemed to enjoy the sound of his voice and his animated gestures as he described the difficulties of this first journey home.

"I remember, during the winter preceding my first solo journey, the land was blessed with generous amounts of snow and rain. The waters of the rivers ran higher than normal, forcing me to seek higher ground, making it necessary to make my way home through the mountains piercing the sky. The slow, twisting path was like a treacherous sidewinder patrolling its hunting ground." Pausing momentarily, he sighed. "But, I was younger, and climbing mountains was much easier for me to accomplish."

As tired as he was, the old man would gladly have done it all over again in order to experience that night once more. He returned to his memory in silent reverie:

It took several days to lead the horse, heavily laden with its cargo, into the mountain peaks, and through the land of the fiery spouting waters. Reaching the summit well before sunset, he chose a campsite on a grassy area near a trickle of water. This ripple, making its way down the plateau toward the valley below, will become a stream. In its pursuit of the lowlands, it will join many other streams, until they eventually merge into the churning water of the river, snaking its way through his village.

This view always created a strong emotional reaction in White Wolf. Even as a young shaman, who had seen it many times before, it remained breathtakingly beautiful to him. The sky was endless. The air possessed a mysterious reddish tinge, adding to the aura of other-worldliness. The sun was high in the sky, allowing its rays to reflect off the river below, transforming it into a shiny, silvery, twisting ribbon of light. Thousands of feet below, on either side of the wide, shallow body of water, lay the village of his people. Hundreds of tipis were scattered across the valley, with wisps of smoke lazily drifting upward from the campfires below. He had arrived on time, as he promised Running Fox and Skipping Bird. That night he watched the Grand Father's Tears from the high plateau. It was the night his cousin's son, Flaming Sky, was born.

White Wolf's thoughts returned to the present. The old man had been walking since dawn and was in need of rest. Stopping, he took a few sips from one of the water bags before giving some water to his horse. Leading the animal to a cactus patch, White Wolf tied its reigns to a plant, positioning the animal in such a way as to create a little shade. After hobbling the horse and laying the deerskin on the ground, he rested in his self-made shade. Taking some water, he carefully poured a little over the top of his head. He felt the water seeping through his hair, dripping onto his face and shoulders. There he sat, cooling himself as best he could. Once he was more comfortable, his thoughts revisited the night of the fiery sky.

The Quest

He decided to make camp early that night, even though it would be a while before darkness spread across the sky. It was not possible for him to complete his descent into the valley before losing the sun's light, and becoming stranded half way down the cold, dark mountain in the middle of the night was certainly never a part of his plan. No. He built his fire, ate some roots and the remainder of the dried rabbit from his food supplies. He removed his store of plants and herbs from the packhorse, before staking the animal to a small scrub oak, within light of the campfire.

He was delighted with his three new carrying pouches, which allowed him to pack and unpack the horse very quickly. The design was simple and easily employed. First, he untied the rawhide strips securing the large bag, which were tied to the horse's back. Next, he released the ropes connecting the two containers that were on either side of the animal. Each pouch was approximately the size of an average child, just before its last growth into adulthood. Because of the increased size of the newer pouches, White Wolf gathered larger reserves, thereby reducing the need of traveling as frequently into the dangerous southern deserts.

On that night so long ago, as he watched the sun approaching the western horizon, the valley below was already in darkness. The sight of the campfires burning on either side of the river put him in mind of hundreds of swarming fireflies. Before settling in for a safe night's sleep, White Wolf offered up his evening prayers, as he always did. He painstakingly prepared and lit the pipe. Smoking his pipe and praying, he offered up his thoughts on the sacred smoke. Taking long, slow, deep draws of the bowl's mixture, he exhaled, releasing his prayers with the smoke, which he watched expanding forever, ultimately disappearing into the night sky.

After completing his evening devotions, he rewrapped the pipe, carefully returning it to its storage place. Adding more wood to the fire, he pulled the animal skin up around his shoulders. Even though it was summer down below, at this elevation the nights were winter cold. He quietly settled down next to the fire, gazing into the infinite distance.

Charles Richard Latona

Twilight was just giving way to darkness when he spotted the first star streaking across the northern sky.

White Wolf's mind returned to the here and now. He was well rested and feeling the need to proceed upon his travels. Carefully rechecking his herb bags, ensuring they were secure, he finished his packing by replacing the deerskin on the top of the third container. Content that all was well, he headed eastward. Once he reached the foot of the piercing mountains, he would change to a northerly direction, eventually switching to a northeastern course, leading him directly to his ancestral lands. The journey ahead of him was long and dangerous.

The sun was high overhead when he first sensed their presence; he felt them out there, somewhere. He smelled them in the scorching desert winds. They were coming, heading directly toward him, taking their time, as they were not in any hurry to overtake him. Lacking the courage to attack him before sunset, like thieves, they would try sneaking up on him in the dark. He knew this to be true, as this is the way the cowardly always fight and…make no mistake about it… his pursuers were cowards.

Stopping momentarily, he surveyed the terrain. To the northeast lay the hills holding the entrance to the great mountains. At his present rate of travel, he would arrive at his destination long before sundown, with more than ample time to pitch camp and prepare a welcome for his uninvited guests. He gave a gentle tug on the hemp rope. The horse, neighing, shook her head from side to side, and briefly shuttered once or twice, as she willingly followed the new course charted by the old man. The air was quiet and still. The only discernable sounds were the muted footsteps of White Wolf, the soft hoof-beats of the horse, and the swishing sound made by her tail as she flicked at the flies continuously landing on her chestnut-coloured rump.

Off the two of them went, at a slow, easy pace, as it was hot and they were extremely tired. Except for their short rest, they had constantly been on the move since first light streamed across the

The Quest

desert basin. White Wolf was certain there would be water waiting for them up ahead. This morning, like every other, he arose at dawn, and watched the morning flight of the birds, just as he watched their twilight flight every evening.

"If you know how to read the signs, the birds will always point out the way to water by the direction of their flight," the old shaman explained encouragingly to his burdened horse. White Wolf had been reading these signs his entire life. "At nighttime they fly toward water, to replenish themselves for the night, after a day of searching for food. In the morning, they quench their thirst before beginning their day's foraging. They fly away from the water when returning to their feeding grounds…but, then," he paused, reflecting, "you probably know all of this already."

The sweat was soaking through his headband, his eyes stinging from the burning sensation of the salty water leaking down from his forehead. There was enough water left in the containers to get them to the watering hole…but, just enough. Spotting a large rock, he turned the pony toward the welcoming shade it afforded them. Upon arriving at the boulder, he tied the horse to a nearby tree.

Once the pony was secured, he hesitantly approached the rock, his eyes searching for any danger hiding in the underbrush, or slithering between the rocks and crevices. Carefully poking with his lance, he searched until he was satisfied the area was safe. After retrieving his horse, the two of them settled into the sparse shade as best they could. It was not often White Wolf was given the opportunity to cool himself during his hot, desert trek. Later, he would water the horse and have a drink himself; but, for now, it was time to rest. The horse contentedly grazed on the meager vegetation she found growing nearby, while the old man peacefully napped.

Thus they quietly passed the time as the sun continued its westward journey. The savages were decreasing the distance between themselves and White Wolf. Even sleeping, the old man remained mindful of their steady approach.

Chapter 2

THE SAVAGES

There was ample daylight remaining as White Wolf led his pony to the mouth of the canyon. Pausing for a moment, he inhaled the moist water smell suspended in the air. It was a scent he and the animal had been following for a while. Carefully he surveyed the gullies splitting off from the main canyon, while walking his pony leisurely toward the scent of the creek. As he approached the stream, his eyes were constantly examining the terrain for the most inviting place to establish camp. It did not take long for him to find the perfect cove, noting the narrow entrance, which would work to his benefit later.

He tethered the horse in a grassy area just inside, where the shelter widened into a small box canyon. The passageway appeared to have been carved deeply into the earth by an ancient, longforgotten river. With the ground slanting slightly upward, ending at the base of the cliff, he found the contour to be ideal. The small canyon was approximately one-hundred-and-fifty paces deep by about seventy to eighty paces wide. The outer walls and the narrow passageway would serve as shelter for his campfire, protecting him from the cold night wind.

The Quest

After unpacking the horse, and storing his precious merchandise on a small shelf where it would be safe, he tended to his pony. When he was finished, he went about setting up his camp as usual. He located a grassy area protected by several large boulders, presenting him with an ideal site for his campfire.

"Large rocks reflecting the warmth of the campfire back upon itself," he mused aloud to himself, "… between the warm rocks and the fire, the perfect place for an old man to sleep,"

Feeding the fire was easy, as he was surrounded by an abundance of dried twigs, small branches, and sagebrush. Once he sparked the kindling, White Wolf built a good-sized fire. Although it was larger than usual, it was still suitable for cooking. Taking two long, strong twigs, he skewered some of the fresh deer meat, suspending the uncooked meat over the flames, close enough to cook, yet far enough away not to burn. As the meat roasted, he scrutinized his chosen sleeping area.

Taking the furs and blankets serving as his bed, he carefully arranged them on the grass between the rocks and the campfire. Gathering sagebrush, he stacked it on the bed, which was a safe distance from the fire. Next, he covered the sagebrush with one of the furs. Picking up a small branch he purposely set aside earlier from the firewood, he tied the two ends together with a strip of rawhide, approximating the look of a bow, which he leaned against the rocks.

Turning his attention to his weapons, White Wolf removed his arrows from their quiver and placed the empty receptacle on its side, close to the makeshift bow, angling it so its emptiness was hidden by the shadows. He completed his display by laying his lance across a log next to the fire.

Before completing his task, he stopped long enough to take a quick glance at the meat roasting on the fire. After surveying his handywork, he stashed his bow and arrows on the dirt surface directly behind the boulders. In addition to keeping his weapons out of sight, the rocks also hid a shelf leading to a steep pathway, which led to the canyon rim. Inspecting the shelf, and satisfied with its stability, he scrambled down the path and back to his camp. Checking himself, ensuring his tomahawk and knife were securely tucked into his waistband, he paused for a moment, carefully surveying the area. Content that all was in readiness, he settled down next to the fire.

Prior to his evening meal, White Wolf graciously thanked the Great Spirit for providing him with food and shelter before nourishing himself with the warm food. He ate slowly, his mind calculating the estimated arrival of his uninvited guests, which was more than enough time to finish his meal unhurriedly, and offer up his ceremonial evening prayers. "However" he observed, "after sunset, when they are convinced I am asleep, these predators will most assuredly attack."

Understanding the minds of the savages as well as he did, White Wolf touched into their thoughts, thereby comprehending their strategy. This advantage made it easier for him to repel the attack, which would surely be launched after the sun has gone to rest. Of all the tribes, the savages were the only ones who would defile a shaman. All of the remaining tribes revered healers. Although most of the tribes were not openly friendly to each other, their reverence for a medicine man was strong, even when their people were making war on each other. The combatants always remain non-hostile and respectful of a shaman. By far the most vicious and the least spiritually evolved of all the known tribes, the savages were the only ones who would dare raise their hand against the Great Spirit by assaulting a Wicasa, a Holy One, One who is sacrosanct to all…all, that is, except them.

Finishing his meal, White Wolf purposely left meat cooking on the fire as he went about preparing the prayer pipe for his evening meditation. Completing the blending, and looking longingly into the twilight sky, he lit the pipe. Smoking it, he prayed, asking for strength and guidance to sustain him throughout the ordeal ahead of him. As a warrior, he knew what must be done; and, as a warrior,

The Quest

he would do it. As a spiritual leader, however, he deeply regretted having to do it.

Completing his nightly ritual, he added more wood to the fire, peacefully sitting while watching the last rays of the sun painting the sky. The meat on the fire was close to burning, and the night air was permeated with its aroma, adding to the further enticement of his predators. Although this was a small scouting party, the old man was certain that the main body of warriors was not far behind them. He was estimating the war party was, at most, a day's ride behind the scouts. Yes, there was more than ample time at his disposal before the main band of warriors would catch up to his pursuers.

The last of the day's light finally faded. The rising full moon was a huge reddish-orange sphere, gently easing itself over the mountaintops. The stars were taking their place in the once deserted sky, slowly manifesting one by one. He was sure the anticipated attack was near at hand. Adding buffalo chips to the fire so it would continue burning long, slow and hot, he rechecked his bedding, assuring himself that it certainly appeared as though he was asleep. With everything in readiness, he slipped to safety behind the large rocks. He gathered his hidden weapons and his waiting robe. Slinging the bow over his shoulder, he grabbed the small bundle of arrows fastened together with rawhide and secured them onto his back. Draping the robe over his shoulders, leaving his hands free, he made his way up the shelf leading toward the ridge of the canyon.

As quietly as possible, he crept stealthily over the soft, sliding shale and crumbling rocks, hearing the crunching sound of the shifting surface giving way beneath his feet. Deliberately, he edged his way up the slippery pathway. The climb was steep, making it difficult for him to reach the ridge. Once arriving at the crest, he rested momentarily, taking the opportunity to inventory his weapons. Everything seemed to be in place. The arrows were still bound tightly, resting comfortably on his back along with his bow. His tomahawk and one knife were securely nested in his waistband, the other knife safely tucked into his buckskin boot. Taking care not to drag the robe, he silently proceeded on his mission. The place chosen was close by, only a few short paces away.

His high-post lookout was located approximately halfway between the gateway into the small canyon and his double, peacefully sleeping by the fire. He took shelter behind a small mound of earth, which provided him with safe shadows, hiding him from the bright, full moon. He untied his arrows and laid them on the ground next to his bow. Wrapping the robe snugly around his shoulders to protect him from the cool night breeze, he quietly engaged in his nocturnal vigil. He did not have long to wait. As he had foreseen, they came as soon as they thought he was asleep.

Sitting motionlessly in the darkness, White Wolf listened to the muffled hoof-beats of the approaching ponies being led in single file by the savages. Peeking over the ridge, he spotted them. He was right; there were five of them. He continued watching them deploying, remaining true to their normal, cowardly pattern. It was obvious by now, even to the five of them, that they were trailing one man…just one man…and he was an old man at that.

Spotting his horse just inside the canyon, they un-hobbled her, and led her away. Consistent with their tactics, one of them guided her out of the small canyon to where their horses were attended by the youngest warrior. Retying the stolen pony, the young savage resumed his assigned post. The four other braves quietly slithered into the camp. Once past the mouth of the canyon, a second savage dropped off as a rear guard to protect his companions. White Wolf sat motionless, patiently watching the three warriors doing their best to silently sneak up on their lone victim.

"It will not be long now," he thought. He was poised, ready to strike the instant they shouted their battle cries, signaling the commencement of their cowardly attack on the sleeping shaman. "Brave Warriors, indeed," he sneered.

The Quest

The leader let loose a blood-chilling scream, his battle cry signaling the attack. Rushing toward the *sleeping old man*, the leader was promptly joined by the other two savages. They sped headlong past the campfire, charging their victim. Whooping and hollering as they came, they hoped to intensify the fear and immobilize their overwhelmed opponent.

Stepping to the edge of the ridge, White Wolf quickly inserted an arrow into his bow and let it fly. Making a low-pitched whistling sound, the arrow cut through the quiet night air, directly on course toward the guard standing watch outside the camp. It made a soft, thumping sound as it ripped its way into the young savage's chest. White Wolf watched him standing immobilized, a stunned look on his face, grasping at the shaft in his chest. His legs gave way as he slowly went slumping to his knees, his frantic eyes staring wildly into space. Then, like a limp doll made of rags, he fell face-down into the stream next to the tethered ponies.

Scooting as fast as he could, White Wolf ran back over the ridge to a vantage point where he could oversee the entire small canyon. The second brave, standing guard just inside the canyon, appeared to be slightly distracted. He might have heard something; but, with all of the shouting, it was impossible for him to determine exactly what had attracted his attention. As the guard moved toward the entrance, a second arrow came winging its way through the darkness, finding its home slightly below the guard's right shoulder blade. The force threw his shoulders back into an arch, as the momentum of the impacting arrow sent him sprawling into the narrow entryway.

Still unaware of the loss of their two rear guards, the advancing three savages attacked the *sleeping old man* with all the savagery of a pack of starving wolves about to devour its prey. First shooting arrows into the blanket, they then bludgeoned the hide-covered sagebrush with their tomahawks. When there was no resistance to the force of their blows, they finally realized something was very wrong. Enraged, the leader threw back the cover, exposing White Wolf's treachery.

They were angry, and they were embarrassed at having been outwitted by a solitary, old man. In their fury, they tore the camp apart searching for him.

At that moment, forgetting how well they were lighted by the campfire, they presented themselves as clear targets. White Wolf launched a third arrow winging its way in their direction. The projectile appeared suddenly out of the darkness. Stunned as they were, they could only watch the arrow burrowing deeply into the stomach of the lead scout. He slumped to the ground with a look of agony on his face, still alive, but aware he was a dead man. It would take a long time for the gut wound to kill him; but, eventually, it would. A fiery pain was burning in his intestines, as if he had been pierced with a hot metal lance. His lower abdomen was bloating from his own body waste, which was poisoning him. There was nothing he could do except lie on the ground, doubled up in pain, waiting for the slow, lingering end to come.

The two remaining savages dashed for refuge behind the boulder just beyond the campfire. They did not know exactly where White Wolf was hiding, but they were sure he was somewhere in the darkness above them. Crouching behind the rocks, they were hoping to avoid any more of the old man's death missiles.

White Wolf was aware their eyes would soon readjust to the shadowy darkness. After that, it would be just a matter of time before they discovered the narrow pathway leading to the ridge. Once they found the path, White Wolf would become vulnerable to their counter attack. It was imperative for him to make his way back to the boulders as fast as he could, if he was going to cut the savages off before they worked their way up the ledge and attacked his flank.

Running in a crouched position, making himself as small a target as possible, he headed toward the path. Carrying his bow and his last arrow in one hand, while using the other to help maintain his balance, he went running along the ridge. Suddenly, sniffing a stench in the air, he came to a stop. The enemy had found the path and they

The Quest

were making their way toward him; he smelled them moving in his direction. Scanning the area quickly, White Wolf saw there were not any hiding places to shelter him. If he allowed himself to be caught out in the open like this, outnumbered two-to-one, his chances of survival were nil.

His only possibility of getting out of the situation alive was to make his way up the ridge to a point above the path. The savages would be lighted by the campfire, and with the bright, full moon shinning behind him, plus a little good luck, he just might be fortunate enough to escape with his life. Standing straight up, he raced along the ridge as fast as he could. His legs, which had long since been young, were aching as he frantically dashed to the top of the canyon rim.

He was consciously breathing through his mouth, trying to fully energize his body. Just as he was about to be clear of the danger, he slipped on the loose shale at the end of the pathway. Looking up at the sound, the savages saw White Wolf crashing against the rocks. Although his hand was bleeding, he was unaware of the pain. Grabbing his bow, he pulled back on the bowstring. It was then he became aware of the throbbing in the hand holding the bow. Thinking his hand might be broken, he let fly another projectile, this time missing his mark.

The first savage turned, facing him, as White Wolf's arrow struck his enemy in the shoulder, certainly not a fatal wound. As the savage spun sideways from the impact, his companion managed to get off a shot, striking the Sioux warrior in the leg. The pain sped up his leg in a burning frenzy. Pushing his way past his wounded comrade, the remaining savage launched his attack on the old man. He let loose a bloody scream, while viciously swinging his tomahawk at White Wolf, who absorbed the major impact of the blow with his arm. Whirling around, the savage maneuvered himself into a standing position over the shaman. Deliberately moving toward the wounded brave, he prepared to administer the fatal blow.

His blinding hatred for the Sioux shaman may have been the reason he did not notice the Wicasa sliding the knife out of his boot. As the savage raised his arm to its full extension, White Wolf sprang forward onto his knees, driving the knife deep into his enemy's soft, yellow underbelly. Twisting the knife, the old one rolled on his side, avoiding the force of the blow from the wounded warrior's tomahawk. The savage remained standing stunned, his hands holding his bleeding stomach, his eyes glazing over as a shocked look covered his face. The dying man attempted one last swipe at the old warrior, but failed to connect. Sneering at White Wolf, his strength gave out as he slumped to the ground. The victor stood over the dead man. "I wonder," he thought. "Was his last thought before passing over that he died by the hand of a solitary, wounded, old man?"

Pausing to catch his breath, White Wolf collected his senses. He heard the savage with the shoulder wound talking to his dying companion. Although he could not decipher everything they were saying, the old man understood enough to know the battle was definitely not over. If he were to survive, he needed to come up with a plan, and he had to do it quickly.

Below, the campfire was burning itself out, increasing the darkness and making it even more difficult for the savage to locate White Wolf's perch in the shadows. The old man had only one chance of escaping alive. Moving quickly, he put his knife back in his boot and removed the dead savage's headband. He wiped the war paint off the dead man's face, then stripped the body to the waist. Taking off his own blouse and snakeskin headband, he hurriedly placed them on the bloody body. Calling upon all the strength at his command, he dragged the lifeless form closer to the top of the narrow pathway. Reaching his position, he wedged the dead warrior into an upright position in a crevice within the rocks. There was nothing more he could do except wait in the semi-darkness for the inevitable attack.

The savage with the shoulder wound had re-armed himself, and, carrying his lance in his good hand, was working his way up the path

The Quest

toward his adversary. White Wolf watched the shadow of his enemy moving carefully toward his position. Crouching behind the fake Sioux warrior, White Wolf remained waiting. Timing was the key to the trap he had laid. Peeking over the dead man's shoulder, the old man watched as the savage spotted the mock medicine man. It was at this instant that White Wolf pushed the body out of the crevice in the rocks. In the faint light, the corpse appeared to be lunging at the savage, who, in turn, speared his deceased companion in the chest with his lance. The weight of the body slammed into the attacker, knocking him to the ground. Believing he killed the shaman, the savage allowed himself to relax a little. This was the mistake for which White Wolf was waiting, and he was determined to make the most of his opportunity.

The savage, poking at the body with his foot, turned his face toward the fire, leaving his back unprotected. Quietly scampering, White Wolf worked his way to the bottom of the pathway. Turning and directing his attention to the source of the sound, the savage had just enough time to realize White Wolf was the source of the tomahawk blow shattering his left temple. The chilling sound of crushing bone resounded in the darkness for a very long time. Finally, the savage crumpled to the ground in a limp pile.

Standing over him, exhausted, White Wolf realized he was soaked in blood and covered with small bits of gray brain-matter. Suddenly, the pain came rushing in on him. The fire in his leg was vying for attention with the sharp, throbbing sensation in his hand. He was most certainly wounded, but he was definitely alive, which was more than could be said for four of the five savages who had been foolish enough to attack him. The fifth savage, lying by the fire, unable to defend himself, was no longer a threat.

The savage was dying, of that there was no doubt, and there was nothing the medicine man could do for him except make him comfortable while awaiting his death. White Wolf took the precaution of tying the wounded man securely before offering him aid. Taking a piece of rawhide, the shaman tied it to the injured brave's arm, and wrapped it around his prisoner's chest and back before attaching it to his other arm. Thus secured, the warrior could move his hands, but not his arms. White Wolf broke off the arrow shaft in the front, leaving the arrow lodged where it was. This did the savage no harm, whereas removing it would only increase the bleeding and the pain. Giving the dying man herbs designed to dull the pain, the old healer had done all that he could do. Exhausted, he eased himself down on the grass next to the fire to rest. After catching his breath, he turned his attention to dressing his own wounds.

Ripping off a piece of cloth, he bound it tightly around his leg, slightly below the knee. Slowing the bleeding allowed him to take inventory of himself and his situation. As he was able to move his hand, he concluded it was not broken. Taking his pouches of plants, he stirred the pain-easing herbs into a small, clay jar of warm water sitting by the fire. Sipping the mixture slowly, he soon felt the potion bringing relief to his body, and clarity to his mind.

Cleanly bypassing his shinbone, the arrow had penetrated his calf, where it remained lodged in the muscle. With his injured hand he held the front of the shaft, and snapped off the feathered end of the arrow with his good hand. Placing the broken shaft between his teeth., he bit down hard, while, with his good hand, he grabbed the protruding end of the shaft. In one quick jerk, he pulled the rest of the arrow out of his leg. His mind was growing dark and hazy as he struggled to remain conscious. Taking a small stick of fire, close to the same thickness as the shaft which created the wound, he shoved the ember tip into the wound, while, again, biting down hard on the piece of the shaft between his teeth. Using a second similar stick, he inserted it into the wound from the opposite side.

By this time, he was nauseated by the smell of his own burning flesh. Taking what was left of the potion, he added more herbs to it, thickening the mixture for use as a poultice for the wound. Removing the cauterizing sticks, he applied the poultice to both the entry and

The Quest

the exit wounds. He untied the headband and removed it from the body of the dead savage lying next to him. After checking the thickness of the herbal mixture, he soaked the headband in it, then wrapped it tightly around his wound. Upon finishing the dressing of the wound, he released the tourniquet.

The old man rested for a little while before checking the other four savages for any sign of remaining life. He found none. One by one, he dragged their dead carcasses closer to the campfire and dumped them there. Noting he had a long time remaining before dawn, he added fuel to the fire, and checked his wounded prisoner once more before settling down for the night. By now, his own wounds were feeling much less painful. Easing his weary body onto the blanket, he collapsed in a heap. The instant his eyes closed, the old man drifted into a much needed sleep.

Chapter 3

THE DISGRACED ONES

When White Wolf finally awakened, he was uncertain as to how long he had slept; looking to the east, he saw it was nearly sunrise. During the night, the campfire had burnt down, and was in need of attention. Observing his silent enemy was still breathing with great difficulty, White Wolf went about his morning chores. Shivering in the predawn chill, the old man added larger pieces of wood to the fire to warm himself and relieve the stiffness invading his body.

Standing up slowly, he carefully tested the strength of his wounded leg. There were no signs of fresh bleeding and, after several attempts, he was eventually able to exert his full weight upon it. There was no doubt it would be sore for several days; but, happily, the wound was clean, and the injury should mend free of any major complications. He was able to walk with an apparent limp, but at least he was capable of walking. Flexing his painfully swollen hand several times, he was pleased there were no broken bones, and grateful the damage was not more extensive than it was,

The Quest

Obviously it was going to take longer than he originally anticipated to complete his return trip; however, he was certain he would finish his task in time. Taking inventory of the property captured from the savages, he discovered three useable lances, six knives, in addition to five horses, and an equal number of bows and arrows. Under normal circumstances, this collection of weaponry and ponies would have been a treasure worthy of taking back to the Sacred Hills; but, these were extraordinary circumstances. Determining he could salvage some of the weapons and an extra pair or two of moccasins, he went about collecting the items. Unfortunately, the horses, clothing, and the rest of the weapons would have to be sacrificed.

It did not take long for the surviving savage to comprehend the fate awaiting him and his four dead companions. His face was ashen, watching White Wolf meticulously stripping the bodies, which he had gathered and dumped by the campfire. First removing all of their outer garments, White Wolf tore some of the clothing into long strips for later use. The rest of the clothing had to be discarded… all, that is, except for a couple of un-bloodied blouses and two pairs of moccasins. These he set aside for himself. Gathering all the arrows he could find, he stacked them in a pile, including the ones removed from the dead savages' bodies.

"A couple of extra quivers of arrows just might come in handy," he thought. Taking their knives, along with one of their bows, he added them to his increasing collection. The remaining clothes, along with the bows, tomahawks and lances were destined for the fire.

Painfully kneeling next to the naked bodies of his defeated pursuers, he withdrew the knife from his waistband with his good hand, while grabbing the first corpse by the hair with his wounded one. He went about cutting the first scout's hair, making short, quick strokes with his knife, sheering the dead man's hair as close to the scalp as possible. The cut hair and the headband joined the weapons and clothes being consumed by the flames. White Wolf found the stench of the burning hair so foul that he had to move upwind to avoid smelling it. Returning to his task, he repeated the sheering process on each of the deceased.

Finishing the hair cutting, and picking up a stick of fire, he glanced at the dying savage. The man knew he would be dead long before the old man completed preparing the physical remains of his comrades. Slowly moving the burning stick over each of their heads, the remaining hair crackled, smoked and shriveled under the flame of White Wolf's torch.

"No one, not even a savage, would dare attempt entering the land of the spirits without his warrior's locks." he said solemnly to the dying warrior. "Your shame is now apparent for all to see, both in this world and in the next one. You are all cursed to wander endlessly throughout time, lost forever between the land of the living and the land of your eternal ancestors."

The slowly dying savage could only respond with groans of horror at the thought of his own fate as he watched the Holy Man preparing the others. And so he moaned throughout his remaining time. Seeing the terror in his eyes, White Wolf knew he was anticipating the eternal fate of the journey on which he was about to embark.

Once the four bodies were prepared, White Wolf decided it was time to check his captive. The light was almost gone from his eyes and, from the sound of his heavy, laboured breathing, it was apparent the savage had only a few breaths left in him. "You lay there groaning loudly, clutching your belly, like a frightened squaw in labour," he said disdainfully to the dying man.

White Wolf took this opportunity to retrieve the horses from the mouth of the canyon, allowing the savage a private moment to die alone with a remnant of dignity. Considering the desert devil's ultimate fate, this was a small act of charity on the old man's part. By the time White Wolf returned to the campfire with the ponies, the savage was, indeed, dead. Gingerly limping over to the dead warrior, the old man untied his ropes.

The Quest

"Allowing this last savage to witness his companions being prepared for eternity may seem cruel," mused White Wolf to himself. "However, now he will carry this knowledge with him into his dark eternity. As the five of them embark upon their endless wandering, at least he will be able to inform the others of what happened to them…why this was done…and by whom." Pausing, he addressed the fifth warrior. "You are learning an ultimate truth. No one may insult the Grand Father by ignoring His wishes. No one is allowed to raise his hand against one who has been touched by the Great Spirit. No one." This knowledge was the last act of charity imparted to the five dead men by the old Wicasa.

White Wolf proceeded with the final preparations for their journey into forever. Working quickly, he stripped the last warrior's body, adding his clothes to the rest of the burning rags. He had become quite adept at hair cutting by the time he finished trimming the fifth dead man. Tossing the long black strands of hair into the smoldering flames, White Wolf was glad he moved upwind of the foulness of the fuel on the fire. There was only one thing left for him to complete. Dragging the last body to where the other four corpses were lying, he dropped it face-down on the ground.

He removed a small burning stick from the campfire, the tip of which was a dancing, red flame. Using the stick as a branding iron, he etched the symbol of the Wicasa into the flesh of the dead warriors. It took time and several pieces of burning wood to mark all five corpses. Each of their backs bore a clear representation of the Holy Man's totem. The image was a universally clear message to all who might see it:

"These dead warriors have violated the sanctity of one chosen by the Grand Father," he shouted to the night air. "By so doing, they have raised the ire of the Great Spirit, thus condemning themselves.

Their punishment is just."

Working quickly, he led the ponies, one at a time, to a ledge next to the remains of the dead savages. He stationed the first pony next to the low ridge. Dragging one of the corpses up the dirt and shale to the ledge parallel to the horse's back, he pushed the dead man onto the horse. When he finished arranging the lifeless body, it appeared to be straddling the animal. Once completed, he guided the horse a short distance away from the others and hobbled it. He repeated the process four more times, working until all of the bodies were mounted on their ponies and ready to ride. To ensure the lifeless riders would not fall from their steeds, he would have to tie each securely to his mount.

Taking the remains of their shredded blouses, he fashioned the rags into ropes. In turn, he wrapped each of the dead man's arms around the horse's neck. Gathering longer pieces of the makeshift rope, he bound each of the savage's hands together under the animal's chin. Then, tying the end of each rope to a rider's right leg, he crossed the rope under the horse's belly, attaching the loose end of the rope to his left hand. This completed, he tied the left leg, again crossing the rope under the pony and then tied the opposite end to the corpse's right hand, thus assuring a stable ride for his vanquished enemy. Meticulously, he repeated the process four more times, until all five bodies were fastened safely into place, and the horses were ready for their journey. The most difficult aspect of the plan having been successfully completed, the old man took a moment to relax.

White Wolf went about repacking his horse, ensuring that the weapons he had gathered were safely packed, along with his supplies and herbs. Carefully taking the horses two-at-a-time, he led them out of the small shelter and into the main canyon, where he hobbled them on a grassy area by the bank of the stream. Once all six ponies were secured, he returned one last time to the campfire. Sitting quietly, he watched the flames consuming the last traces of the savage's possessions. When the fire completed its work, he returned to making the final preparations for his homeward trek.

He thoroughly extinguished what was left of the campfire, smothering it with several scoops of sand and dirt. Then he poured a

THE QUEST

large container of water over the smoldering mixture, stirring it until all of the heat was eliminated. Taking a deliberate and careful look around before picking up his bow and arrows, he slung them over his back and slowly limped toward the main canyon, where the horses and their passengers were patiently awaiting him.

Taking a long piece of hemp, he tied it around the lead horse's neck and its rider's upper body. Using a second piece of rope, he tied one horse and it's rider on either side of the lead animal. He completed the process by tying the fourth and fifth horses to the two ponies flanking the lead horse, forming a pattern of a flock of flying geese. With his own horse at his side, White Wolf led the string of ponies to the east, rather than north. The main war party should arrive at his deserted campsite sometime before the sun completes its daily journey. He was well aware that he had gambled with precious time; however, if his plan succeeds, it will have been time well spent. If his strategy fails, he will not have time to waste upon regrets and second-guesses.

White Wolf headed for home, constantly scanning the terrain ahead, looking for a flat area of rock or solid shale. The throbbing in his leg continued growing more severe with each step. Once the clearing he was seeking was located, he could safely rest for a little while. The sun was directly overhead and, after walking in the day's heat for a very long time, he stopped long enough to take a sip of water and to water the animals.

Spotting a small mesa within walking distance, the old man breathed a sigh of relief. Determining it was not advisable to approach the plateau straight on while leading the string of ponies, he decided to take the longer, easier route to the top. At this point, safety was more crucial than speed. There was ample time, and it was imperative that he arrive home with all of the cargo intact. Once arriving at the top of the mesa, he would be able to see far to the west. From this vantage point, he could observe any signs of the approaching pursuers.

He was utterly exhausted by the time he reached the top of the high mesa. Removing his blouse, he tossed it aside, enjoying the cool breeze flowing gently over his sweating torso. Not only was the soft wind refreshing, but he was sensing a difference in the air, a calmness which had been missing until now. Not exactly sure when he passed beyond the borders of the land of the savages, he was certain that, in fact, he had. The distracting throbbing in his leg was now joined by the pounding pulsation in his temples. It was safe for him to remain here, but only for a little while, long enough to rest briefly and care for his wounds.

Unwrapping the cloth from around his wounded leg, he saw signs of new bleeding. However, considering the distance he had covered walking, it was an acceptable exchange. After tying the horses to a small dried scrub oak near the trickling creek a short distance away, he proceeded attending to his leg wound. Sitting on a small rock, extending his injured leg straight out in front of him, he was hoping to relieve the throbbing pain.

From this vantage point, White Wolf had an excellent view of the land just traveled. In the distance he saw a small cloud of dust, slightly to the west of his last campsite. He calculated the trailing marauders would reach his old campsite shortly before dark. How they interpreted the signs would determine the speed with which they pursued him. But no matter how they read them, sooner or later they would come for him, being much too proud to allow their prey to escape. The warriors would be forced by their own arrogance into proceeding with the hunt, no matter what the final outcome.

Slowly chewing on some of the dried deer meat, White Wolf gazed upon the open prairie stretching endlessly ahead of him. Out there, not very far away, was the beginning of the land of the Comanche. They were among the majority of the tribes respecting the Great Spirit's chosen ones. It was safe for White Wolf to cross their land.

The Quest

Conversely, his enemies approaching from the west will be risking death if they dare follow him. Strength of spirit versus arrogance and pride held the key to his hopes of successfully eluding his pursuers.

The sun was midway between its zenith and the western horizon when the old man decided it was time to renew his travels. Painfully struggling to his feet, White Wolf leaned on his lance, surveying the western expanse for any sign of the enemy. Observing they did not appear to be any closer, he concluded they had not yet left his last campsite. He was unsure as to whether they would continue pursuing him before the sunset, or if they would wait until tomorrow's dawn. The truth was, it really did not matter. In either case, it was imperative he move on tonight, putting as much distance between himself and the tracking savages as possible.

Gathering up the horses and leading them eastward, White Wolf followed the rim of the mesa, walking for a while before reaching the end of the loose rock and shale. The surface beyond was a combination of sun-baked earth and gravel, which, after a distance of approximately forty to sixty paces, blended into the grasslands of the endless prairie. Tying the lead horse to a low tree branch, and lining the other four horses behind it, he checked, making sure each corpse was firmly attached to its mount. The task completed, he hobbled his own horse a safe distance from the other five ponies. Returning to the disgraced warriors, he completed the last preparations before sending them on their final journey into the prairie, and eternity.

After ensuring the ropes connecting the horses to each other were secure, White Wolf carefully cut the hemp one-third of the way through, thus weakening the connecting ropes between the number two and three horses and the lead pony. Satisfied with his handiwork, he proceeded cutting halfway through the ropes attaching the second and third horses to the fourth and fifth ones.

Gathering up nearby sagebrush, he attached it with rawhide to the tails of the four trailing mounts.

Carefully he removed the diamondback rattle from his medicine bag. This rattle was considered to be strong medicine and, right now, he was desperately in need of strong medicine. His life depended upon it. Gently and quietly, he tied the rattle to the crossed hands of the dead rider on the lead horse, with the rattle resting underneath the animal's neck. Releasing the lead pony's tether, he escorted the group of riders to the edge of the plain, very carefully moving a safe distance behind the horses.

Picking up a sharp rock, he hurled it at the lead horse's rump. His aim was true. Rearing up on its hind legs, the horse angrily pawed the air, it's head jerking up and back, causing the rattle to shake. The sound of a rattlesnake terrified the horse. Panic stricken, the animal frantically bolted, galloping full-speed toward the prairie, dragging the other four horses along behind it. The sound of the dragging brush added to their fear and confusion. Off they went, blindly racing eastward toward the homeland of the Comanche. White Wolf stood watching the horses and their riders fading completely out of sight.

If the old man estimated correctly, the two trailing horses should break away from the first three ponies sometime around dawn. After that, it would only be a matter of time before the other two broke free of the lead horse, running wildly until someone or something stopped them. In any event, the disgraced ones would receive no honour at the hands of the Comanche, understanding White Wolf's clear message.

"The main war party of the savages will, no doubt, follow their dead comrades into the land of my allies. Assuming they are foolish enough to do so, they will indeed be taking a journey to their deaths. The Comanche will not allow any members of the war party to survive," mused White Wolf. "The punishment of the savages will be slow in coming, and extremely painful, their deaths an obvious warning to all who are tempted to violate Comanche land…or disrespect the sanctity of a Holy One serving the Great Spirit!"

Chapter 4

THE NIGHT OF FIRE

Safely out of harm's way, White Wolf became less intense, but no less vigilant. Although he was experiencing pain in his leg, the discomfort was tolerable. The wound had only caused him a slight delay; however, due to his injury, the return journey would take even longer then usual. In the spring, he rode the pony all the way into the southern deserts. Once he began collecting the herbs and plants, his days of riding were numbered. He was slowed down even further by the heavy burden carried by his pony. This had been a bountiful harvest, and he was well pleased with the outcome of his journey. The limping man and the horse struck out on the long journey north, walking at an easy gait on their homeward trek.

He was hoping the southern pass would be clear when they arrived. Based upon their present pace, the old man calculated they would be there within eight to ten sunrises. Even though his leg might be healed by the time he reached the southern range, he would not be any younger. "No," he thought. "Mountain climbing must be avoided whenever humanly possible."

The next several days were uneventful. The air was constantly growing cooler the farther north White Wolf traveled. Despite the fact it was nearing midsummer, the winds rebounding off the mountains were always icy. The old man's leg was progressively mending without incident; however, his hand remained stiff and somewhat achy, lacking flexibility and full strength.

White Wolf maintained a constant surveillance of their wake. After a period of time without glimpsing any sign of trouble, he was more at ease. Accordingly, he allowed himself to camp a little earlier than usual that night. The site he chose was one of his regular campgrounds along the route, an area well supplied with clean, flowing water, tall rocks for shelter, and a supply of fresh tender shoots for the horse. It was the perfect place for relaxing, and reflecting.

Since it was not yet sunset, he took advantage of the opportunity to set up a proper camp. Corralling his pony in a shallow inlet between two small hills, he relieved her of her precious cargo, leaving her free to leisurely wander and nibble the young, spring shoots. Having attended to the needs of his horse, White Wolf set about gathering wood for his evening fire, and replenishing his water supply from the clear stream. These tasks completed, he enjoyed a leisurely meal of deer meat, fresh roots and crystalline water. After storing his remaining food supplies, and carefully packing his pipe, he began his evening prayers. Drawing deeply of the mixture, and slowly releasing the smoke, his mind drifted backward to that memory of long, long ago, his thoughts carrying him back to when he had been camping on the plateau overlooking his village…the night he witnessed the sky exploding with fire. In his reverie, he reexperienced that night as clearly as if it had just occurred.

It was approximately the same time as now, nearing midsummer. Despite the summer season, it was cold, as always, in the high plateaus. This was especially true after sundown. Having finished his evening chores and devotion, he stoked up his campfire, providing warmth against the

The Quest

chilling mountain winds. Relaxing, he watched the sun moving slowly toward the western horizon, as the vast sky turned a deep blue. Little white points of light were making their appearance overhead in the deeper patches of dark blue. Wrapping his blanket more tightly around his shoulders, he patiently scanned the blackening sky.

Finally they came, sporadically streaming across the sky, disappearing almost before he was aware of having seen them. As the night grew darker, the tears of fire increased in intensity as their numbers grew. He watched them shooting across the northern horizon. Their faint, white tails first created dozens, eventually hundreds, of bright lines streaking through the summer sky, arriving so fast, they overwhelmed White Wolf with their sheer numbers and speed. They continued increasing in brightness and speed, multiplying beyond his ability to count, filling the sky like swarming fireflies.

While this wonder was filling White Wolf's eyes, the entire sky burst into one enormous, blazing, white light. The shooting stars appeared to be hurling wildly in all directions. He felt his spirit drawn from his body, his entire being enveloped in the brilliant, exploding light. The following deafening silence shielded him from the calling of the earth, beckoning him to return from the sky. Slowly, the bright light dissipated into a gentle, enticing, vibrating glow.

Deep within the silence, he heard it, initially starting as a small rolling sound, struggling to free itself from it's unearthly void. The din grew louder and louder, until it became a thunderous roar, shaking White Wolf and the earth on which he stood. It was a quaking so intense that it extended well beyond the plateau, spreading in all directions. His body resonated to the frantic rhythm of the swelling cadence engulfing him.

Suddenly, he saw them manifesting in the brilliant light, flooding the prairie, and rushing straight toward him, a sea of brown flesh. There they were, thousands and thousands of buffalo, stretching out in all directions as far as he could see, and beyond. Endlessly they poured from the north, the home of Tatanka, far beyond the Sacred Mountains, their numbers stretching beyond the edge of the southern deserts. He watched in awe as they flowed passed him…wave after endless wave. This bounty provided by the Great Spirit was the source of his people's food, shelter and medicine, as well as their tools and weapons. He stood there witnessing the lifeblood of his people streaming past him, disappearing into the glowing night. Within a little while, the image slowly faded into the thundering light from which it had come.

White Wolf remained sitting quietly, as the swirling sparks zigzagged across the deep sky, contemplating what he had seen. At last, all once more was silent. New images were taking form in the shimmering light…visions of very strange beings. Although they stood erect like people, they were obviously quite different. Their bodies were extremely hairy, appearing more animal-like than human. Despite their bear-like appearance, they possessed hands rather than paws. Their lighter coloured hair was matted, and much shorter than anything he had ever seen. Their faces, like their bodies, were covered with fur. Due to the hairiness of the beasts, the only facial feature he could clearly distinguish was their eyes, which were strong and determined. Their skin, although somewhat tan, was much lighter in colour than that of his people. However, he had yet to see the strangest thing of all. They carried long sticks, which spoke with the voice of quiet thunder, with puffs of white smoke escaping from the ends of the weapons at each shattering blast issuing forth from the fire sticks. White Wolf continued watching the animal-men as they drifted away into the night, ultimately disappearing like the wisps of smoke drifting from his campfire.

"Who are these creature?" he had wondered.

Unfortunately, before he could ponder the question any deeper, a new image was drawing him into the mist. Grey clouds were spreading across the Black Hills, blocking out all of the mountain peaks. Small round droplets were descending endlessly from the clouds, suffocating the prairie. They were not raindrops, but rather small, hard objects similar to hail stones in size. Vengefully they came, pouring relentlessly down from the black sky. They deluged the mountains and saturated the prairie like an evil, grey fog, flowing like molten liquid, oozing across the plains and

The Quest

well beyond the southern deserts. Soon everything in sight was covered with the small cold, hard, grey spheres.

The grey hail stones melted into the landscape, eventually vanishing altogether. The shaman felt the earth shaking. He watched in horror as the ground cracked open, creating long wide furrows in the prairie. Large, bright, white objects were exploding out of the earth, spreading like locusts across the terrain. The objects pushed their way across the prairie, leaving huge mounds of white debris. Suddenly he realized he was gazing upon endless horizons of bleached, white bones...mountains of bones, smothering the entire prairie. Bones. Buffalo bones. The blood of the great beasts was absorbed into the prairie soil, turning it into red mud.

Helplessly, he gazed upon enormous mounds of rotting buffalo meat, decaying under a relentless sun, as the spoiled flesh festered under the attack of millions of egg-laying flies. He watched in horror as the hatching eggs turned into squirming maggots within the decomposing flesh. The foul stench rising from the decay filled his nostrils, suffocated him, gagging him as he felt the queasiness erupting from within the depth of his bowels. The meat turned disgustingly black, disintegrating as it returned to the earth from which it had come.

At that moment, he was inexplicitly flooded with a sense of despair, leaving him sick in his soul. The ghastly image filled with the muffled sound of thousands of lamenting voices sending up a futile cry, echoing endlessly in the deadly stillness of the night.

The shaman remained quiet, listening, lost in the reverie of his vision. He continued pondering the vision for a very long time. He would never be certain as to the exact duration of the phenomena. The grisly images remained for a very long time before finally passing into nothingness. Once they vanished, he found himself staring into the black night filled with the Grand Father's Tears endlessly speeding across the sky, like a barrage of exploding fire arrows. The falling stars presented a much more soothing, peaceful sight than the stark, barren images he had just been shown. There he abided, in the bittersweet silence, overwhelmingly lost in the spectacular beauty of the night of raining fire. White Wolf remained haunted by the foreboding images overshadowing that night, images which would haunt him throughout the remainder of his lifetime.

The raining fire was fading in intensity as the sun made its presence felt. A little at a time, through the mist, he felt himself summoned back into the world of morning light. Thus the shedding of the Grand Father's Tears came to its end. During the course of its reign, the night blessed the people with many new births, new ones who made their entrance into the world of man on the wings of the fiery tears. One of those newly arriving braves was his cousin's son, Flaming Sky. White Wolf had, indeed, made it back in time for the birth of the boy, thus keeping his promise to Running Fox and Skipping Bird. He had correctly foretold them of the birth of a son. It was his right and responsibility as the shaman to name the important children of the tribe upon their birth. This was a task he would willingly perform once he returned home.

Within a short time, having mustered his strength, he began descending the path leading down the side of the plateau and into the valley below. The journey was treacherous and slow, as the path was narrow and steep. In time, it led him back to his village, where he properly welcomed his cousin's son into the tribe.

Leaving the puzzling images from the past unresolved, the old man drew his thoughts into present time. Re-centering his mind in the here and now, he took stock of himself. Checking the bandage on his leg, he saw that the bleeding had stopped. The throbbing of the wound was giving way to a constant dull ache. The wound was healing quite nicely, despite the possible danger of infection due to the long distances of walking. The pain in his hand was completely dissipated. However, it remained stiff, and he lacked the full strength and use of it. The night was advancing as the medicine man felt the tiredness of his body weighing heavily upon him.

Before preparing for sleep, White Wolf added kindling to his fire. As the flames consumed the smaller pieces, he added several larger

The Quest

pieces to the fire. He supplemented the wood with chips, which burnt long, hot and slow, keeping him warm throughout the cold night that lay ahead. Spreading a blanket over a soft, lush, grassy area close to the campfire, he eased his tired body gingerly onto his bed. Pulling up his buffalo robe, covering himself to the neck, the old man, safe and warm, slept peacefully this night.

White Wolf awakened shortly after dawn, feeling stronger than he had in several days. The morning air had a crisp edge to it. The flames were low and in need of tending, and the old man set about rebuilding the fire in hopes of eliminating the deep chill within him. Once he was warm, he gathered his possessions in preparation for his departure. After he completed collecting his cargo, he sat close to the fire, eating dried deer-meat and precooked roots. Finishing his meal, he proceeded to pack his horse. Content that all was in order, he went about changing the bandage on his leg. He thoroughly extinguished the campfire with dirt and water. Once satisfied the fire was safely out, he rechecked the area, making sure he had not forgotten anything of importance. With an obvious limp, White Wolf led the pony northward, toward home.

Graciously, the next several days were dull and monotonous. With the passing of each day, his strength grew as his leg continued mending. All things considered, he was making good time. With no further signs of danger from the war party of savages, he was free to concentrate upon the tasks awaiting his return.

"If everything has gone well, the boys will be returning home within the next few days," he thought. "Then I will resume my responsibilities of leading them through the last phase of their initiation into manhood. All four of them possess the potential to become brave warriors, of this I am sure. However, one question remains: 'Which one of them should I choose to become the next shaman?' The Grand Father will select the next Wicasa, but it is I who must decide upon our medicine man."

White Wolf had been one of their most important teachers from the time they were young boys. For many winters he trained them, watching them daily learning and growing. Nonetheless, he was extremely concerned as to which of them, if any, would be the one to replace him. This was a question he repeatedly asked himself. "So far, no answer is forthcoming," he said, half smiling.

Re-evaluating each of the four boys in his mind, the old man's immediate tendency was to eliminate Standing Elk. White Wolf intuited that this boy will, in time, become a great warrior and, no doubt, a renowned war chief. "However," he mused thoughtfully, "his way does not appear to be that of a shaman. Standing Elk's destiny lies along a different path. The boy is strong of body and will. There is no doubt the young warrior's future is to become an exceptional leader of the tribe, but it is highly unlikely he is destined to become their shaman. He can be taught to set bones, but his heart is not the heart of a healer." No. White Wolf was sure that Standing Elk was not the one he was to train to become the next medicine man.

Thinking aloud, he went on to reconsider Standing Elk's younger brother, Lone Feather. "Not only is Lone feather less aggressive than Standing Elk, he is also less decisive. He possesses the skills of a potentially good warrior and, as a protector of the people; he will win honour. However, he lacks the physical and mental strength of a great leader and, as such, can never be a great shaman."

Pondering hard, he affirmed to himself, "A medicine man must embody not only the physical attributes of a Sioux warrior, he must also possess the leadership qualities of a chief. A shaman, in his own right, must be the equal of any chief within the tribal council." He asserted aloud, as if to reassure himself, "He must always have confidence in his ability to accurately read signs, and correctly interpret symptoms. A shaman must be extremely sure of himself and have the strength to stand up to any resistance, no matter its source, including the council, itself."

THE QUEST

White Wolf affirmed quietly and thoughtfully, "Despite Lone Feather's many good qualities, he is lacking the necessary strength of spirit. It is highly doubtful Lone feather is the one I am seeking."

Directing his attention to the third candidate, White Wolf reevaluated the qualities of Short Bear. "He is the dullest among the four boys, slow physically as well as mentally. Although even tempered, he is definitely a follower, not a leader." Pausing momentarily, he continued aloud, "On the positive side, he does possess a natural ability with herbs and roots. It is quite possible that this talent may have been inherited from his father, Thunder Eyes." With a furrowed brow, he questioned himself, "What else might he have inherited? Is his blood tainted by the corruption of his father?"

Only time would reveal the answer to that burning question. However, White Wolf was unsure as to how much time it might take and. more importantly, the old man was concerned he might not have enough time left to find out. He ended his evaluation by acknowledging that the chances of Short Bear becoming his successor were extremely remote.

Once more, White Wolf was left with his most promising candidate: his cousin's son, Flaming Sky. "The son of Running Fox is quick of mind and strong of body, and is a fast learner. Despite being a free spirit, he possesses great potential of becoming a strong and wise leader. His skills as a warrior are equal to those of Standing Elk. His relationship to the healing resources of nature is obvious. He has already learned the secrets of many of the plants from his mother, Skipping Bird. Someday, he, too, could become a great chief among our people, as is his father, Running Fox."

Of the four, Flaming Sky was, beyond doubt, the best prospect as White Wolf's choice to become his replacement. What constantly troubled the old man was the boy's high-spiritedness, and whether or not it could be tamed, or at least controlled. The last thing he wanted was to see the boy's spirit broken. "A shaman must be independent, but remain available to the wisdom of others. It will be imperative that I help him attain and maintain this balance. As always, my cousin's son appears to be my best prospect. Hopefully," he thought, "my final choice will be revealed to me during their rites of passage."

After the sun traversed several cycles, and was descending on the horizon, he reached the southern end of the mountain pass. Although its height lay too far in the distance for him to be completely sure, from this vantage point it appeared to be clear. White Wolf would have to wait until he caught a closer glimpse of the canyon before he could be absolutely certain. However, it was looking very promising. Here and there, small patches of snow scattered throughout the half-frozen terrain were reflecting the bright sunlight like hundreds of miniature stars. In places, the terrain was so slick, White Wolf had to walk carefully to guard against slipping and falling.

The winds of the north were cold, very much colder than those of the desert he recently abandoned. Pulling his robe tightly around his chest, he bent forward, trudging headlong into the harsh winds of the canyon pass. It was clear, and it was cold, but it was easily traversable for the old man and the horse. Once he arrived at the other side of the valley, he would follow the river north until it veered off sharply to the west. When he reached the bend in the river, the walk to his village would be less than a day.

When White Wolf reached the other side of the pass, there was just enough sunlight left for him to find a campsite capable of sheltering him and his pony from the gusty winds ripping through the canyons. Building his usual evening fire, he leisurely consumed the last of the dried meat. He drank slowly, enjoying the cool, clear water from the river. In the morning he would refill his water containers. Unpacking the pony and hobbling her for the night, he settled down, quietly smoking his pipe and meditating, as was his nightly routine. Finally, curling up in front of the campfire, before drifting into sleep, he

The Quest

thought about the boys whose initiation into adulthood he was to oversee upon his return.

It was the Wicasa's responsibility to prepare the boys spiritually for their last tests. He was also the one who would instruct them in interpreting any of the visions they might experience along their way. Visions often foretell the true path, while sometimes even revealing the fate of the warrior. The ability to correctly interpret messages from the spirit world is an important part of every young warrior's training. Although it is true that the Wicasa is responsible for the spiritual well being of the tribe, each man and women is solely accountable for his or her own soul. White Wolf was keenly aware that his function was to facilitate their spiritual awareness, not control it. The responsibility for this task is always left to the individual.

White Wolf knew the spirit of three of the boys was strong. It was Short Bear's apparent lack of spiritual strength that was of constant concern to him. He was not completely sure, himself, as to why he allowed Short Bear to study with him. Maybe it was to give him safe space away from his father, Thunder Eyes, whose uncontrollable rages were well known to all. Only White Wolf, because of his status as a Holy Man, could step in between a father and his son; and, mind you, it was a step that had to be taken very carefully. White Wolf may have also chosen Short Bear in an attempt to help heal Thunder Eyes' self-anger for having betrayed the trust invested in him.

"Maybe," the old man often thought, "…maybe, allowing his son to walk this path, at least for a while, will bring Thunder Eyes some peace."

It was a good seed he planted; sadly, it had not yet taken root. White Wolf was far from giving up on Thunder Eyes. However, the safety and well being of the boy was of primary importance in the old man's considerations.

"After all," he thought, "a tree receiving some sunshine while it is growing is healthier than a tree completely deprived of the light altogether. Who knows," he mused, "maybe someday this tree may grow strong enough to fight its way out of the darkness and into the light of day."

The truth was, he was uncertain himself as to exactly why he had taken Short Bear under his watch. However, he was positive it was not to train the boy to be the new shaman. His choosing of the other three boys was less selfless. "One of these three, hopefully, will be the one," he sighed wearily. "I have been waiting a long, long time. The one I choose will have to undergo very intensive training, and there is so much I must teach him."

White Wolf was ever aware of his own time constraints. He would be allowed to take three of them only to a certain level, but not beyond. Despite the fact that, from then on, he would concentrate his energies and efforts on the one, the other three will have profited from their training. Knowledge of the healing properties of herbs and plants is useful to any warrior after battle, or hunting accident. They will be given respect by the other warriors, in deference to their training under his tutelage.

Such were the thoughts consuming his mind by day, and flooding his dreams by night. He always knew Standing Elk and Flaming Sky were the only real possibilities. Nonetheless, because of their similar strengths, he found it difficult choosing between them; but choose he must. "I will appoint and train a shaman. but only the Great Spirit selects His Holy Ones. The tribe will have a new shaman; I will see to it!" he affirmed. "However, as far as a new Wicasa is concerned, I trust in the Grand Father and allow His visions to direct my actions. If He so wills it, I will recognize the chosen one."

Most frustrating to White Wolf was his inability to find a connection between the eagle in his vision and any one he knew. "The eagle is a symbol of bravery, strength, and wisdom," he muttered as he continued exploring the thought. "This very general description applies to all Sioux warriors, including the four initiates presently in my charge. I must remain patiently waiting for the answer to this mystery to reveal itself when the time is right."

The Quest

With White Wolf's mind thus occupied, the days passed swiftly. Every step was taking him closer to home. Walking with just the slightest sign of a limp, he was aware of a little tenderness making itself known whenever he found himself getting tired. The trip was taking longer than usual, due to the wound he received in the battle with the savages. In truth, a few days one way or the other was of no real consequence.

The final ceremony could not take place until White Wolf and the four boys all returned to the village. The preparations for the final steps in their initiation were not to take place until after the boys complete their purification rite. It is during this time, when their spirits are the strongest, that they will make their vow to the sun. They will be called upon to demonstrate their willingness to suffer, sacrifice, bleed and to die, if necessary, for the preservation of the people.

"Yes," he thought, "it is here they will show their courage and expose their hearts. I will see the true strength of their spirits, and recognize our new medicine man. The four of them will perform the dance to the sun, as our ancestors have done for countless generations, and as our descendants will do for endless generations yet to come."

Approaching the bend in the river, his thoughts returned to the present. "From this place, it will take only one-half cycle of the sun for us to make our way safely home," he announced to his pony. The animal made no reply. Undaunted, the old man continued, "The river curves and twists its way around the base of the mountains, before eventually flowing past our village, so following the river any farther north will be a waste of our time and energy." Again, the horse remained silent. Refusing to acknowledge the lack of response, White Wolf continued, "It will take much less time for us to cut straight across the valley, rejoining the river near home." He was relieved his journey was almost at its end, and he would soon be safely in the shadows of Paha Sapa, the Sacred Black Hills.

Due to his tiredness and his aching injuries, he decided to make camp one last time, rather than continuing. Tonight, after tending to the pony, and eating his last meal alone, he will smoke his pipe and gaze upon the Great Spirit once more. He will sleep, and he will dream, hoping his dreams will clarify the meaning of his vision of the flaming eagle.

Chapter 5

THE HOMECOMING

The sun was high overhead when White Wolf reached the outskirts of his village. The air was becoming progressively warmer, as the old man continued making his way home. Approaching the river, the aroma of fresh roasting meat carried on the breeze from the village met his nostrils. He concluded by the smell filling the air that the first spring hunt had been successful. The scent permeating the camp assured a bountiful supply of new buffalo skins, which, along with the other animal hides, provided the needed clothing for the tribe. The bones provide the materials necessary for sewing clothes and fashioning new tipis, and for repairing the existing ones.

"It is a good day to be home," he grinned.

Leading his horse closely behind him, White Wolf leisurely strolled into the center of camp. The women, turning away from their chores, and the men setting aside their labors, quietly and respectfully encircled the old man, as he made his way to his cousin's tipi. Their Holy Man, their Wicasa, was safely returned to them, and they were thankful to the Great Spirit for his arrival. In silence, the crowd multiplied until the entire village joined the procession.

It was customary for White Wolf to first greet his cousin, Running Fox, immediately upon his return. Since White Wolf and Running Fox were of the same grandfather, each was the others only adult blood-bond existing between them. The blood binding them was as strong as between any brothers, possibly even stronger. The fact that Running Fox was a war chief, who was soon to become chief of all the Lakota, added honour to this connection. The last few steps of White Wolf's journey were the physical manifestation of his love and his respect for Running Fox. Even though White Wolf was the elder of their bloodline, his cousin was his chief; therefore, this honour was due Running Fox.

Customs are the lifeblood of the people. These old traditions will serve as an example in guiding the comportment of the four young boys upon returning from their journeys. As an act of honour and respect for their tribal leaders, upon his arrival, each boy will display reverence for his leaders in the following fashion: First he acknowledges Running Fox, his chief. Next, he pays his respects to his Wicasa, the Holy One. The last member of the council visited is his shaman, the medicine man. In this case, as White Wolf is the Wicasa and the shaman, one visit accomplishes both. Finally, upon completing the telling of his tale, he is free to greet his parents and family.

Once the boys are considered sufficiently recovered from their journeys, they continue preparing for the next rite of passage into their status as warriors. First, each relates his adventures to the elders gathered around the council fire, who weigh the value of his story in terms of learning and truth. If the story is found acceptable, the council grants permission for the boy to advance to the purification phase of initiation.

The art of story telling is and always has been a crucial element in the lives of the people. From these legends, new totems are painted on

The Quest

their tipis and shields, as a visual footnote to their history. However, the verbal legacy is of the greatest importance. These tales of valour are forever told and retold in detail, eventually becoming an intricate segment of tribal history.

This first relating of White Wolf's story was to his cousin, whom he greeted with a warm, firm embrace. His greeting was returned in kind by Running Fox, as they remained silent for several heartbeats. They ended the silence by taking one step backward, before engaging in this important exchange of information. Each, in turn, listened to the other's recounting of the events transpiring since they were last together.

The old man listened attentively to Running Fox, briefly describing the tribe's homeward journey, following an early spring thaw. The chief's retelling of events did not take long. "Thanks to Wakan Tanka, our return home was without major incident," Running Fox stated. "The hunting was good. The tribe is healthy and well fed. The women have an abundance of skins, ensuring the people will be warmly clothed."

After a brief pause, the chief went on with his story. Every now and again, White Wolf politely asked a question or two, for his own clarification. But, other than an occasional inquiry, the old man stood in silence, memorizing the tale Running Fox was telling. The story was of the people safely surviving an extremely severe winter, worthy of becoming a part of their collective history.

Having finished relating his account of the tribe's return to summer camp, Running Fox motioned White Wolf to be seated next to the fire, across from him. After the men were comfortably settled into a cross-legged position, facing each other, the shaman recounted his story. "The plants were plentiful, and the harvest abundant. All went well, and the Grand Father was generous. One night he answered my prayers with a vision." Continuing, he related the story of the giant, flaming, bird of prey…an eagle surviving, unharmed by the fire consuming it. Reverently, he spoke of the injured deer. He recounted his encounter with the savages at length, going into minute detail describing lashing the bodies to their mounts before sending their corpses on a death ride into Comanche territory. Nodding his head approvingly, Running Fox listened, as White Wolf resumed relating his adventure. He told of etching the mark of the Wicasa into the savages' skin. The Chief smiled with ironic amusement, listening to the old man spinning his tale of retribution.

His story completed, White Wolf inquired of news of the boys. Unsure as to how long they had been gone, he was anxious concerning their anticipated return. The two men discussed the four boys until Running Fox inquired about the seriousness of the wounds White Wolf sustained on his journey.

"Even though the wounds are healed, I am still suffering a certain amount of stiffness and loss of strength in my hand." He assured his chief, "The weakness is not enough of a deterrent to interfere with my ability to use it. It is, however, enough of an annoyance for me to be constantly aware of it," he acknowledged to his cousin. "Due to my endless days of walking," he explained, "my leg is taking longer to heal than I originally estimated. It bothers me enormously when I am extremely tired, such as I am right now. Other than these occasions, the limp has disappeared."

For all intents and purposes, he had regained the full strength and the complete use of his leg. Pleased that his cousin was in relatively good health, Running Fox bid him farewell. White Wolf turned toward his own tipi, taking the final thirty paces leading to his own shelter, and the conclusion of his journey.

As White Wolf was unmarried, it was the duty and pleasure of a few widows to attend to his needs. Some of the women who were without a husband or an adult son to provide for their needs were selected to care for their Wicasa. The four presently serving were chosen from among the available women. They pitched his tipi,

The Quest

built his campfire and prepared his meals. In addition, like all of the women, they helped with the autumn harvest, and the buffalo hunt. In return, he shared the food given to him by members of the tribe, as well as any fresh game he shot on his own.

It is the collective responsibility of the tribe to ensure ample food for the children. After the children's needs are met, the welfare of their shaman comes next. This was the wisdom passed down from their ancestors, which influenced the customs of the tribe.

"As the shaman serves the tribe, so the tribe serves the shaman."

Thus, White Wolf was liberated from the constant need of seeking food, freeing him to address the tribe's spiritual needs. This also allowed him the time needed to train the four boys. Unencumbered with his own survival needs, as shaman, this enabled him to administer to the sick and wounded in need of his restorative herbs and prayers.

White Wolf eased himself down by the fire in front of his tipi, while two of the women tended to his horse and stored its precious cargo. The third woman brought him some freshly roasted buffalo meat. The fourth wrapped a blanket around his shoulders, sheltering him from an afternoon breeze carrying the sting of ice. Taking the plate of meat, he cut the contents into smaller pieces, more suitable for consumption.

"The taste of fresh buffalo meat…Oh! How I have missed it!" he exclaimed.

Eating slowly, savoring every morsel, he pulled the blanket tightly around his shoulders, moving a little closer to the fire. Contentedly, he sat relaxing, breathing in the comforting scents of home. Assured they had successfully seen to the old man's comfort, the helpers returned to their chores.

In a short time, requests for his intervention will be brought to his lodge by the families of those in need. In deference to the old man's age, the families always wait until White Wolf has sufficient time to eat and recuperate. Shortly after he completes his nightly prayers to the Great Spirit and sleeps for a little while, they will come seeking his knowledge and power. Of this, there is no doubt. But, for now, it is time for his body to rest, and his mind to enjoy its peacefulness.

Morning Star waited a respectable time after White Wolf left the tipi of Running Fox before running to see the parents of Flaming Sky, hopeful of hearing news of her future husband. Running Fox and Skipping Bird smiled as they watched her rushing across the camp to their lodge. She was very attractive, with a strong body and a quick mind; however, she naïve in the art of subtlety. Her eyes were asking questions long before her lips formed the words. Smiling sympathetically, Flaming Sky's parents could only shake their heads, "No."

Stunned and disappointed, she could only stand there. She was hoping for news…anything…some word of Flaming Sky. Casting her eyes downward, her heart felt like a cold rock in her chest.

"I was aware that the chance of hearing any such news would be extremely unlikely," said Morning Star respectfully, "but in spite of this, I held on to the hope of receiving some information pertaining to your son." The fact that they had to remain separated for another winter only enflamed her desire for him. She was longing to know if he felt as strongly about her as she did about him.

It was past sunrise when White Wolf returned from his healing rounds. During his absence, the spirit helpers, as he liked to call the four women, sorted and properly stored the newly collected herbs and plants in a separate tipi. It was an accommodation constructed solely for this purpose. They were most careful to ensure the freshest harvest was placed at the back of the tipi, behind the older herbs already stored there. The old man, exhausted, entered his lodge, where a small fire was removing the chill from the morning air. Politely, he refused the food offered to him by one of the women. His only desire was to sleep; but, for now, sleep would have to wait a little while

The Quest

longer. He was hearing Short Bear's name called repeatedly, as the weary boy stumbled into camp.

Stepping out of his lodge, White Wolf watched the boy presenting himself to Running Fox. The chief and the initiate talked for quite a while, with Short Bear remaining animated and excited as he relayed his tale to Running Fox, who listened intently until the boy completed his story. Smiling his approval, the chief gave him permission to leave. Wearily, the boy slowly walked across the clearing to where White Wolf stood waiting outside his tipi. After Short Bear paid his respects, the old man requested him to recount the story of his journey.

Nodding his head in acknowledgement, he began, "Lacking the talent of Flaming Sky in making bows and arrows, I had to find other ways of surviving. My main source of food was snared rabbit and speared fish, providing a majority of my meals, along with tender willow buds and bird eggs," he said proudly to his teacher. "In my travels, I met a band of Sioux, who were heading to rejoin their tribe at summer camp. Knowing I was doing survival training, they offered me nothing that made my test any easier. The only thing they gave me was friendship, words of encouragement and a temporary place by one of their fires."

The proud boy standing in front of White Wolf was physically drained by the time he finished recounting the entire story. Short Bear had done well, and was pleased with White Wolf's approval. Puffing up his chest, the boy grinned broadly. It was the first time the old man recalled seeing this degree of pride or confidence coming from Short Bear.

"You have done well, Short Bear," reassured White Wolf. "You are free to go to the lodge of your parents and greet your family."

The shaman watched Short Bear enthusiastically repeating his story to his eager parents. The boy was even more excited than when he recounted his adventures to either White Wolf or Running Fox. Short Bear was always intimidated by the majesty of the two cousins.

However, he was not the only member of the tribe who felt that way. These men were great leaders among his people, whose presence demanded respect, while simultaneously conjuring up a certain amount of fear among the younger braves and maidens.

Running Fox was a great chief. Everyone was cognizant of this fact, and when the time comes, the council will choose him to replace the old chief of chiefs. White Wolf was not solely a shaman; it was obvious he was blessed by the Great Spirit, and was truly a Holy Man, a Wicasa. There was a dominating force and an air of confidence radiating from the two leaders. Despite their different energies, each in his own right commanded the esteem and admiration of the people.

White Wolf watched approvingly as Short Bear concluded telling his tale to his family. Smiling broadly, the old man turned, disappearing into his own lodge, aware of the tension in his neck and shoulders. The muscles were drawn as tightly as a bowstring, and he was feeling the aching heaviness of his legs. The burden of the spiritual well being of the tribe was weighing heavily upon him. His body depleted, the old man desperately needed rest.

Spreading a buffalo robe on the floor and reaching for a second robe, he covered himself and stretched out lazily in front of the friendly fire. Closing his eyes gently, his breathing quickly became deep, calm and regular. His strength spent, the old man drifted into a silent sleep. It was the most peaceful rest he experienced since first leaving the tribe, many moons ago. He intended to sleep until his tired body regained its strength and his mind recaptured its clarity. Sleeping straight through the remainder of the day and the entire night, he did not awaken until the following dawn.

The next few days passed monotonously for the old man. White Wolf went about his daily caring for the sick and injured. Luckily, a majority of the ailments were minor in nature or, at least, easily diagnosed and treated by him. He set a few bones, while attending to

The Quest

an inevitable variety of cuts and bruises. There were scraped elbows, dislocated fingers and, of course, an assortment of fevers requiring his healing touch. Except for Thunder Eyes, the spirit of the people was healthy and, therefore, not in immediate need of his intervention. Dispensing the herbs, he went about healing his people as he had been trained to do, so many countless winters ago. At night, he recited his prayers and sang the chants.

The fact that he was not only the shaman, but also a chosen Holy Man, may have contributed to his patients tending to heal more quickly than normally anticipated. It was highly probable that a good deal of the magic of White Wolf's medicine lay in his calm demeanor and easy, confident manner. The old man was extremely pleased, having only non-fatal wounds and minor illnesses to treat. It meant his people were not only spiritually strong, but physically healthy as well. Due to the relatively light demands made upon his attention, he possessed the time necessary for properly processing the fresh herbs and plants recently gathered. It also granted him the opportunity to recuperate from his latest journey.

White Wolf's spirit helpers were responsible for the initial drying and storage of newly harvested herbs and plants. Completely trusted by him, they were also involved with the processing of the dried plants, but only up to a certain point in their preparation. Only White Wolf, himself, could complete the final steps necessary before storing the herbs for future use. He alone knew the correct prayers to say and which songs to chant to release their true healing powers. These sacred elements must be introduced at precisely the right moment of the curing process, infusing them with the sacred words of the Grand Father, increasing their potency and their purity. The four women alternately worked with the old man, allowing each of them to possess knowledge of the healing properties of specific plants, herbs, and roots.

Charles Richard Latona

He depended upon the spirit helpers to administer to the physical illnesses of his people whenever he was absent from camp. It was their honour and shared responsibility to assist White Wolf in attending to the welfare of the tribe. They served as midwives, ushering new life into the world. It was they who guided the young women through their pregnancies, teaching the expectant mothers to understand the mystery of a woman's body, preparing them for the birth of their children. At least one of the four was always present when a young woman was giving birth. It was the duty of these women to ensure a safe, healthy delivery for the mother and the newborn. These spirit helpers were truly loved and respected by the people.

The stability of repetitiveness and the boredom of the slow passage of time was finally interrupted. The incident occurred early in the afternoon of the third day after White Wolf's return to camp. He was inside his tipi, chanting, while grinding roots and herbs, when he was suddenly distracted by the sound of excited voices shouting, hands clapping, and the shrill, piercing whistles filling the air. "Another one of the boys has returned home!" he exclaimed to the spirit helpers.

From the intensity level of the crowd, White Wolf was positive that it was either Standing Elk or Flaming Sky. Ceasing his chanting, the old man placed the herbs and roots aside. Stepping outside of his lodge, he clearly observed Standing Elk walking across the campsite toward Running Fox's tipi. The large group gathered around was accompanying him to his chief, who stood silently, awaiting the approaching boy.

White Wolf watched the animated boy reporting his adventures to his chief with great enthusiasm. Running Fox, listening intently, occasionally smiled broadly, while nodding his head in agreement. The old man could tell by observing them that Running Fox was extremely proud of the boy, and was obviously favorably impressed by the tale the young initiate was relating.

The Quest

Finishing his story, Standing Elk was granted permission by Running Fox to relate his adventures to White Wolf. The boy raced the short distance to where the old man was waiting for him. After properly greeting his Wicasa, he was invited to sit with White Wolf and describe his journey. The boy's tale was destined to be told and retold around the campfires for generations to come, a living record added to the peoples' oral history.

The boy's story, as he related it, started a few days before his tribe's return to summer camp. "I was away from the village for six risings of the moon before becoming comfortable with being completely alone. It took this long for me to adjust to the absence of human voices. During the first few days, I continuously spoke out loud, especially during the long dark nights," related Standing Elk, who clearly enjoyed talking, as evidenced by his ease and pleasure in relating his story. "After a while, I stopped talking altogether, becoming comfortable with the constant silence," he continued.

"At first, I struggled, trying to keep my attention on establishing the needed new markers along the trail, which would guide me home on the return trip." He went on to explain that, with the passage of time, he eventually learned to deal successfully with his fears and solitude, allowing him to diligently refocus his attention on the tasks at hand.

His self-discipline, along with the regaining of his skills, were accomplished none too soon. "To my surprise, sitting directly in my path, blocking the trail like a huge dark boulder, was a fully-grown black bear. It was gigantic!" exclaimed the boy. "The bear sat there, leisurely nibbling on wild berries, completely unaware of me. I, however, very much aware of the bear, came to an abrupt stop." Acting out his story, he stared wide-eyed, as if in a state of shock.

"The bear remained sitting there, peacefully, until it noticed something different in its environment. Cocking its head to the left, the bear let out a terrifying, rumbling growl, sounding like the sky was shattering all around me," shuddered Standing Elk. "Rocking itself back and forth, ending up on all four paws, the bear slowly lumbered in my direction. The bear, persistently sniffing the air, was snarling and roaring angrily as it advanced toward me. Even at this distance, I was able to smell the stench of death on its breath." Hesitating for a few calming breaths, he continued his story. "Stopping, the bear reared back on its hind legs, growling and slashing the air with its deadly claws."

The boy had always been instructed not to run away, as this act was an invitation for the bear to attack. He remembered hearing these instructions reverberating in his mind, having heard them repeatedly: *"The best way to defeat a bear is to play dead. Let the bear smell you. If you are able to control your fear, the bear will pass you by, unharmed."*

But Standing Elk was born to be a warrior, and as all warriors instinctively know, *"When one is under attack, the best defense is the counter-attack. Use the weapons of surprise and speed. Confound your enemy. Confuse and distract him. Do the unexpected: attack."* And attack he did.

Waving his arms wildly in the air, Standing Elk told White Wolf, "I yelled my most aggressive war whoop, while jumping up and down and shouting as loudly as I could. Lowering my head, I charged straight at the bear. The creature was completely taken aback by my tactic, unable to comprehend what was happening. Surprised and confused, the animal reacted by growling even more vigorously. Running as fast as my feet could carry me, I went speeding directly toward my predator."

Standing Elk explained, "Just as it appeared that I was about to make contact with the beast, I veered off to its left side. Ducking underneath its dangerous claws, I thrust my elbow into the bear's kidney, as I went darting past the irate animal. The beast let out a howl of pain. Stretching its neck around, it searched frantically, looking for its elusive quarry…me! For an instant, I was safely behind the bear, temporarily out of its visual range."

The Quest

Standing Elk went on to describe how he quickly surveyed the area before he headed at top speed toward a grove of intermeshed oak trees. He remembered being advised: *"Never climb a tree. The bear will follow you up the tree and trap you."* In his clearly focused plan, this was exactly what he was hoping the befuddled animal would do.

"Before I reached the grove, the bear, having turned, spotted me running and swiftly gave chase. Grabbing a low growing branch," he continued, "I pulled myself up into the tree, climbing as quickly as I could. By the time I was halfway up the tree, the angry bear was clawing its way up the trunk, snarling and snapping right behind me.

"Having climbed many trees in my life, I was certain that, once I climbed high enough, the small branches would support my weight, but not the weight of a fully-grown black bear. Approaching the top of the tree, I worked my way farther out onto the thinning branches, with the bear closing in behind me. Coming to a place where the boughs of two trees were intermeshed, I reached across to the branches of the neighboring tree and transferred to it.

"In the meantime, about four paces below me, the bear was scaling the trunk of the first tree. Digging deeply into the tree with its rear claws while extending its body upward, it implanted its front claws ever higher up the trunk of the tree. Pulling itself up, while clawing into the tree, it continued ascending in vengeful pursuit.

"By the time the bear reached the same height as I was, the branches were becoming much too thin and weak to support the bulky animal. The bear gingerly tested a limb, pulling back as the branch began giving way under its weight. The infuriated animal was savagely clawing at me but, by this time, I had made it safely into the neighboring oak."

Continuing to excitedly relate his plan and execution of it to White Wolf, Standing Elk explained how he carefully worked his way around to the back of the second tree, constantly attempting to keep himself hidden from the bear's view. He remained out of sight of the bear for a time. However, fearing the beast may have lost interest in its next meal, the boy again exposed himself to the roaring animal.

"I riled the bear even further by shouting at it, while pelting it with acorns. Then I retreated and waited. When it seemed the bear was again losing interest in the game, I jumped up and regained the animal's attention by showering it with a fresh supply of acorns," he grinned.

"When the bear finally became completely enraged and totally out of control," continued Standing Elk, "I made my escape, leaving the animal pawing angrily at a prey that was no longer within its grasp." He told White Wolf, "I very carefully climbed down the back side of the tree, steadily making my way toward the ground. Eventually reaching the bottom-most branch, I laid down on it and, wrapping my arms around the branch, I slid out of the tree, dropping safely onto the ground. Looking up, I could see the frustrated animal still roaring and tearing frantically at the leaves of the trees.

"Once solidly on the ground," he said, "using the other trees as shelter from the animal's view, I ran immediately into the thickest part of the grove, leaving behind one very hungry and very hostile bear. Not seeing any signs of his prey… me," he said, pointing at his chest, "the bear was ultimately left with only one decision, which was to scoot down the tree without its dinner."

By the time Standing Elk reached this part of his story, White Wolf could no longer hold back his laughter. He smiled a broad, warm smile of approval, which crinkled the lines around his eyes. Once the old man regained his control, they resumed discussing the rest of Standing Elk's experiences which, compared to the bear story, were quite mundane.

Standing Elk continued his quest without further incident. Like Short Bear, he too came across a friendly hunting party, "but I did not spend much time with them. Although I could not accept food or weapons from them, I was overjoyed at seeing people, and hearing the sound of human voices. I was content with the comfort of their

The Quest

company, and the warmth of their fire for one night, and I did not break any of the rules of initiation. I ate my own food and drank from a cold, running spring flowing near the campsite."

He told the Dakota warriors of his adventures and they, in turn, shared some of their own stories. All in all, it was a very pleasant interlude for Standing Elk. "The next day," he said, "I resumed my journey as I started it…by myself…alone." However, his enthusiasm had returned, and his spirit was rekindled. He felt renewed.

Things had gone well, except for one minor mishap overtaking him a few days later, occurring when he was crossing a small, swiftflowing river. The force of the water caused him to slip a little and lose his footing. He was not injured. The only negative result for the boy was an icy bath. Having completed his story, and receiving White Wolf's permission, he departed, proceeding directly to the lodge of his parents for the last time.

From this time forward, until they each took a wife, he and the other three boys would sleep in the lodge of the unwed warriors. Only after finishing the entire initiation was a young brave allowed to take a mate. A maiden could be promised to a young man, but he could only bond with her after passing his final test of manhood… and then, only if he was capable of paying the father's asking price for his daughter.

The value of a maiden's hand was determined by her parents. The amount was calculated in part by the importance of her father within the hierarchy of the leadership, and the overall status of her family. Other factors considered included her skillfulness in the domestic arts, her physical attributes and, most importantly, her childbearing potential. Although Standing Elk was not yet promised to anyone, he, like all of the boys, was looking forward to the day when he would take on the ultimate responsibility of a warrior, with a wife and a family to provide for and protect.

After Standing Elk left, the old man smiled approvingly at the young brave's ability as a story teller, as well as his capacity for quick thinking. The tale of his adventure would surely become a favorite of the tribe. White Wolf then returned to his ritualistic chores of preparing the healing plants awaiting him within his lodge. The work, with the help of the four women, was progressing very efficiently.

While laboring, he wondered how Lone Feather and Flaming Sky were faring on their journeys. He was most concerned about Flaming Sky, who chose to travel deep into the southern prairies. It was the most dangerous of the four routes taken by the boys. White Wolf was proud of his cousin's son's decision to do so. Nonetheless, his confidence in the boy was not quite strong enough for him to completely release his concerns. He was confident that Lone Feather would be safe, barring any unforeseen accidents. The boy was brave, and had already demonstrated strong survival skills during his earlier training.

"No. The two remaining boys will be fine," he thought. White Wolf was aware, deep within his soul, that no harm would befall them. The old shaman did not have to wait very long before receiving his first confirmation of their safe return. Shortly before dark, he heard the crowd gathering as Lone Feather came dragging his very tired, slightly bruised and scraped body into camp.

By the time he made his way to the lodge of Running Fox, Lone Feather was exhausted, and on the verge of collapse. Due to the boy's weakened physical condition, Running Fox chose to sit, inviting Lone Feather to do the same. There was no shame in accepting the courtesy of his chief. The boy's story did not take long for him to tell.

Like the other two boys before him, it had taken several days to become comfortable with complete silence and aloneness. "I found a plentiful supply of roots and plants, which sustained me early in my quest," he said proudly to his chief. "A day or two later, I completed making some weapons. Using the bow and arrows, I was able to bring down a small deer. I used the cured deerskin for warmth at night, and smoked a majority of the meat to preserve it for the rest of my trek, supplementing my diet with an occasional catch of fresh fish."

The Quest

All in all, everything had gone well with him…that is, until two days before returning to the village. Lone Feather was climbing a steep hill, attempting to get his bearings for the last stretch of his homeward journey. He was scrambling through some loose shale when it happened.

"Just as I was about to reach the top of the hill, a large bird came swooping down, seemingly out of nowhere, heading directly toward me." He told of how the bird's attack startled him, and he flung his arms wildly at his assailant. "Unfortunately, in so doing, I lost my balance when the shale gave way." Moccasins over headband, he went tumbling down the hill, coming to rest on a large flat ledge, about ten paces below the ridge. Other than a few scrapes and bruises, added to some very achy muscles, he sustained no serious injuries.

"Looking around for my attacker, I spotted it in time to see it diving directly at my head. I dashed for the protection of the ledge just before the bird of prey completed its second pass at me. Catching an updraft, the eagle held a stationary position in the air current, directly overhead, watching me.

"Slipping the notch of an arrow into my bowstring, I took aim, as the bird prepared its next assault. Just as I was about to let loose the arrow, the eagle quickly changed direction. Down it sped, diving straight out of the white-hot sun,. The light temporarily blinded me, causing the arrow to go sailing well off its mark," Lone Feather related painfully. "The last thing I saw was the bird of prey winging its way into the sun, beyond the mountain peaks. I watched the eagle being consumed by the flames of the sun, only for it to come out the other side unscathed," he said solemnly, with a concerned look of confusion on his young face.

Lone Feather explained that he gathered himself up, and returned to his task of scaling the hill. He worked his way carefully through the shifting shale, until he reached the summit. From this vantage point he saw familiar signs, confirming he was nearing the village. He rested for a little while, checking his minor wounds. When he finished attending to his injuries, he continued onward toward his destination. He completed the final stretch in only two full suns.

Upon finishing his story, Lone Feather was graciously dismissed by Running Fox. The boy proceeded directly to the lodge of White Wolf. Immediately, the old man sat the boy down, gently cleaning his cuts and bruises, while encouraging him to repeat the story to his Wicasa.

The Great Spirit had been kind to the boy. He was free of any major injuries or broken bones. Slowly sipping the potion given to him by White Wolf, Lone Feather proceeded to recount the story of his journey. While the boy was telling his tale, White Wolf soothed the boy's larger cuts and scrapes with his herbal preparations. Once treated, he wrapped the wounds in clean bandages. White Wolf was justly proud of the boy. He had done well. Lone Feather was very tired but, despite his fatigue, he went to pay his respects to his parents. From there, he joined his brother, Standing Elk, and Short Bear in the lodge of eligible young men.

Several more nights came and went without any word from or about Flaming Sky. The chief and the shaman shared their mutual fears concerning the boy's safety. However, they kept these concerns among themselves, speaking only words of encouragement and comfort around Morning Star, who grew increasingly anxious with each passing day. The two men spoke to her of their faith in Flaming Sky's ability to return home safely and unharmed.

Her mother, Snow Bird, and Skipping Bird encouraged Morning Star to resume the preparations for her official betrothal, and the wedding that would eventually follow. There were skins to clean and sew into the coverings for the new tipi she would share with Flaming Sky. She had ceremonial clothes needing to be fashioned, including her own marriage dress and Flaming Sky's wedding shirt. A great many tasks remained to be completed, but these chores only acted as temporary distractions, failing to hold her full attention for

The Quest

very long. And so she, White Wolf, Running Fox, and Skipping Bird waited, praying for the safe return of Flaming Sky.

A few days later their prayers were answered. Just as the sun was warming the morning air, an outburst resounded throughout the village. In addition to the usual whistles and shouts, the sounds of war whoops were echoing throughout the camp. White Wolf knew this much clatter could only mean one thing: the people were hailing Flaming Sky's return.

"But why the war whoops?" he wondered.

Determined to satisfy his curiosity, he went rushing out of his tipi to witness the boy's return to his people. White Wolf, expecting to find another very tired, very hungry, young man, was astonished with what he saw. In the midst of the crowd was a well-fed, well-rested, proud boy sitting astride a Pawnee pony. Standing next to them was a very happy Morning Star, smiling up at the young man who was to become her husband. Reaching up to him, she held his hand as they waited for his father, the chief, to make his appearance.

Running Fox was as shocked as White Wolf at what he saw. Although he was very pleased, he was also stunned by the sight in front of him. In addition to his amazement at his son's appearance, Running Fox was overwhelmed with a sense of joy and pride. His son returned home safely, completely uninjured and mounted upon a liberated Pawnee pony, no simple feat, by any means. Even more astonishing was the fact that there was a scalp hanging from his waistband.

Releasing Morning Star's hand, Flaming Sky dismounted his horse. The father and son embraced each other in a warm greeting. Skipping Bird, who was near tears, stepped up to welcome her son home with a firm, loving hug. It took a long while for the excited villagers to calm themselves. Running Fox and Flaming Sky entered the tipi, and, when the camp finally grew quiet, Flaming Sky related his story to his chief. The telling of his experiences took a great deal of time. After receiving his father's approval, Flaming Sky proceeded to the lodge of his Wicasa.

The Holy Man listened intently to Flaming Sky recounting his adventures. White Wolf was especially curious and deeply concerned over the presence of the scalp. He knew many of the savage, southern tribes engaged in this vicious practice but, until now, he had never seen the proof of it. Finishing the story, Flaming Sky presented the scalp to White Wolf, knowing the shaman would give it a proper burial in the sky, thus allowing it to be reclaimed by its former owner. This ritual will bring peace to the dead warrior to whom the scalp belonged.

Upon completing his story, the boy and the man exchanged embraces before Flaming Sky left the presence of his Wicasa to call upon Morning Star and her parents. Later, he would join his three friends in the lodge of the unmarried men.

BOOK II THE PATH

Chapter 1

THE FOX AND THE WOLF

There was nothing exceptional about the boy himself. Nor was there anything unique about any of the children who made their way into the world that night. No, but the night itself was extremely rare and special. It was the time of the Grand Father's Tears. It was a nocturnal event so unique that only the most ancient of the living members of the tribe had ever experienced one like it in the dawn of their early youth.

Although White Wolf was unaware, this extraordinary evening was to see the birth of the warrior destined to walk the path of the shaman. At first, he will walk in White Wolf's footsteps. In time, the boy will walk beside the man. In the end, he will walk alone, replacing his master as the tribe's medicine man. This was the promise of the Grand Father, another one of His generous gifts to His people.

Names have a meaning within each tribe's history and folklore. Special events, omens, and spirit animals are among the most common and useful sources of names for the newborn. This night, many parents would name their children in remembrance of this brilliant display of falling fire. Tonight the big sky was to be filled with flaming lights from an endless meteor shower. The following dawn would usher forth a vast bouquet of new names, like Fire Tears, Rain of Tears and Heavenly Fire, for the infant maidens. The braves would bear names such as Sky Fire, Fire Rain and Fire Eyes. But the one destined by the Great Spirit to replace White Wolf, was to be called Flaming Eagle.

Names are power and, as such, must be chosen with great care and wisdom. Everything in nature is a potential guide, teacher or inspiration; therefore, the earth and its creatures have always remained a valuable source of namesakes. Time passes. New events occur, thus altering the destination of the traveler.

Circumstances impact individuals, transforming their experiences. As the growing being flourishes within the constantly changing environment, the person's name is often modified, usually by the shaman, reflecting this important growth. So it was with White Wolf.

The story of his renaming came about because of an event which occurred in the early days of the long sun, shortly before White Wolf was to see his fifth winter. *The warm, still air hung heavily over the valley, as twilight was quietly spreading throughout the peaceful village. The entire landscape was speckled with lights from hundreds of campfires burning in front of the tipis. In the darkening sky, the first of the brightest stars were making their appearances. A full moon, looking like a small orange sun, was ascending into the eastern sky. Fading beyond the mountains, the sun coloured the sky and the earth with an eerie, reddish-brown cast. All of the signs were present. This night was exceptional; even the sunset possessed a magical feel. This was a night of strong medicine.*

Adding to the dream-like quality of the scene were the mournful sounds of two wolves, at opposite ends of the campsite, calling to each other. Their long howls and short yips echoed, resounding clearly throughout camp. It was one of those extraordinary nights foretelling rare occurrences. White Wolf, the boy, was sitting in front of his family's lodge, tending the

The Quest

fire while his parents went about their evening tasks. He was unaware of the animal approaching him cautiously through the darkness. She remained motionless, hiding in the shadows, carefully observing every movement the boy was making. Her eyes glowed like two large sapphires in the reflecting light of the fire. Uttering a soft whimpering sound, she hesitantly began making her way in the direction of the young boy. Her white fur glistened in the soft firelight as, slowly, she came limping out of the black night. Carefully edging her way toward the light, she timidly crept closer, cautiously keeping her eyes on the boy. The skin on her left front leg was torn and bleeding.

Sensing her presence, the boy turned away from the fire, directing his attention on her. She stopped. She did not retreat, but was no longer advancing. The she-wolf was staring into the eyes of the boy who, in turn, was gazing back into hers. They remained transfixed, looking into the core of each others being. At last, the wolf slowly advanced toward the boy, who was now standing, stretching his opened hands out to her. Accepting his invitation, she guardedly resumed edging her way closer to him.

Instinctively, she sensed he was trustworthy. Lying down on her stomach in front of him, she fearlessly waited. The young boy moved to her and, sitting down next to her, he reached out, gently stroking her fur, while reminding her how pretty she was. By the time the boy was ready to examine her leg, she was comfortable enough with their friendship to allow him to do so. Slowly reaching toward her, taking her left front leg, he held it gently in his hands. He sat motionless, talking to her in a soft, soothing tone of voice. Renewing her approach, she crept forward, a little at a time, until she was close enough to rest her head on his lap. There she lay, obviously feeling safe in the boy's company.

Unwrapping one of his wristbands and pouring some water on it, the boy used the wet cloth to gently clean her wound. She whimpered some, but did not withdraw, thereby allowing him to complete the job. When he finished washing out the dirt, he searched for something to apply to the gash. Only a short time earlier, he watched the medicine man applying an herb to a warrior's cut arm. His sight came to rest on the wood he was using to fuel the flames.

"That is it," he thought. "The green growth on the wood…this is what the shaman used."

While holding the she-wolf's paw with one hand, using his free hand, he crumpled a small handful of the moss.

"It is alright." he spoke softly. "We are safe with each other."

Gently, he placed the pieces of moss on her wound. Rinsing off the cleansing cloth, he carefully wrapped it around the moss, fastening the bandage securely to her front leg. When the boy finished, he returned to gently stroking her head and scratching her behind the ears. There she lay, contentedly wagging her tail.

How long the two of them remained sitting together, no one really knows. Nor is it possible to guess how much longer they might have remained that way, had they not been interrupted by the young boy's mother. The she-wolf, startled by the woman's emergence from the tipi, jumped up and, with a very slight limp, scurried back into the protective blackness of the night. Dumbfounded, the woman watched the wolf quickly retreating from the exposure of the campfire.

Once the wolf was safely out of firelight range, she slowly came to a stop. There she stood in the darkness, looking back at the boy. Although the boy could not see her, he sensed her presence close at hand. Eventually turning, she made her way back to her lair. The boy heard the soft padding of her paws on the loose gravel along the riverbank, listening until the quiet sound no longer echoed in the night air.

The story is, from that day forward, the she-wolf constantly watched over the boy, who was thereafter known as White Wolf. No matter where he went, she was always close by, acting as his personal guardian. Others only caught occasional, fleeting glimpses of her in the distance, or perhaps the flash of a shadowy, white streak running through the trees. It is said she used to take the boy to her lair where she kept her litter, allowing him to play with her pups. No one really knows exactly when she died, or if she

THE QUEST

was actually dead. Shortly after White Wolf completed his initiation into manhood, she simply disappeared and was never again seen by anyone.

The telling of the tale of White Wolf's renaming always ended with the fact that he forever remained a brother to her children. It was rumored he possessed the ability to communicate with the children of the night. This was the first tale of White Wolf to become a part of his people's history. It was the first story of his exploits, but it was, most certainly, not the last one.

Skipping Bird and Running Fox waited a long time for her to become fruitful, and to bear them a son. She knew immediately when she conceived. It was during the time of the falling leaves, with the first icy gust of wind blowing from the white mountains of the far north. The reddish-orange moon appeared much larger and brighter than usual, marking the season when the tribe put the finishing touches on their preparations for their annual journey to winter camp.

The hunt had been good, and the harvest plentiful. An aroma of fresh, roasting meat filtered through the chilled autumn air. They were blessed with an abundance of new skins for the making of clothing and boots. There was more than an adequate supply of rawhide and bones from which to fashion their tools and weapons. They possessed a plentiful supply of bear grease, used to protect their bodies from the harsh winter elements. In addition to the generous supply of eagle feathers collected, there was a large assortment of animal teeth, claws, and horns from which to make their ceremonial decorations. The Grand Father had truly smiled upon His people. For Skipping Bird and Running Fox, it was a time of special blessings. It truly was a time for rejoicing and gratitude.

The journey to winter quarters took half a moon cycle to complete. There was nowhere they could go to escape the constantly falling snow. However, with good shelter, they were able to avoid the bitter northern winds raging wildly across the plains, like a starving wolfpack on the hunt.

Skipping Bird was a big, rawboned woman, with high, strong cheekbones, and was spotted with more freckles on her round face than usually found among her people. She possessed full lips, and glistening dark hair that flowed all the way down to her firm buttocks. Her ample breasts were firm. However, her most appealing features were her easy, warm smile and her soft, throaty laugh. She was plain, yet she was very loving and caring. Her dark eyes were two black spheres, challenging the universe. Along with all of her other treasures, Skipping Bird possessed the secret knowledge of the healing properties of plants and herbs. She was taught to understand the secret mysteries by her mother's mother, before the old woman passed over to the spirit land.

Her husband, Running Fox, was given his name when approaching the sixth winter after his birth. Even as a very young boy, he took great pleasure in running and playing with the small animals of the forest. He especially enjoyed the company of the baby foxes. Over many passings of the seasons, they had slowly grown to trust each other. As he grew older, he roamed the woods and valleys as one of them, learning their ways and, in time, coming to understand their spirit wisdom. The fox became his medicine animal, his spirit guide, and his helper. It was this relationship with his forest brothers that earned him his name, Running Fox. Even now, in a foot race, he was one of the fastest warriors in the entire tribe if not, indeed, the fastest.

Running Fox was of average height for his people, but he was as solid as a tree trunk. He possessed a round, barrel-like chest with a long body and short, strong, muscular legs. His jaw was rather square, and his long, black hair hung down to the middle of his broad shoulders. Normally, he wore his hair pulled back, bound on either side with strips of snakeskin to keep it from flying wildly in the constantly blowing prairie winds. At a young age, he earned the right to be appointed as a war chief.

THE QUEST

This coming winter would be the second one that Running Fox and Skipping Bird shared the same tipi, as they were married a full changing of the seasons before the tribe moved from summer quarters. Although their first winter was a rapturous time for them, this one held the promise of being even more joyful. They possessed soft buffalo skins in which to wrap themselves for a comfortable, warm sleep. Ahead lay the long grey days, with nothing to do except enjoy each other. They were young, healthy and expecting their first child…indeed, they were truly blessed.

The previous winter had moved all too swiftly for their pleasure, and much too slowly for their patience. In addition to enjoying the long, cold nights together, they discovered pleasant diversions in their daily activities. When the weather was fair, Running Fox and the other braves went hunting and fishing. Skipping Bird and her companions gathered wood for the fires, and dug up edible roots for food. When not otherwise engaged, the people enjoyed sitting outside by the small fires, talking together. The men smoked their pipes and told stories of great deeds, whose greatness grew greater with each retelling. The women attended to the mending and making of new clothes, while gossiping among themselves. The less true the gossip was, the more intriguing the topics became. At the end of their day's activities, Running Fox and Skipping Bird retreated to the peacefulness of their own private world, remaining warm, safe, and tranquil.

During the long, snowy days and icy, cold nights, they remained within their shelter. Running Fox and Skipping Bird took turns rubbing each other's naked bodies with warm liquefied bear grease to protect them from the harsh weather. They warmed the grease in a wooden bowl which they always kept near the small fire. In a slow, deliberate motion, they each smoothly rubbed the melted grease lightly onto the other's skin. The thin coating of liquid absorbed into their flesh, leaving a warm reflecting surface on their skin, which shone like a shiny, wet beaver. With their bodies lightly coated with bear grease and wrapped in buffalo robes, they sat serenely and contentedly by the small, warm fire. Talking and dreaming, making love and sleeping, they enjoyed the pleasant, long nights of winter, grateful for the time they were given. Come summer, their lives would be forever altered.

The first signs of spring were appearing through the slow, ebbing clutches of winter, and the snow was falling less often. When it did fall, it was usually much lighter. Days remained frigid, although, occasionally, the sun made its presence known. A little at a time, the skies became more blue, and free of the drab gray. As the days grew warmer, the tribe returned to a more socially active life.

By the time the grass was growing and radiating a brilliant green, and the streams started rippling through the blue ice, signs of new life were showing everywhere. This, of course, included the stomach of Skipping Bird, who was a full six moons into her pregnancy. She was due to deliver in mid-summer, during the time of the ripening cherries …and so she would, on the night of the raining fires.

The legend says, *"On this night, the Great Spirit weeps for the misdeeds of his children. His tears streak through the dark sky, like a never-ending shower of sparks from the great campfire in the Spirit World,"* a world that remains invisible to the people. Their shaman,

White Wolf, made them aware of the approach of this special night before embarking upon his long, dangerous journey into the southern deserts.

Since White Wolf and Running Fox were of the same grandfather, it was only natural the older man once more entrusted the ceremonial pipe for safekeeping into the hands of his cousin, Running Fox. Although his annual journeys were often quite long, White Wolf promised Running Fox and Skipping Bird he would complete his harvest and rejoin them in the Sacred Hills in time for the birth of their son.

The Quest

Before White Wolf left on his southward journey, he and Running Fox found an opportunity to go on a small hunt together. It was too early in the spring for them to find any large game; however, a few winter rabbits are always an appreciated source of fresh meat. So it was the cousins went hunting together this day, returning in the late afternoon with four freshly killed rabbits. That night, the three of them feasted on the meal prepared by Skipping Bird. They talked. They smoked the pipe. They slept. In the morning, they prepared for the separate journeys laying ahead of them.

Although their paths were destined to remain different, their purpose was always the same: *to serve the people.* Each of them, following his own path, had faithfully done so, and they would continue to do so throughout their lives. Running Fox was to return to summer camp in the land of his ancestors. Here he would hunt with the other braves and replenish the tribe's food supply. White Wolf, on the other hand, would make the dangerous trip into the southern deserts to gather the needed roots and cacti native only to that area.

White Wolf made this particular trip once every three or four springs, as it was a dangerous undertaking. It was imperative he retrieve the maximum cargo one horse was capable of carrying on it's back. Whenever a man, even a Holy Man, ventured into the land of the savages, the risk of death was naturally accepted as part of the decision. The fewer the trips, the longer the life expectancy.

White Wolf rode his horse southward, staying close to the protection of the mountains. Once arriving at the great valley nestled between the mountains, he headed southwest toward the land where the Great Spirit speaks with a hot breath, and shearing winds constantly purify the precious plants he intended to harvest. Reaching the desert was easy compared to the return journey, when the horse is over-laden with cargo and unable to support the extra weight of a rider. Leading the pony on foot the entire trip home always increased the risks involved, but it was White Wolf's choice to accept them. For him, it was much easier for one man to control one horse than for the same man to try to control two horses. No. He would make the long journey home on foot, as he had always done. Even under these conditions, he had more than enough time to complete his task and successfully return before his cousin's son was due to arrive.

Running Fox and Skipping Bird enjoyed a much shorter and safer journey to summer camp. Along with the rest of the tribe, they traveled at a steady, unhurried pace, thus allowing the men to hunt, and giving the women the time they needed to maintain a camp and attend to the needs of the children. As the nights remained cold and the days short; there was no need for them to hurry. Included in the migration were newborns, and many women, like Skipping Bird, who were awaiting the birth of a child. The people were in good spirits as they began their pilgrimage back to the Black Hills and the endless sky of home.

Later, after settling into their campsite, Running Fox and Skipping Bird had plenty of time to prepare for the arrival of their son. All things, including the birth of a child, come about as scheduled. Time would pass, and the day would come…of this they were certain. Occasionally they grew impatient, as most young couples do when expecting their first child. Now and then they wondered whether or not White Wolf would actually return on time. Always, before, he kept his word, and there was no reason to doubt him on this occasion.

The son born to Skipping Bird and Running Fox that night was marked for greatness. White Wolf knew this to be pre-destined, but not even he was aware of the child's true path. The boy's inheritance included the compassion and love of his mother and the bravery and skill of his father flowed within him, just as surely as the flame of the spiritual truth of White Wolf was reflected and amplified within this boy. He was named Flaming Sky by his father's cousin.

Chapter 2

THE SNAKE AND THE POSSUM

Flaming Sky came to an abrupt halt, frozen by the sound of danger hanging in the breathless air. Listening, he heard the repeated rattling. Turning his head very slightly to his left while maintaining his statuesque body stance, he spotted the serpent coiled approximately three paces away. He saw the deadly, poised diamondback. The snake's head was moving, first back and forth, and then from side to side. The tongue was unceasingly lashing the static air in front of it, as the lidless, yellow eyes remained focused on the motionless boy. Judging from the length of its rattle, the snake was obviously an extremely old and wily adversary.

Almost unnoticeably, Flaming Sky moved steadily backward to a safer distance from his enemy. Thoroughly surveying the immediate area, he located a stick that served his purpose. Safely out of the rattler's striking range, he calmly made his way over to the twopronged branch. Picking it up, he broke off the prongs to a length of approximately three-fingers each. Thus armed, he turned, facing his unblinking challenger.

The boy was stalking the predator, which had now become the prey. Carefully, slowly and deliberately, he circled his cunning foe, the snake's hissing and rattling increasing in direct proportion to Flaming Sky's menacing approach. Stopping short of two paces from the serpent, the boy extended the pronged branch toward his adversary. Rattling furiously, the snake feigned a strike. Recoiling quickly, it then lunged directly at the boy, who instinctively jumped backward, even though he was safely out of range.

Stopping for a moment, Flaming Sky took a deep breath, holding it before blowing it out through his mouth. He inhaled again, this time taking a slow, deep breath through his nose, releasing his breath lightly, as he straightened up to his full height. Extending the branch toward the snake, he started poking at it. Taking one or two small steps forward, ceaselessly jabbing at the snake, he attempted to pin it's head to the ground with the prongs. It was a strange and dangerous dance they were dancing, with each one bobbing, weaving, striking and withdrawing…and then striking again.

The serpent's strike was a flash of lightning. The boy's response was somewhat slower, but the outcome of this deadly game was to be based upon something more important than speed. The boy had seen eagles catching snakes from the back side, grabbing the vipers with their claws just below their triangular shaped heads. Ensnared by the bird's talons, the snake would be rendered totally helpless and completely incapable of protecting itself. Flaming Sky realized that, if he was going to be able to successfully maneuver the snake into a vulnerable position, he must first find some way to safely distract it.

Backing away from the engagement momentarily, Flaming Sky visually searched for something…anything that might prove helpful to him in confusing the viper's senses. Quickly, but carefully, surveying the area, he didn't see anything that he could put to use. There were rocks, vegetation, dirt, tree bark and twigs, but nothing

The Quest

holding out any promise of the results he was hoping to achieve. The boy continued looking around, desperately trying to locate something to further his cause. His eyes finally came to rest on, of all things, his own wrists and hands.

"Yes," he thought, "this just might do it."

Quickly he untied the rawhide strips binding the cloth wristbands to his skin. Setting the rawhide aside, he unwound the two sweaty cloths wrapped around his wrists. Slowly and deliberately, he rubbed the cloths on his arms and chest, soaking them in his body's sweat, allowing them to absorb his human scent. As soon as they were completely drenched, he tied the two pieces of cloth into a knot, leaving the ends sticking up like a set of rabbit's ears. He fastened the two pieces of rawhide securely together. Then, attaching one end of the rawhide to the cloth decoy, with the other end held firmly and securely in his hand, he looped it around his wrist.

"Let us see how you like this, my friend," he said, returning his attention to the hissing diamondback, which was maintaining its poise to do battle. "You must be the grandfather of all snakes. Your skin will make a fine pair of headbands. Come and get it!"

Thus prepared, he confidently rekindled his intention toward this unanticipated foe. Picking up the forked stick in one hand and the knotted cloth in the other, he carefully advanced on his opponent. Circling slowly to the left, he poked the stick at the snake, thus drawing its attention. As the serpent's head turned, following the jabbing stick, the boy tossed the cloth out with his other hand so that the bait landed less than one pace from the twisting snake.

When the diamondback withdrew into a coiled attack position, the boy backed off, carefully watching the snake. Flaming Sky stood motionless, listening as the snake's rattles vibrated even more violently in the still air. In the meantime, it's tongue was wildly sweeping the air. It did not take the viper long to spot it's cloth victim, a prey smelling very human. As the snake recoiled, preparing to strike, the boy gave a slight tug on the rawhide…just enough to cause the cloth to move slightly, as though touched by a small gust of wind. Shaking its rattle vigorously, the snake vehemently hissed at the decoy.

With that, Flaming Sky gave another tug on the rawhide, causing the lure to jiggle ever so slightly. As it moved, the serpent launched its attack; when it struck, so did the boy. The snake bit the decoy, sinking its fangs deeply into the ball of cloth and rawhide. The force of the serpent's thrust caused it to uncoil, rendering it vulnerable.

It was exactly at this moment that the boy made his move. Holding the stick firmly in both hands and raising it above his head, Flaming Sky let out a fierce war cry as he lunged, driving the prongs directly toward the spot immediately behind the snake's head. One fork lodged firmly into the dirt next to the rattler; however, the other prong, missing its mark, ended up pressing deeply into the viper's back. His trap had not worked well; at best it was only partially successful.

Applying as much pressure as he could with the stick, he cautiously approached his prey from behind, as the diamondback continued it's frantic attempts to withdraw its fangs from the decoy. Due to the constant pressure applied by the boy, the snake remained incapable of retracting them. Standing over the struggling rattler, he stepped on the back of its head with his foot. Once Flaming Sky secured the viper, he released the stick. Pulling his knife from his waistband, he knelt down, his knee adding to his captive's discomfort. However its distress was short lived, for in one quick, straight, backhand stroke, the boy cleanly severed the head from the snake's twisting body.

With the serpent dead, it was now safe for Flaming Sky to allow himself to relax. Feeling the intensity of the battle draining away, he paused, taking slow, deep, deliberate breaths, as he returned to his normal breathing pattern. Removing his foot from the decapitated head, he stood there victoriously viewing his defeated adversary. The rattle was indeed a worthy prize; but, his pride of victory was soon relinquished, as his need for food was a higher priority. Its meat would provide him with several hardy, hot meals.

The Quest

The serpent, minus its head and rattle, was greater than the length of an arm span. Although freeing the meat from a snake is a very simple process compared to skinning a large game animal, he was extremely careful and exacting, as he intended to preserve the snake's skin intact. He was soon to become a warrior and, as such, he had a very special purpose in mind for this particular skin. It was to serve as a part of his transition into manhood.

Flaming Sky's rite of passage was presenting him with a variety of opportunities for testing himself, not only as a warrior, but as a potential leader of his people. His mind was developing with every feat he accomplished during this time of proving his abilities, as his thoughts were on purpose as well as actions. He remembered White Wolf teaching him, "Anyone can easily learn to hunt or to make war against his enemies. The only thing necessary for a person to be willing to hunt is hunger. Accordingly, it is only necessary for him to feel fear, hate or outrage, in order to voluntarily participate in war. However, a true warrior has to be more than just an adept killer of his enemies. He must possess the skills to recognize the real enemy, to correctly identify with whom he will do battle, and to understand his reasons for choosing to do so. It is up to him to determine the time and place where he will engage. These things must be decided with a clear, unemotional mind. Even his choice of weapon is a crucial part of the warrior's responsibility: *The correct weapon for the circumstances.* If the cause is just, a warrior is honour-bound to accept the challenge. He does not have a choice. His duty is always to preserve the life of the tribe, to provide food, and to defend his people from all potential enemies…even unto his death."

In these matters, the old man knew Flaming Sky most assuredly possessed the skill and heart of a warrior. His father, Running Fox, trained him well. No, this aspect of his training was never an issue. The true challenge for him lay beyond the physical attributes of a warrior; it was testing the strength of his spirit.

He had been charged by his father and his father's cousin to take the first step in a crucial quest, a journey allowing him the opportunity of exploring the very depths of his soul. Agreeing to make his way south would enable him to retrieve the sacred plants needed by White Wolf, treasures only found deep within the heartland of the savages. The goal: Find the plants and herbs and return with them, alive.

Flaming Sky had often proven himself valiant on the field of battle by having helped defend the village, on more than one occasion, from marauding war parties of the Pawnee and Crow. For one so young, he was a formidable warrior. There was no need for him to question any of these abilities. He was a master in the art of knife throwing and a good marksman with a bow and arrow. Although he was slender, and a little light for his age of thirteen winters, he had inherited from Running Fox the gifts of strength and speed.

If he were to be successful on this quest, he would have to avoid all contact with the savages, at any cost, despite the circumstances. He was well aware that the death of a few savages would not have any long-range effect on the course of his people's history. On the other hand, his own death and failure to return with the healing plants would undoubtedly be detrimental to the health and welfare of his people.

Sharpening the end of the pronged stick, converting it to serve as a small lance, Flaming Sky added his trusty forked weapon to his increasing arsenal. He left the village two days earlier, armed only with a knife, and carrying the small empty leather pouches that were to be used to store the flora he was to gather for his shaman. After having his fill of cooked snake meat, he gathered the materials necessary to make arrows from the surrounding woods.

The area abounded in smaller pieces of light wood, which were perfect for making the shafts. In addition, there was an endless supply of shale and flint, which he could easily shape and hone into arrowheads, as well as a generous supply of bird feathers scattered throughout the forest. All of the materials necessary for him to make

The Quest

arrows were at hand. He knew that the difficulty of the process lay in his uncertainty of finding the right type of wood from which to make the bow. But for now, he gathered the gifts readily available to him, and was most thankful for having them.

Since this was the farthest Flaming Sky had ever traveled from the village on his own, he decided to make camp a little early, thereby taking advantage of remaining within range of familiar territory that he could use for markers when he continued the journey in the morning. Remembering the things of importance he had been taught, his first thought was to seek out a place sheltered from the wind to build his night fire. He gathered dried brush and small pieces of wood from around his chosen campsite. Within a short time, the fire was burning with a warm, crisp, crackling sound. On a night like this, a fire was needed more for light and protection from night prowlers than it was needed for its heat. After gathering some larger pieces of wood to feed the flames, he picked up the rudimentary elements of the weapons. Then, sitting comfortably in front of the fire, he began his evening's work.

Flaming Sky's hands went about their tasks without any need for him to be consciously involved with the process. His mind went soaring with the soft evening breeze, breathlessly suspended in the night. Once more, his thoughts were pulled backward in time to that place, and to the memory of the girl. The remembering, itself, was always a mixture of honey and salt, never measured in equal proportions. The salt usually dominated the final tally. The image was perpetually unchanged in his mind, and the question forever remained unanswered. At times, he was almost willing to concede the possibility of having created her in a dream, and she was, in fact, nothing more than a hallucination.

"No. She was real," he affirmed. She was as real as the emptiness and pain he carried in the very core of his being. She was as real as the small scar he bore on the inside of his left wrist. She was a real as the beating of his heart. He allowed his wandering mind to drift more deeply into their experiences together:

To the best of his recollection, Flaming Sky just completed his seventh winter. It was a warm day, and he had been out in the woods most of the day, hunting small game…mainly squirrels and rabbits. Of course, he was using a bow which was the appropriate size for his height. Thus armed, he went sneaking through the woods, as quietly as an enraged bear. His legendary hunting stealth, coupled with his fabled marksmanship, tended to place the odds overwhelmingly in favor of his prey. He was more than slightly annoyed at himself for having badly missed all of the shots taken thus far that day.

Although his mood was grey, the day was not. The sky was a deep blue, drifting outward forever, stretching out in all directions. The air was especially sweet smelling, and he found the summer breeze warm and comforting on his bare skin. With the exception of his hunting skills, it was truly a perfect day…a perfect day that was about to become even better.

At first she appeared to be unaware of Flaming Sky's presence. Approaching her from her left flank, he may have been outside the range of her peripheral vision. Her long, shining, black hair was braided on both sides, and tied in place with small strips of brightlycoloured cloth. Her soft skin was the hue of warm sage honey. Having placed her footgear right next to her, she sat, barefooted, on a large, flat rock in the middle of the stream. Pulling her skirt up to her knees, she watched the swirling water, feeling cool and soothing as it gently bathed her bare feet. She was too young to wear a headband, as she was not yet a maiden.

Slowly, she turned toward him, softly smiling as she did. For a long while, they remained transfixed…motionless…just staring at each other. Her warm, easy smile was intoxicating, even though she was very slightly buck-toothed. The attribute was hardly noticeable; in fact, he found it to be very enhancing rather than in the least distracting. Her dark brown eyes reminded him of the Sacred Hills on a moonless night during the dark times of winter.

The Quest

A strange sense of relief and peacefulness flowed through his entire being, filling him with a feeling of warmth and happiness. No, it was not happiness, but rather a wave of joy and anticipation…an expectation of something far beyond his comprehension. In fact, until this moment, he never possessed the remotest idea that such emotions even existed.

The two were instantaneously drawn to each other. He remembered being the one who was effortlessly moving to join her. She did not rise as he stood next to her, but simply extended her left hand. He responded by slipping his right hand into her upturned palm. Almost unaware of what he was doing, he eased himself down comfortably next to her. There they sat in silence for an imperceptible amount of time, saying nothing, doing nothing other than contentedly holding hands and gazing into the swiftly flowing waters. Finally she spoke.

"I am Sleeping Possum," she said.

He sat there, completely dumbfounded. He tried speaking, but he could not believe the stammering words slipping out from between his lips.

"Of course you are," he replied, embarrassed by the awkwardness of his insightful response.

Smiling, the girl looked back at him before lowering her eyes to the stream. He never could recall very much of their conversation, only that her name was Sleeping Possum, and she was a Northern Cheyenne. The thoughts and feelings he experienced when they were together were all he could reclaim. Being with her made him feel like he wanted to laugh and cry simultaneously. For the first time in his young life, he felt completely whole. This was odd, considering he had never been aware of the existence of the void before meeting her.

As far as facts about her were concerned, he could summon only a few. Her parents lived in temporary quarters at the far northwest edge of the encampment. He never saw nor met them. In fact, he never even knew their names. The only thing he was aware of was finding a person who made him feel complete, and she was the only one who would ever be capable of making him feel that way.

As the memory of Sleeping Possum faded away, he became aware of his present surroundings. His hands were effortlessly making the hunting arrows, fashioning them perfectly, one at a time. Although he did not yet possess the correct wood for making a bow, he decided it was wiser for him to have five arrows complete and ready for his use than to have ten arrows incomplete and unusable. Once he located the correct wood, the making of the bow would go swiftly. Even from the very beginning, when he started undergoing his training as a warrior, Flaming Sky's skill as a weapons maker always brightly outshone his skill as a hunter. However, over time, his two abilities tended to even themselves out.

Absentmindedly, he returned to his weapon-making. Searching for the softness of Sleeping Possum's voice led him backward in time, returning to the mixed images of that place, and her. Flaming Sky never knew for sure how many times they met at the stream. He possessed a clear image of their first meeting. Unfortunately, after that, it was impossible for him to determine if he was seeing a blending of a few memories or the combination of a few hundred. To him the experience always felt rather short lived. Maybe it was one moon, or possibly two or more; however, deep inside himself, he suspected it probably was less, rather than more.

Another image clearly retained was the memory of the day when the young braves first tested their potential as providers and defenders of the people. The aspiring warriors were given the opportunity to demonstrate their skill with the bow and arrow. Even though Flaming Sky's prowess as a hunter was less than legendary, his aim was always truer when he was shooting at a stationary target. He flowed easily into the experience:

The day was warm, the breeze was gentle, and the boys were nervous. They had each made their own weapons, under the guidance of their elders. In order to move forward along their path to becoming warriors, it was necessary for all five of their arrows to embed in the target. Each

The Quest

boy's skill would be carefully evaluated, based upon the placement of his arrows in relationship to the center of the target.

Flaming Sky and his three closest friends were among the seven who were participating in the contest that day. Each boy was allowed five shots at a mark stationed approximately thirty paces away. Their accuracy would determine their positions. This was an extremely important day in all of their lives. He remembered it as clearly as if it had just happened yesterday.

Flaming Sky carefully placed the arrow notch into the bowstring. Taking a deep breath, he pulled the string back to its full extent, steadily raising the bow before returning to target height. Resting his backhand lightly on his cheek, he steadily sighted along the arrow's shaft. Continuing to hold his breath, he loosed the arrow with a slight arch in its flight, in order to compensate for the light breeze and the distance it needed to travel. One by one, the sound of the seven arrows cut through the still air. His aim was true. The arrow bored deeply into the target, approximately a hand's width from the center. His friends, Short Bear, Standing Elk, and Lone Feather, were also accurate with their first round of shots. The villagers watched in transfixed silence.

The contest only lasted a short while, each boy shooting in his turn, at his own pace. Remembering what Running Fox taught him, Flaming Sky knew he would have to block out the distractions of the environment, in order to be successful. He must become one with the bow, the arrow, and the target; therefore, each shot was to be a focused meditation.

One by one, the arrows continued flying through the air. The only audible sounds were the arrows singing in their flight, followed by the soft, dull thud they made when striking their mark. Flaming Sky sent his final arrow directly into the heart of the target. It was his best shot of all his efforts. The silence was shattered by the sounds of cheering, clapping, and the shrill high-pitched sound of wooden whistles.

All of the boys had done well. After the judges inspected each target carefully, they lined the initiates up according to their marksmanship. Flaming Sky came in second to Standing Elk. Lone Feather placed fourth, with Short Bear finishing off the group in seventh place. However, the most important thing was that they all passed their first test. The overall positioning of the boys was fairly well anticipated by everyone in attendance. The only unanswered question in the minds of the spectators was: "Which of the two boys will place first, Flaming Sky or Standing Elk?" Now they had their answer.

After a few moments of watching the boys' jubilation, the audience returned to their chores, leaving the archers to continue celebrating among themselves. Flaming Sky and his friends were excitedly talking, when, out of the corner of his eye, he caught a glimpse of Sleeping Possum moving casually toward him. For some reason, she appeared to be slightly different. Her carriage was more confident and her gait was intent and purposeful.

She walked directly toward him, coming to a complete stop right in front of him, face to face. He felt his heart racing, making him feel breathless. To say that he suspected what was about to transpire would not be an entirely truthful statement. Stepping forward, and closing the distance between them, she firmly, yet gently, wrapped one arm around his waist while resting her other hand comfortably on his back. Leaning into him, she gave him a memory that would never leave him. Her lips were warm, extremely soft, and moist. In response, he slipped both of his arms around her waist, returning her embrace, and her lingering kiss. In retrospect, Flaming Sky suspected that, in truth, their hug most likely only lasted a few seconds. The duration of the kiss was probably even less. But, in his mind, the moment remained timeless.

If not for the undeniable small scar on his left wrist, he might have dismissed the memory of Sleeping Possum as a hallucination, or a reoccurring dream. However he could not do that, as he carried the tangible proof. Smiling wistfully, he glanced at his wrist, returning to his memory.

His male pride would like to have taken credit for the idea, but the truth of the matter was, it was Sleeping Possum who actually brought the knife. Flaming Sky always carried a knife on him, but it was hers

The Quest

that they used to perform the ceremony. With pieces of rawhide from her braids, they bound their left wrists together, allowing their two bloods to blend into one. They were looking deeply into each other's eyes, which were speaking their silent pledge. He was sure he winced a little when the sharp stinging of the knife's blade sliced through his flesh. Despite the pain, neither of them cried out. In fact, he was unable to recall any words they might have spoken.

In his reasoning mind, he suspected their blood ceremony took place a short time before Sleeping Possum and her family moved on to wherever it was they went. This particular image was especially unsettling for him. Knowing they silently vowed their love for each other only served to increase his sense of loss. These feelings still haunted him. The aching in his chest never completely deserted him. It never would. Like a wild stallion cornered in a box canyon, he was trapped by these memories. Their forgotten words held no answers, no clues, and no escape. They contained only the bitter repetitiveness of the inevitable surrender to the immutable barriers of the past.

Try as he might, it was impossible for Flaming Sky to conjure up any other images of Sleeping Possum. When was the last time he saw her? He was never completely sure. Remaining unaware of any other specific encounters between them before she left, he knew they were together almost daily. With the exception of three specific memories, the day of their meeting, the kiss occurring after the archery contest, and the blood pledge, the rest of their time together was a gentle picture of the two of them silently sitting side by side and holding hands.

He was able to feel her, and could easily see her, but remained unaware of what they talked and laughed about together. He had long since been unable to clearly recall the sound of her voice, let alone remember any words that she may have spoken to him. No matter how hard he tried, the rest of the memories of her remained in a void, always slightly beyond his reach. The void was, once again, filling him.

"One day, she was simply no longer there," he said out loud, incredulously. "She just vanished!"

Flaming Sky wondered whether or not they even kissed again. Had they been given the opportunity to say goodbye? That was the most disturbing, unanswered question of all. Even now, continuously searching his mind for any other recollections, he felt the onslaught of the emptiness that was his constant companion. Beyond these three specific images, the only other thing he clearly remembered was pain, and he allowed himself to embrace and fully experience it.

He felt the disapproval of their relationship by many of the adults. Sleeping Possum and Flaming Sky were considered much too young to be feeling, let alone displaying, the emotions they were experiencing. To some of their elders, their open display of affection for each other was unacceptable at any age, but especially at theirs. It was at this point that his mind painfully jolted him back into the present. By the time he was completely back in the here and now, the sun was setting. He continued working on his weapons, while putting aside the wood shavings from his newly made arrows. They would make good kindling for his morning fire.

Adding fuel to his campfire, he made his preparations for the night. Before settling down to sleep, he ate a little more of the snake meat. He was glad to be moving on in the morning. Hopefully, tomorrow, he would find the right wood from which to make his bow. With a little luck, within the next day or so. he would be eating fresh meat. For the time being, he was content and grateful to be full, safe, and warm. Curling up next to the fire, listening to the hooting of a nearby owl, he soon drifted into a peaceful sleep. As he slept, he dreamed, as he often did …of Sleeping Possum.

Chapter 3

THE ANGRY MAN

Flaming Sky's day started as the first slivers of dawn came creeping across his campsite. He had slept well, despite his awareness that, by the end of this day, he would be venturing into unknown territory. This was the farthest he had ever traveled from the summer camp, and he was doing it alone.

For the first time, he wondered how his friends were faring with their own initiation paths. Lone Feather ventured northward toward the frozen mountains, while Standing Elk headed due east, across the endless rolling prairie. Short Bear took the path leading toward the western lands. At the end of fifteen suns, if they are successful in their quests and safely home, they will take the next step in preparation for their final rite of passage. They will dance to the sun the way it has always been danced since the dawn of the people.

Flaming Sky quickly went about the business of eating. Finishing his hurried meal, he gathered his possessions in preparation for the continuation of his journey. Assuring himself that the fire was properly extinguished, he resumed his trek into the unknown. His father, Running Fox, assured his son he would have no trouble finding the wood he needed to make a bow. Beyond that comforting thought, he remained ignorant of what was awaiting him in this new land.

The sun was bright by the time the boy returned to his southerly path. If he was reading his surroundings correctly, he was positive he would find the needed wood by midday, at the latest. Meanwhile, there was time for him to think, to remember, recalling the early days of training, when the four friends were originally taught by their fathers. The older men took them on group survival trips, with each of their fathers taking an active part in preparing the boys to face their tests of manhood. Although they were training together, each would be judged independently when it was time to be evaluated upon their merits.

Running Fox, being an extremely gifted maker of bows and arrows, taught the boys to survive in the wilderness by making weapons from materials they could easily find in their immediate environment. He showed them how to choose the best shoots of wood for making arrows, and the proper wood for crafting bows and lances. They were taught to recognize which stones were suitable as arrowheads and lance tips. It was he who instructed them in skillfully feathering the arrows, ensuring a swift and true flight to their mark. From him, they learned the technique of binding the weapon tips to the shafts with thin strips of wet rawhide. As the rawhide strips dry, they contract and tighten for the proper attachment.

It was Thunder Eyes' responsibility to instruct the boys in the proper technique and the art of wielding a deadly weapon. When in charge of himself, he was a fearsome warrior. He taught them to use their lances as spears for fishing the streams. Once they learned to compensate for the refracting effect of the water, they became quite proficient as fishermen, confident in their ability to fend for themselves as long as there was a stream nearby. If they could feed themselves, they could always provide for the tribe.

Like his father before him, Flaming Sky quickly earned a reputation as a skilled maker of weapons. This talent was envied by many,

The Quest

including some of the older braves. Although his skill as an archer was acceptable, it could hardly be called spectacular. His ability with a knife, however, was an entirely different matter. He quickly learned the proper method of releasing a knife with just enough wrist snap for the correct number of rotations needed, determined by the distance, to propel it to the target. Braves considered expert with the knife could fling a blade from a distance of seven paces with consistent accuracy. Flaming Sky's proficiency extended beyond twelve paces, sometimes even to fifteen. Beyond that distance, hitting a target was a matter of pure luck.

Swift Hawk, the father of Standing Elk and Lone Feather, was their instructor in the art of hand-to-hand combat. He taught them how to fight with small weapons and with no weapons at all. Swift Hawk was a tall, lean man, possessing a soft, firm voice. His legs were long, slender, and muscular, and his upper body well proportioned for his height. His chin was weak, with a nose almost too small for his round face, but in combat, his eyes remained cold and unflinching. It was his responsibility to evaluate each boys' skills in full contact fighting. The top match was always between Flaming Sky and Standing Elk, as the other two boys were never their competitive equals.

Standing Elk was the oldest, the biggest and the strongest of all of the boys. Flaming Sky, on the other hand, although younger, was faster and smarter. He learned more quickly than the other boys, giving him a distinct advantage, which he hoped to maximize in triumphing over Standing Elk. They used sticks for weapons rather than real knives or tomahawks, thereby leaving marks on their opponent's body without causing any permanent damage. Thus were their tests for proficiency judged.

The contest between the two boys was even, both fighting well. When the match was finished, the decision was declared a draw. Standing Elk used his height advantage and strength to win the hand-to-hand fighting without weapons. Flaming Sky fought valiantly, but was unable to overcome the disadvantages of Standing Elk's weight and reach. However, due to his lightness of foot and natural speed, he outmaneuvered his adversary, and won the bout fought using small hand-weapons. They were well-fought encounters, and Swift Hawk was justly proud of their performances.

This, however, was not the fight Flaming Sky was dwelling upon in his memory. The combat between himself and Standing Elk was a contest with a clean, purposeful intent behind it. No. The conflict preoccupying him and playing upon his mind was the fight occurring many seasons earlier, when he and Short Bear were in their sixth winter.

Flaming Sky was the older of the two by a grand total of three days. Their families were friends for many moons before the birth of the boys. From that time forward, their campfires were always built close to one another. Considering the strength of the bond existing between the families added greatly to Flaming Sky's confusion concerning the incident. The two boys often fought on their own, countless times, with Short Bear forever coming in a very poor second; but, their friendship remained unimpaired. The outcome of their sparring was never even close. Everyone knew this, including Short Bear's father, Thunder Eyes.

"Could it be that this is at the core of the problem?" the boy wondered to himself.

Because of Flaming Sky's youth, villagers were careful not to discuss Thunder Eyes' situation in his presence. However, even with the passage of a mere six winters, the boy overheard enough to know Thunder Eyes was possessed by his own special demon.

"He is touched by the righteous wrath of the Great Spirit," he thought, remembering what he had heard White Wolf saying to Running Fox.

"The trouble originated during the time when Thunder Eyes was in training to become a shaman. It was while studying the secret powers of the plants that he strayed from his purpose. His misuse of the sacred ceremonial herbs was common knowledge. As a punishment, the Grand

The Quest

Father gave him a sickness of the mind. Despite the fact that the power of the herbs clearly turned against him, he persisted in misusing them, growing more unpredictable and volatile with the changing of the seasons. Within a short time, he was experiencing periods of lapsing time, in addition to episodes of complete loss of emotional control."

The incident still haunted Flaming Sky. Searching the past, he was hoping to find something allowing him to unravel the confusion surrounding this incident. He was desperate to make sense of it, but was never able to remember exactly how the fight started. The boy drifted into a familiar reverie of objective recalling:

The two friends were outside together, standing near their parents' tipis. He was not sure if they were playing or just talking to each other. The only thing he remembered hearing was Thunder Eyes' angry voice demanding that Short Bear attack Flaming Sky. The raging man repeated the command over and over again. In between shouting at his son, he railed at Flaming Sky. Even after all this time, the boy was uncertain as to precisely what it was that Thunder Eyes was hollering. The exact wording was not nearly as important as the hatred and loathing in his voice. Even now, he felt the contempt spewing forth from the foul mouth of Short Bear's irate father.

At first, both boys stood there, frightened by the intensity of Thunder Eyes' uncontrollable fury. Short Bear immediately realized he was caught in an untenable position, ensnared in a foolproof trap, and on the verge of panicking. Although afraid of fighting Flaming Sky, he was even more terrified of the consequences awaiting him if he did not assault his friend.

Increasing his verbal tirade against the boys, Thunder Eyes became physically threatening toward his son. Short bear was being forced into making a decision. He knew full well he would be subjected to his father's ire, as the outcome of the fight was predestined. Short Bear knew that fighting Flaming Sky meant losing to him again, after which he would still have to face Thunder Eyes. If he did not fight Flaming Sky, the consequences would be even worse for him. So, having run out of options, he advanced on his friend and, lowering his head, charged, swinging his arms wildly from side to side as he did.

Flaming Sky responded by putting his arms up in self-defense. Although he easily defended himself, he did not return any of Short Bear's blows, fearing the rage of Thunder Eyes. Slowly circling his opponent, Flaming Sky moved to his left, trying to stay far away from his foe's flaying arms. The boy was well aware he could quickly and easily end the fight with Short Bear any time he wanted. The only thing stopping him from doing so was his fear of what Thunder Eyes might do to him if he did. He was feeling as helpless and vulnerable as his terrified friend. There was nothing the boy could do but continue circling Short Bear. He tried to protect himself, while always doing his best to know the location of the crazed one, fully aware that it would be dangerous for him to get too close.

By this time, the boys found themselves surrounded by a small group of their neighbors. The observers were unaware how the fight started but, nonetheless, it had. By custom, once a fight began, the adversaries were usually allowed to finish it. Of course, the elders could intercede, but only did so after a clear winner was established, thereby ensuring the safety of the losing combatant.

So the fight went on, with Flaming Sky protecting himself from Short Bear's attack by constantly moving out of his range, and continuously pushing his opponent backward with his left hand. Flaming Sky did not counter attack. He held his punches, frantically searching for a way to escape the situation. The boy was finding it very difficult to keep his eyes on both Short Bear and Thunder Eyes, while desperately scanning the area for a safe path of retreat.

Finally, out of the corner of his eye, he saw Running Fox stepping out of his tipi. The chief said nothing. He did nothing. He only stood there, evaluating the situation. This was all that was necessary for him to do, as Flaming Sky knew he was now safe from retaliation by the unstable Thunder Eyes. Once seeing his father watching over him, the threat of Thunder Eyes was nullified, and the complexion of the encounter rapidly

The Quest

and dramatically changed. Flaming Sky immediately went on the offensive. Advancing on Short Bear, he finally started throwing punches of his own. Now, instead of merely blocking Short Bear's wild blows, he was returning them. Flaming Sky pressed his advantage, forcing Short Bear to back away, holding his hands high, trying to protect his face.

The instant Short Bear retreated, Flaming Sky accelerated his attack, viciously landing two or three hard blows to Short Bear's stomach and ribs, causing him to drop his hands in an attempt to protect his body. His face presented an easy target for Flaming Sky, who threw two more lefts at his opponent's face. One of the blows landed on the right side of Short Bear's nose, causing it to bleed profusely. The blood came gushing out, flowing over his mouth and chin. Flaming Sky next released a straight right from the shoulder, landing solidly on Short Bear's jaw, sending him awkwardly reeling backwards. As his prey desperately tried to maintain his balance, Flaming Sky advanced. Feigning with his left, he followed with two clean rights to the boy's stomach.

Flaming Sky stopped attacking when he saw Short Bear was defeated. He was standing there, stunned and breathless, his arms dangling uselessly at his sides, obviously unable to defend himself. His dazed eyes stared straight ahead as he slowly sank to his knees.

Slumping to the ground, clutching his stomach, he curled up in pain.

Flaming Sky, standing over the vanquished boy, realized Short Bear was incapable of getting to his feet. The instant the fight was finished, Flaming Sky anxiously looked around for Thunder Eyes. He was safely several paces away from the angry man, who was railing at his son, giving him a vivid, verbal description of the punishment awaiting him for his repeated failure to defeat Running Fox's son. The young Flaming Sky took advantage of this opportunity and slowly backed away, all the while keeping his eye on the ranting Thunder Eyes. Carefully and deliberately, he made his way back through the crowd to his own tipi, where Running Fox was quietly waiting for him.

Unable to recall any words of the conversation between him and his father, he remembered only trying to tell Running Fox what little he *knew about how the fight started. But, try as he might, then as now, Flaming Sky was extremely confused and baffled as to why Thunder Eyes possessed such hateful feelings toward him. The issue was not resolved that day. No matter how many times he reviewed the incident in his mind, he could never remember the details, and the question always remained unanswered, "Why does he hate me so?"*

Still haunted by the question, and the memory, the boy returned to the present, pondering the event in his reasoning mind. Flaming Sky and Short Bear remained friends, but their relationship was never quite the same. Running Fox and Thunder Eyes continued hunting and fishing together, as if the fight never occurred. The incident was never talked about openly, at least not to Flaming Sky's knowledge. However, from that time forward, the wary Flaming Sky made a conscious effort to stay as far away from Thunder Eyes as he possibly could, never allowing himself to be caught in a situation where he was trapped and alone with the raging man.

The sun was high overhead when Flaming Sky refocused his thoughts in the present time. There was a small stream nearby where he could rest in the cool shade. He was becoming aware of the hunger steadily building up inside of him, and was looking forward to some food, fresh, clean water and a little rest before resuming his journey.

Flaming Sky refilled his water skin with fresh water before continuing on his way. He was unsure how far he might have to travel before reaching the next source of water; therefore, it was necessary to carefully limit the amount of water he consumed. This was an important part of his survival test. In the past, he survived for several days on little or no water when it was scarce. Since this territory was new and unknown, he determined it would be prudent for him to be extremely conservative with his meager supplies.

If he remembered Running Fox's words correctly, he was sure to come across the correct wood from which to form a hunting bow.

The Quest

After a short amount of walking, the boy spotted a small grove of young saplings of the type well suited to his purpose. They were exactly what he was looking for to construct a bow. Carefully scanning the woods, he searched the area for the most appropriate sapling. He needed one that was slender, and straight…one that could tolerate the stress intended to be exerted upon it, without splitting or cracking. Most of the young trees were easily eliminated as potential sources of material for bow making. He often stopped, closely examining the more acceptable candidates, only to reject them, moving on to the next prospective choice.

It did not take long for his careful search to yield a sapling with excellent possibilities. Immediately, he went about the business of cutting the small tree free from its taproot. The choice was perfect. The barrel of the shoot was of a consistent thickness for a total length of approximately a full arm span. It was strong and flexible, bending without shattering under the force exerted upon it.

"Yes," he thought, "this will do quite nicely."

He went about trimming away the twigs and fashioning a rough weapon, etching deep cuts into each end of the sapling before attaching the bowstring into the notched ends. Retesting its strength and flexibility, he was satisfied with the bow's resilience. Slipping his arm through the string, he slung the weapon onto his back, joining his quiver of newly made arrows. His plan was to rework the bow, attending to the final shaping of the wood later, after making camp for the night.

Before moving on, he carefully searched for a second shoot to use as a fishing spear, replacing his forked stick. He cut another sapling of equal quality. Not only would the new spear allow him to fish but, being similar in attributes, it would make an excellent replacement for his new bow if the need should arise. Although he was taught to travel lightly, he was also trained to think ahead.

"Anticipate what the future might bring and prepare yourself for it," he said aloud to himself, comfortably reciting the words of Running

Fox. "This spear will double as a walking stick, in case I encounter any steep inclines."

Skillfully, he whittled one end of his spear into a fine, sharp point. Like his cousin, the brown bear, who freely roamed the woods, he, too, could now snatch fish out of the clear, icy streams and brooks. Proudly in possession of a walking stick, a spear, and the makings of a replacement bow, he was well fortified for the remainder of his journey. Hopefully, he was properly prepared for whatever future might await him.

As soon as the sun started drifting below the horizon, Flaming Sky searched the area for a suitable campsite. He was entering the foothills containing the passageway leading into the southern desert. The land was already becoming less hospitable, a tendency that would continuously increase as he traveled southward. He was aware that he would soon be able to start gathering the harvest he had come to collect for his father's cousin, White Wolf; but. for the time being, he needed to find shelter from the cold night wind. Knowing the path to the south would be more easily found in the bright light of a full sun, he decided to camp for the night and wait for the light of dawn before seeking the southern passage.

His eyes came to rest on a welcome sight. A few hundred paces ahead was what appeared to be a possible haven for the night. At the base of one of the foothills, he spotted a small cavern, with a path leading upward toward the entrance, leveling off at the mouth of the cave. Carefully approaching, he observed it was shallow, probably no more than twelve to fifteen strides deep. The entryway was approximately twelve paces across and nearly ten paces high, enough to easily accommodate a warrior on horseback. The interior consisted of a combination of stone and earthen clay. Best of all, the opening was facing the opposite direction of the breath of the chilling night wind.

He placed his weapons, including his partially fashioned bow, just inside the mouth of the cave, keeping only his knife with him for

THE QUEST

use as a possible weapon as well as a tool. There was enough daylight left to gather the necessary firewood for his campfires. He gathered dried sagebrush, small twigs and several larger pieces of dried wood, storing the fuel against one of the walls of the cave.

The first fire he built for warmth, located in the center and well inside the opening of the cave. He set the fire far enough back to allow the heat to reflect off the walls, yet shallow enough to enable the smoke to be drawn out, dissipating in the night air. This was the fire built to fight off the night chill. The second fire at the entrance of the cave was intended to ward off prowlers that might wander his way during the night. With both of the fires properly set, he gratefully consumed the last of the snake meat. His present supply of water was adequate, for the time being. Finding food, rather than water, would be the main item on his agenda come morning.

Picking up the piece of freshly cut sapling, Flaming Sky returned to fashioning it into a hunting bow. Having done this so many times in the past, it was as natural to him as breathing. His hands swiftly went about their work, as his thoughts drifted forward to the time when he and the other boys return to their village.

"Here we will complete the final rite of passage, allowing us to be declared warriors of the Lakota, defenders of the people," he thought aloud, with a sense of pride welling up within him. He felt the awe of one who is about to partake in the highest rituals of his people. "When we successfully complete the survival test, we will undergo the passage into adulthood…separately, but also together as brothers. After fasting for four days and nights, we will take the ceremonial cacota, and purify ourselves in the sweat lodge, meditating and awaiting the visions." Upon completion of the vision quests, initiates allow themselves to be offered up as sacrifices for the protection of the people. "Then we will perform the ritual dance to the sun, the ultimate test of our manhood!"

A sound cutting across his thoughts drew his attention back into the here and now. Listening, he very carefully waited for the noise to be repeated. He did not have to wait long before hearing it slicing through the silent night. It was the cry of a mountain lion and, from her intonation, she was very close, and none too friendly. For the first time since leaving his village, the boy was truly afraid. The lioness continued growling, and, by the intensity of her roar, he surmised she was no more than a hundred paces from his shelter. She was definitely not happy.

"Is she smelling the smoke or me?" he wondered to himself. In either case, she sounded increasingly angry and agitated.

As her growling continued, Flaming Sky's fear intensified, and he knew he needed to do something…but what? He considered building up the fires and hiding himself deeper within the cave.

"Hopefully," he thought, "if she does come looking for me, the fires will scare her away. But hiding? No. That is the act of a coward."

Although he was not yet a warrior, he was Sioux and, therefore, he was certainly not a coward. Even though he was frightened, he refused to cower in the cave like a helpless trembling animal.

"What are my options?" he questioned himself? "I can go out there and confront her in peace, showing her I am not her enemy."

Listening to the angry sounds of her voice, he decided this was neither a wise nor a prudent choice. He was aware that confronting her was unnecessarily dangerous, as well as an extremely stupid idea on his part.

"If, in fact, she is wounded, or protecting her young, it is highly unlikely that she will be in a cordial mood. What else can I do?" he questioned, realizing he could not allow himself to hide from her in the cave.

Debating internally, he wondered aloud, "What would White Wolf do under these circumstances?"

After pondering this question in his mind for a few minutes, he heard White Wolf's voice clearly speaking to him. *"Make peace with her from here."*

The Quest

He turned the answer over repeatedly in his mind. "Certainly, I do not have to take a foolish risk in order to keep myself from acting cowardly."

He sat down between the two fires, and inhaled deep, relaxing breaths, slowly calming his mind. With his mind clear, he focused his thoughts on the lioness.

"Considering the time of the year," he suspected, "she is most likely protecting her young." Besides, he was not hearing the sound of pain in her voice. "No, this is only threatening anger."

He reached out to her, sending calm, peaceful, thoughts, intermixed with images of her young ones lying undisturbed, safely next to her. His thoughts were telling her that he was neither a threat to her nor to her cubs. "I am not your enemy," he assured her. "I will not infringe upon your space." Quietly, he promised not to bother her in any way.

Waiting for a while, he sent her another image. This was one showing Flaming Sky remaining inside the cave throughout the entire night, promising her he would not intrude upon her terrain, in turn suggesting she remain within her own territory, a safe distance from him. Repeatedly he sent her the message.

Within a short time, she was sounding calmer. Although she continued calling out to him on the night wind for a while, it was not long before she became completely silent, for which he was enormously relieved. Apparently, they had reached an agreement of mutual respect. With his emotions more subdued, and his mind clear, he ceased sending images to the she-lion. They agreed to keep a reasonable distance from each other, going about their individual business without any fear or threats on either side. With the problem thus solved, he released his attention from her, once again freeing his mind to contemplate the trials awaiting him and his friends.

The vision quest intrigued him the most. It was through such visions that his life's path could be laid open to him. "What other things might be revealed? What mysteries are waiting to be solved? What universal truth waits to be learned?"

But, of course, there was always the other side to be taken into consideration. He contemplated the disappointing possibility of learning absolutely nothing. "A vision quest is exactly that: a quest. It is a search for insight, and enlightenment. It is the hope of discovering the life path that one is to pursue. From time to time, there are braves who receive nothing from their experiences. They are more fortunate than others, whose search often leads them into ugly visions of a distorted reality… a reality where they are forced to remain trapped forever in the chaotic madness of their own creation."

Even though the details were hard to come by, over many seasons Flaming Sky had come to the awareness that something like this must have occurred with Thunder Eyes. He knew Thunder Eyes served as an apprentice to the same shaman who trained White Wolf. The boy was told Thunder Eyes was a very eager student, but also an extremely impatient one, and, from what Flaming Sky could glean, it was this impatience that triggered his downfall. He recalled the story White Wolf once told of him:

"Thunder Eyes was in such a hurry to experience the mysteries, he recklessly ignored the safeguards of proper preparation, as well as the correct use of the sacred herbs. He was never able to successfully train his mind to become quiet. Instead, it was constantly filled with strange voices and, more often than not, they were demonic in nature. Without a calm mind and a strong spirit, it was impossible for him to withstand the overwhelming power of the ceremonial herbs."

At this point, the story always became unclear, and more than a little vague. Flaming Sky never learned exactly what occurred. He knew, somehow, Thunder Eyes lost command of his spirit, and from that time forward, was constantly tormented by the fury created within his own rage. Flaming Sky never understood what caused Thunder Eyes to become so unbalanced prior to misusing the sacred herbs. Some say he was beguiled by the herbs even before starting his

The Quest

shaman training. Others whispered, "The man was unstable from the very moment of his birth." In either case, shortly after passing through his eighteenth winter, his training ended disastrously for him. He is lost so deeply in the land of demons that he will never completely return. There he remains, constantly torn between two worlds.

It is not uncommon for a shaman to have more than one apprentice. Young warriors are like spring saplings. Only time will show which ones become the strong, straight trees reaching upward, touching the sunlight. Thunder Eyes was not one of these. He continuously lived in the shadow of the greater trees of the forest, spiritually growing crooked and twisted.

Although no longer traveling the path of the medicine man, Thunder Eyes is a Lakota warrior and, as such, has responsibilities to the people. When his mind is not aflame, he is capable of serving his people fairly well. At times, he is a brave warrior and, when in his senses, a good hunter and provider. He took himself a wife, who gave him three children, the oldest of whom is Short Bear.

"Short Bear," thought Flaming Sky. "I wonder how he is coming along on his survival trip." The thought brought him back completely to the peaceful warmth of the cave. His new bow was finished and ready to be strung. "The wood of the bow is hard and smooth to the touch, strong, and flexible enough to handle the demands that will be made upon it," he said with pride. "It is a good stout bow!" he affirmed, smiling.

Flaming Sky laid it down next to the quiver of arrows and his new fishing spear. As it was getting late, he realized how tired he had become. With a fleeting thought of the lioness, he refueled both of the fires before settling comfortably down between them. Wrapping himself in a blanket and closing his eyes, he quickly drifted into a restful slumber. In the quietness of the cave, the night…as it always did…once more filled his mind with dreams.

Chapter 4

COUNTING COUP

On the eighth day of his journey into the desert, Flaming Sky spotted the first plants whose treasures he had come to collect. He easily recognized the cactus from the drawings White Wolf made for him prior to setting out on his quest. Carefully harvesting the cacti, the boy stored them in the pouch he brought with him for this purpose. Because the plants were scarce and scattered over a large area, it took most of the morning to gather enough cacti to actually fill the leather pouch, which he stuffed into one of the two large bags he brought along to transport the harvested plants. The items in this first bag were to be delivered directly into the hands of White Wolf, for only a Holy One possesses the secret knowledge necessary for their final preparation and proper use in the sacred rituals.

Neither Flaming Sky nor any of the other young braves had the ability to discern the meaning of the words spoken by White Wolf while performing the purification rites. The boys only knew he prayed over them while painstakingly processing them, slowly, over a fourday span of time. So far, none of them were ever taught the

The Quest

sacred words used in that part of the ceremony. These words can only be uttered from the lips of a Holy Man. However, once the Great Spirit chooses a Wicasa to succeed him, this will change.

Their experiences with White Wolf taught the boys one thing: He will have the buttons properly prepared and ready for use when they have need of them after the completion of their cleansing phase. Each boy will freely experience for himself whatever visions might be revealed to him. However, they will all look to White Wolf for guidance in correctly interpreting these images, which could hold the key to the young brave's life path. A clear understanding of themselves is the most important characteristic they can gain in their passage into manhood; therefore, it is crucial for each young brave to correctly comprehend the true meaning of his visions.

Flaming Sky was curious as to what his own visions might contain. "What dreams will I experience? What images might occur along the way, lighting my path to manhood?" he wondered aloud.

Throughout his entire young life, he often experienced misty images, which later revealed themselves as prophetic dreams. His mind was often exposed to pictures while in a peaceful state. Unfortunately, his clarity of interpretation was, at best, average. It was common among his people to receive glimpses of the future; however, only a Wicasa, like White Wolf, is capable of fathoming the deepest truth of their meanings.

"Remember," he had been told, *"the purpose of taking the sacred button is to serve as a catalyst, extending and sharpening the spirit message, not creating it."* "Maybe," the boy thought, "this is where Thunder Eyes went astray. The power of the buttons is seductive and extremely dangerous when misused. The same thing is, to a certain degree, true of many of the sacred herbs used by a shaman, as well as a Wicasa."

Comprehending the graveness of the responsibility, he wondered, "Will it or will it not be my path? Will I be chosen to follow in the steps of my father's cousin, White Wolf? Am I to become a shaman, or will I grow to become a chief like my father, Running Fox?" The possibilities were perplexing.

By the time he finished his chores, the sun was high overhead. He was hot and extremely thirsty. As the water left in his drinking skin was getting low, he decided it was time to seek out a fresh spring. He was hoping to find a stream with a tree or two, offering soothing, restful shade. Once having located water, he was confidant that, with a little luck, there would be game nearby. Armed with his bow and arrows, he was now a properly equipped hunter. The chances of finding prey near fresh water seemed excellent. If nothing else, there should be fish available for spearing.

Pausing briefly, he surveyed the area, searching for the most likely location for flowing water. Easily reading the signs, as he had been taught to do by the older braves, he spotted a small grove of trees in the distant southwest. Even from where he stood, the green growth appeared abundant and lush. So, off he strolled, eagerly heading straight for the cooling oasis and whatever awaited.

In time, he reached the grassy banks of the stream. The water trickled through the rocks, flowing clear and steady. Flaming Sky knelt down by the iridescent liquid, gazing into his reflection. Bending over and cupping his hands, he took long, cool swallows until his thirst was quenched before splashing water on his face, and pouring some over his back and shoulders. Finally, dipping his hands back into the brook, he allowed the cooling droplets of liquid to flow over as much of his body as he could reach.

Refreshed, he sat back, sighing deeply. Eventually, he proceeded with replenishing his water supply. Finishing, he set aside the skins and his weapons. Sitting comfortably with his back leaning against a tree, relaxing, he breathed in the coolness of the moist air. Closing his eyes, he peacefully allowed his mind to drift. It was a common occurrence during such quiet moments for his thoughts to return to the memory of Sleeping Possum.

The Quest

"What ever happened to her?" he wondered painfully. "Why did she not even say good-bye? Is she happy? Does she remember me? Does she ever think about us? Does she remember that short time we shared together?" He had no answers.

Once having run their course, his thoughts refocused on contemplating his immediate future. He would be a warrior, of that he was certain. Beyond that fact, the images of his future were a dancing fog, light and hazy, a mist in which he saw the wispy image of Morning Star. Yes, she was a part of his future. She was an important aspect of his life, impatiently awaiting his return.

Although Morning Star wore the white headband of a maiden, soon she would replace it with a new one of snakeskin, made for her by Flaming Sky. They were to be together, of that there was no doubt. Their parents had decided long ago, when they were very young children. The entire village was anxiously awaiting their forthcoming union. It was only a matter of time, perhaps one more winter. When was not as important as the inevitability of it. It would happen.

Soon he will be a warrior, and eligible to take a mate. However, he must first complete his passage into manhood, a test of courage which not only includes the sacrificial Sun Dance, but the killing of his first buffalo during the autumn hunt. Then, and only then, will he receive an eagle feather as a sign of his bravery. These are the important trials lying ahead of him.

His thoughts turned to Morning Star, the one promised to him. A willowy girl, with small breasts and a delicate waistline, she wears her raven coloured hair loosely around her shoulders, flowing all of the way to her waist. Her eyes are so dark and bright, they look as black as the eyes of a honeybee. Possessing an easy, sweet smile, she always makes people feel comfortable in her presence. Her height is average, and her high cheekbones maintain a natural glow of health and vitality.

"Morning Star is being trained by the older women to become a productive and responsible member of our tribe," he thought aloud, "learning the art of a Sioux woman who will be an asset to her people and her mate." The latter responsibility she happily anticipates, having had her eye on Flaming Sky for as long as she could remember.

"No, there is no argument," he thought assuredly. "It is a good match. She is pleasant to look upon, and gentle of spirit. Oh, she has fire in her veins, but it is a warm, enticingly approachable fire. Morning Star has already proven herself in many areas, as she is wise far beyond her young years. In addition to harvesting the cultivated crops, she has a talent for locating and identifying edible roots and plants, a gift inherited from her mother. She is skilled in attending the campfire, including gathering the proper woods for the preparation of food. Her versatility in making clothes and decorative sewing is highly praised. Furthermore, she is an excellent receptacle of the stories destined to be a history of our tribe, a very handy talent for when we have children of our own to teach." Flaming Sky was well pleased, knowing he would be hard pressed to find someone who could even come close to matching her, let alone surpassing her. He cared as deeply for her as she did for him.

"Yes, it is a good pairing. It is good for us, and for our people," he thought, smiling a little to himself.

Upon his return home, he will call upon her father, Two Claws, officially seeking permission to take her for his wife. This is how it has always been done. The price for her will be high. The payment due Two Claws is naturally commensurate with the rank and status of their families. There is great honour for his family in having Morning Star become his mate. After all, her father is a brave war chief and a highly regarded member of the council. Being so young necessitated Flaming Sky's having to wait at least one more winter before affording her father's asking price. The fact she was already promised to him did not change the way things are done.

Flaming Sky's mind was filled with images of his future with Morning Star. He deliberately removed the stored snakeskin from its leather pouch, first measuring it with his eyes, and then

The Quest

physically holding it against his head and waist. He was convinced, if he proceeded carefully, there would be enough material to make two headbands, a belt, and at least one or possibly even two sets of wristbands out of the skin. The matching headbands would serve as an outward declaration of their mutual intentions, symbolizing their commitment to enter into their new roles as mates and adult contributors to the tribe. By the time they are united, she will have completed the process of transforming herself from a maiden into a woman Of course her transformation, as well as his, will be continuously shaped and molded by the examples of their elders.

Once they are husband and wife, she will always walk beside him, no matter which path he chooses. A warrior? A hunter? A medicine man? War? Peace? To her it does not matter. Once they are joined, they will think, feel and act as one, for the good of the unit, as well as the best interest of the entire tribe. They had been taught the value of family, and the proper respect for the traditions of the people, throughout their entire lives. Walking together as one spirit, they will be several times stronger than the total of two separate ones.

The sound of his empty stomach was strongly drawing his attention to how long it had been since he had eaten. Picking up his bow and arrows to go hunting, he stopped, intently listening to a noise approaching from a distance. He was hearing hoof beats moving much too fast and hard to be grazing deer or buffalo. No.

They were of a steady, even, quick pace. It could only be the sound of horses.

Listening carefully, he estimated there were at least four of them. Aware he had not traveled far enough south to be in the land of the savages, he concluded the approaching enemy was probably Pawnee. In any case, no matter who they were, the last thing he wanted was to be caught out in the open, unprotected.

Quickly slinging his bow and quiver of arrows across his back, he grabbed his spear, the water skins and the leather pouches and went scampering up the side of a large boulder next to the trees. Using the rock as a stepping-stone, he made a running leap up and into one of the taller, fuller ones. He pulled himself up the trunk to the center of the oak. Here the main branches split numerous times, spiraling upward toward the sky.

Frantically searching for the most heavily foliaged area of the tree, he shimmied up one of the boughs, ducking behind a thick growth of leaves. Straddling one of the large main branches, he wrapped his arms and legs around it and lay there, his bare chest and arms bleeding from the rough bark. He waited,. With the sun directly behind him sending blinding light streaming down through the thick foliage, he was hoping his uninvited visitors would not see him. Soon he would learn whether or not he was safely hidden from them.

Here they came, four of them, following the small stream to where it widened at the base of Flaming Sky's hiding place. Grabbing the tree more firmly, he breathed slowly and evenly, attempting to keep himself calm and composed. Watching them approach, it appeared they were tracking something. Since he had come from the north and they were traveling west, he felt safe, believing that, for the time being, they were completely unaware of his presence. They had probably been tracking a deer, or some other game animal.

He listened to them talking loudly as they approached the tree. They were Pawnee, all right. Although he was unable to understand everything they were saying, he made out enough to understand they were intending to set up camp here. The hunters tended to their horses before setting about pitching their camp directly underneath Flaming Sky's tree.

Peeking down, he watched as two of them went wandering off, gathering branches and small pieces of wood for the campfire. One of the remaining warriors busied himself cleaning some fish they had caught earlier, while the last brave set about searching for edible plants and roots. The braves packed the fish in mud and, setting them aside with the freshly gathered roots, they waited until the fire was ready.

The Quest

After they finished preparing the meal, they rested by the campfire. When the food was ready, they talked while eating their fill.

All the while, the Pawnee remained completely unaware of Flaming Sky's presence in the tree above them. He, on the other hand, was very much aware of them, and of his hunger. There was nothing he could do for the present, except wait. Eventually, they would talk themselves out and drift into sleep.

Flaming Sky was beginning to feel the night chill, despite the meager warmth drifting upward from the Pawnees' fire. While remaining as quiet as possible, he shifted himself into a more comfortable position. Despite feeling cramped, tired, and frightened, he discovered himself drifting in between wakefulness and sleep, while desperately clinging to the tree, awaiting his chance to escape. In his mind, he was listening to the echoing of White Wolf's words, reminding him: *"Your mission is to gather the ceremonial herbs, and plants, returning them, and yourself, safely back to our people. This is not the time for you to make war. Your quest is much too important for you to risk your life in a meaningless battle."*

Deciding the old shaman was correct, Flaming Sky knew this was a time to remain still and avoid being detected. Having no choice in the matter, there was nothing he could do except straddle and wait. He remained hiding in the boughs, shivering and clinging to the branches, awaiting the night's inevitable progression towards the dawn.

The long, slow night in the tree gave Flaming Sky more than ample time to evaluate his position. He did not find himself in the best of all situations; he was alone, frightened, cold, hungry, hiding in a tree, and outnumbered four-to-one. In addition, he was inwardly bombarded with conflicting thoughts as to the preferred course of action. The initiate within him wanted to count coup. The boy only wanted to get away, as fast and as far as possible. His warrior voice was calling out for vengeance against an old enemy. *"Attack!"* Fortunately for him an older, wiser voice was counseling discretion. *"Take the first opportunity presented and use it to escape with your life. Leave, and by doing so, you will live to fight more important battles."* Confused with these conflicting urges, he took advantage of the long night to think things through. Now that his adversaries were fast asleep, the time for thinking was over. This was the time for action.

Very carefully and deliberately easing himself down through the thickness of the oak, he balanced himself on one foot while holding onto a bough with both arms. Gingerly, he felt his way down the trunk until he was able to locate a solid limb under his other foot. Little by little, he completed his descent by repeating the process over and over again. Quietly, he continued easing his way down until he arrived safely back on the same boulder he originally used for his ascent.

Once both feet were safely on the large rock, he surveyed the situation from a completely different perspective. His new vantage point allowed him to merge his three conflicting urges into one relatively reasonable plan. If he could manage to pull it off, he would be able to count coup while safely escaping with his life. Especially, his warrior's voice was giving a positive endorsement to his new decision of a more aggressive action.

Carefully setting down his weapons and herb pouches, he placed them out of harms way. The only weapons he carried were his knives, one of which he tucked snuggly into his waistband and the other in his boot, as White Wolf had taught him. The fact that the Pawnees' horses were tethered several paces downstream from the camp was indeed very fortunate for Flaming Sky. At that distance away, the animals were less likely to take notice of him.

From the opposite side of the tree, he listened to the four snoring hunters. Henceforth, he realized circumstances were becoming increasingly more dangerous. It would have been far safer for him to go sneaking off, silently, instead of walking toward the outer ring of sleeping warriors. Taking the necessary precautions not to alarm them from their dreams, he carefully examined the eagle feathers each

THE QUEST

of them wore in their hair. It did not take long to find the best eagle feather among them. The one who appeared to be their leader wore three feathers, which were notched several times and marked with multiple red spots. Using extreme caution, the boy lightly grasped the tip of one of the feathers. Holding his breath, he gently eased it out of the brave's hair. Although remaining in a silent mode, he was inwardly elated. "I have just stolen a Pawnee warrior's feather…and it was taken from the head of their leader!"

With his confidence renewed, Flaming Sky stood up and looked intently at the other three men peacefully sleeping by the campfire. They were completely unaware of his presence. Earlier, the tallest of the three men had been leading a paint pony, which caught Flaming Sky's admiration. "That pony will do very nicely," he thought to himself. The animal was a great prize, in itself; however, he was looking forward to riding the remainder of his journey, rather than walking through the scorching desert. The horse would be the last thing he would take care of before leaving. For now, he had unfinished business with the remaining two warriors.

Squatting down, making himself as small as possible, he advanced on the third warrior. Pausing by the sleeping man's head, Flaming Sky gently eased one of the man's arrows from its quiver. Once he was sure it was safe, he continued making his way slowly around the outside of the camp, arriving next to the final sleeping adversary. The brave's lance lay next to him, decorated with a dozen human scalps. Working quickly and quietly, Flaming Sky removed a single scalp from the warrior's lance. The one he chose was that of a Cheyenne, a friend of his people. He recognized the sign on the rawhide attached to it. Holding the scalp in his hand, he felt his fiery blood cascading through his veins, screaming for revenge.

Once again, Flaming Sky found himself in an internal argument as to what he should do next. Trying to kill all of the Pawnee would bring him certain death. He was not old enough, nor was he experienced enough to defeat all four of them. Of this fact, he was absolutely certain. "No. That type of retribution will have to wait for a more advantageous time and place. Right here, right now, vengeance is not the appropriate course of action," He accepted the necessity of settling for the one Cheyenne scalp, which he planned to give it to White Wolf for proper burial later, trusting the spirit of the warrior who lost it would finally find peace.

Flaming Sky stopped breathing momentarily as the fourth warrior started sputtering in his sleep, appearing to startle himself awake. The boy remained motionless, holding his breath in the semidarkness, awaiting his fate. The sleeping man, remaining unaware of Flaming Sky's presence, opened his eyes, lazily blinking a couple of times. Turning over onto his left side, facing the fire, he mumbled, quietly grunting as he drifted back into sleep.

Oh, how Flaming Sky longed to punish them for their barbaric act of scalping. This disgraceful tactic of removing a dead warrior's scalp was in great disfavor among his people. Unfortunately, this custom was very common among many tribes, especially those of the south and of the east. Struggling to keep his anger under control, at least momentarily, he ultimately accepted the fact: their punishment must wait. His present responsibility was to survive and return safely with the ceremonial plants and herbs he had been commissioned to gather.

"If all goes well," he thought, "the four of them will not even miss the stolen articles until much later. With any luck at all, they will probably assume the items were lost somewhere along the way."

With his three treasures securely in hand, he directed his attention to the ponies. "What a coup it would be if I could take all four ponies back with me. No," he reconsidered thoughtfully. "It is not the wise thing to do. It will be prudent to take only what I have already confiscated, plus the paint pony I am about to liberate from the hapless Pawnee."

Confident with his decision, he perused the possibilities in his mind. "If I am extremely careful, they will believe the animals were

The Quest

not properly tied off for the night, and went wandering away on their own. Even if the braves suspect someone was here during the night, surely their intent will be upon finding their own mounts rather than searching for me. Who knows how long they might spend looking for the fourth missing horse before becoming discouraged and giving up completely?" he wondered, smiling mischievously. His plan had been successfully working up to this point, and there was no reason not to trust it through to the end. So, gathering up his weapons and his stash of herbs and food, he headed downstream, to where the Pawnee ponies were secured.

He eased toward them at a slow, casual pace, being extremely careful not to move too quickly, ensuring his approach remained non-invasive. First, he quieted the ponies by feeding them roots from his own food pouch. Next, gently rubbing and patting their necks, one at a time, he untied all four of the reins from the small saplings holding them.

He slowly guided the horses away from the camp, taking extra care not to leave any of his own footprints for the Pawnee to find and follow. Stepping quietly from rock to rock, he led the animals downstream. The horses' hoof prints in the muddy edge of the stream would be sufficient for the Pawnee to track. He continued walking the creek until arriving at a large rock along the bank of the stream, where he stopped. Taking the ponies to the boulder, he climbed onto the smooth surface. Standing on the rock made it easier for him to mount the horse's back. Holding the reins of the other three ponies in one hand, while using his free hand to steady the paint, he mounted. With the other three ponies in tow, he eased quietly down stream.

There was still ample darkness left before the sun was due to rise. Once he was comfortable that he was a safe enough distance away from the sleeping warriors that they would not hear the horses, he started running them at a full gallop. He intended to run them as long and as far as he could before they tired. By the time the bewildered

Pawnee awakened in the morning, Flaming Sky planned to be very far away from their camp.

True to his plan, the instant he was safely out of hearing range of the four braves, he kicked his pony in the sides with his heels, just hard enough for the horse to understand the command. Off they flew. Flaming Sky was riding the paint at a full gallop, with the other three ponies running at top speed right behind him.

The moon was nearing its full phase, providing ample light for him to make his escape. He headed the horses toward solid ground, away from the stream. They would travel faster and farther on hard, dry earth than in the muddy banks of the stream. At this point, he did not care if they left tracks for the Pawnee to follow. In fact, the truth of the matter was, he was hoping this would occur. The sound of the ponies' hoof beats were echoing louder than normal under the quiet, moonlit sky as he charged into the night.

By dawn, the ponies were played out. Releasing the reins, allowing the trailing ponies to scatter one by one in three different directions, he and the paint leisurely took the fourth direction, resuming his journey south, where the herbs and plants were waiting to be harvested. Assuming the Pawnee would follow the ponies, he was sure it would take them a majority of the day just to arrive at the place where the four horses split up.

After that, he was not exactly sure what the men would do.

"They could each follow a horse," he mused, "sending the warriors in four different directions, thereby weakening them." Then, considering some other possibilities, "They could go directly back the way they came. Maybe they will follow the horses only so far, before giving up. Or, they might decide to continue their hunt, while looking for other ponies to steal along the way."

He was sure there were many other possible combinations of things the Pawnee could do, but they were no longer important to him. He was comfortable at this distance, and more than a little relieved. No matter what they chose to do, the odds were greatly in his favor.

The Quest

As the sun was rising over the mountains to the east, Flaming Sky was still riding the paint. They were traveling at a steady, easy pace. "It will not be long," he thought, "until I can dismount and lead the pony for awhile." The ground continued getting harder the farther south they traveled. He knew he would soon be able to dismount and walk along side the horse without leaving any visible signs of his footprints. Without the burden of a rider, the pony would more quickly regain its strength and stamina. The animal was young, strong, and healthy. Except for being winded, it did not appear to be suffering any ill effects from the draining ride they had taken together.

Pulling the pony's reigns, Flaming Sky brought it to a halt. He slid off the horse, leaving his pouches securely attached to the animal's back. Checking to see if he was leaving footprints, he observed the ground was so hard that the hoofs of the animal were barely leaving scuffmarks on the earth. Certain he was now safe from detection, he walked beside the horse, steadily heading southward, to whatever lay ahead for him.

This was new, unknown territory for him, and he had never ventured this distance from his base camp, even when hunting with the older warriors. With this fact clearly in mind, Flaming Sky carefully studied the landscape, plotting markers in his mind for use later, to guide him on his return journey.

Walking calmly, he resumed his search for the plants and foliage he was committed to gathering. From White Wolf's description, it appeared he was nearing his final destination. "With any luck at all, I should find everything I need to harvest within a few days," he surmised. Soon he would be able to start on his return trip home, riding his brave pony. Along with the plants of his quest, he would be carrying the coup taken in his encounter with the Pawnee warriors. This image pleased him immensely.

This land was indeed the place described to him. During the next two days, he easily harvested a generous supply of herbs and plants.

Finding the plants had not been very difficult, once he identified their natural environment. The time spent here was safe and comfortable. There was absolutely no sign of anyone else on the southern prairie. He often contemplated the fate of the Pawnee as he went about his work in a relaxed, serious manner.

Flaming Sky's shaman taught him "*all living things must be treated with respect…sometimes, even with reverence,*" and so he did as he was trained to do. He said the prayers of thanksgiving to Wakan Tanka while picking the sacred plants and herbs, and digging up the ceremonial roots. He was unsure as to how many plants he should harvest; however, he was aware that everything he was gathering needed to be dried, so it could be easily and safely transported back to the Sacred Mountains. Once there, he would place them in the hands of White Wolf, for the old man to sanctify on another day.

Now riding, Flaming Sky was covering larger areas much faster than he could have if he remained on foot. He and the pony were starting to become comfortable with each other. From this time forward, he was sure they would remain together until one of them died. Someday soon, Flaming Sky would ride the paint on his first buffalo hunt. Thanks to the mobility provided by his horse, Flaming Sky was now expanding his area in search of food. With the help of his new companion, he not only had fresh deer meat, but he was now likely to start his return journey to the Black Hills on schedule… possibly even a little early.

He was well pleased with himself and content with the generous harvest gathered. In order to avoid any stray Pawnee, the boy and his pony first circled widely to the southwest. When he was sure it was safe to do so, he turned the pony straight north…homeward bound.

THE QUEST

BOOK III THE INITIATION

Chapter 1

STORIES

The boys were given a good seven days to rest, allowing them to recuperate and regain their strength. Their resting time now complete, they were ready to proceed. Tonight they will take the initial step of their rites of passage into adulthood. The counsel, gathering in the ceremonial circle in the medicine lodge, will patiently listen as the young men make their claims to manhood, declaring their right to be recognized as Lakota warriors.

After White Wolf completes relating his tale to the counsel, the boys will present themselves, one at a time, first to their chief, and then to their Wicasa. They are to stand directly across from Running Fox and White Wolf, who are always seated next to each other. While facing the two most important members of their tribe, each boy must give a detailed recounting of his adventures, hoping to receive the approval of the elders and chiefs. Each will address the counsel in the same order in which he returned from his journey.

If found worthy, the boy is allowed to advance to the next step in his rite of passage. While recounting the story of his adventures, he will have to prove his valour. If judged meritorious, and found to have acted as a true warrior, he will be allowed to remain inside the council circle until the entire ritual is completed. This will be the first and last time the boy is allowed to be within the sacred circle… that is, until he has earned the right to become a council member, himself. Membership is a privilege earned through deeds of bravery and acts of service on behalf of the people.

Immediately at dusk, as the last light of the sun faded from the sky, White Wolf's spirit helpers set about the task of building a large council fire. They maintained a keen awareness toward detail throughout their preparations. In addition to the fire in the middle of the circle, the council is to be surrounded by torches, as light is a crucially important element in the ceremonial rite of passage. It is imperative that the elders see each candidate clearly, for, no matter what their words may say, their facial expressions and body language speak the ultimate truth within them. Everyone is capable of hiding the truth in shadows; however, light exposes each person's secrets, lying hidden in darkness. So, with the four boys always within the circle of light, the truth is revealed. Hearts, so exposed, are sure to beat rapidly in nervous anticipation. A rare potion, prepared by White Wolf explicitly for this occasion, was to be consumed warm by the members of the council and the boys.

Diligently, the spirit helpers cleared the area of rocks and other debris, assuring the ground would remain comfortable for the elders as they sit through the long ritual. Tonight was to be a night of story telling. Stories, well told, are often incorporated into the tribe's oral history. Tonight, the entire tribe will hear the boys relating their adventures. The braves will sit in an outer circle, a few feet behind the tribal elders. Behind the braves will be the women and the older children. Naturally, the youngest ones are home sleeping. Finishing their preparations, the women seated themselves next to the fire, feeding the flames with fresh fuel, while waiting patiently for the rising of the moon, signaling the commencement of the ritual.

The Quest

At last the moon arrived. Solemnly and quietly, the tribe drifted toward the circle, assuming their positions for the ceremony. The boys, anxiously awaiting their turn to enter the inner circle, were seated directly behind the elders and in front of the braves. The chiefs wore their ceremonial garb, including beautiful headdresses made of eagle feathers, some of which cascaded down their backs, almost touching the ground. Running Fox wore his most decorative headdress, containing fifteen clipped white eagle feathers, each notch commemorating a brave act.

White Wolf, wearing his Wicasa headdress made from a buffalo's skullcap, including the horns, carried the tribe's ceremonial pipe, the same pipe he often left in his cousin's keeping. It was not that White Wolf did not trust the four women, but the pipe must be safeguarded at all cost…even unto the death of its protector. This responsibility was best given to a seasoned and trustworthy warrior. Who better to be its guardian than Chief Running Fox? The ornate pipe was being pressed into service for the first time in many moons. It felt comfortable to the old man as he sat there crossed-legged, balancing the pipe on the palms of his hands. This was the signal for the elders to be seated.

Immediately, the rest of the gathering settled down, quickly becoming silent. White Wolf took a small flaming stick from the council fire and, guiding the flame to the pre-prepared mixture, he lit the bowl. It was the same mixture of cacota, white sage, pompotote and strong tobacco White Wolf often used when offering up his evening prayers. As always, in turn, he offered up the smoldering mixture to each of the four winds. Taking the pipe to his lips, and drawing deeply of the mixture, he asked the Great Spirit to bestow His blessing upon the boys. Softly exhaling, he released his prayer to be carried on the sacred smoke to the Grand Father.

He paused briefly before passing the pipe to Running Fox, who repeated the ritual of offering up the pipe to be sanctified by the four winds before inhaling deeply of the pipe's contents. Releasing the smoke to the Great Spirit, he passed the pipe. The procedure was followed by each of the elders, until the ceremonial pipe made it's way around the circle, eventually returning to White Wolf. Drawing four more times from the pipe, the old man offered up a final prayer to be transmitted by each of the winds. The opening ceremony was complete. It was now time for the recounting of great deeds.

White Wolf stood silently next to the seated Running Fox. Pausing, he took a long sip of the prepared potion before briefly summarizing the first days of his journey. This part of the trip had been uneventful and, therefore, did not take long in the retelling. He picked up his story by recounting his vision of the flaming eagle, symbolizing the one who would replace him as Wicasa. He followed it with the story of finding the ensnared doe.

Going into great detail, he spoke solemnly of the events transpiring over the following days. Only slightly embellishing the account of his encounter with the savages, he related how he had not only outsmarted them, but also outfought them. Step-by-step, event-byevent, he described in detail the bloody battle as it unfolded that night at his campfire. His words remained hanging in the air as he described how he stripped their bodies' of honour, shaving their heads and marking them as cowards for all to see.

Continuing his story, the old man was more in the past at the battle site than in the present meeting at the council fire. As always, White Wolf spoke in a constant tone, animating his story with the motion of his hands. He recounted how he carefully and painstakingly tied all of the dead savages onto their horses before sending them on to their final destiny in the land of the Comanche. He completed his story with the contrasting peacefulness of the remainder of his journey home.

Finished, he patiently waited, watching the reaction of the council. He smiled a little to himself, as they nodded, smiling approvingly at the conclusion of his tale. The reaction of the council clearly indicated the old man just added another chapter to the history of the people.

THE QUEST

He retired to his sitting position, justly proud and well pleased with the impact of his story upon the members of the council.

The ceremony proceeded. Standing, Running Fox invited the boys, one at a time, to enter into the circle, commencing with Short Bear, as he was the first to return. The boy, being the least qualified of the four, was justifiably nervous. Short Bear took a sip of the potion to calm himself. Then, summoning his courage as best he could, he began his story. Although Short Bear's journey was less challenging than the other boys' quests, he was grateful that at least he was able to retell it rather quickly. He recounted the fact that, through his own skills, he lived comfortably on the bounty supplied by the land. The high point of his story was meeting the other tribe. Although his story was uneventful, he had proven his courage and achieved his mission by surviving alone in a strange wilderness, far from the tribe for fourteen days, returning safely home, unharmed. The counsel nodded approvingly at the way he had conducted himself.

A little less frightened, Short Bear smiled wearily as White Wolf handed him the ceremonial pipe. Taking a small draw from the pipe, the boy held the sacred smoke for a short time. Remembering White Wolf's teaching, he offered up his thanks to the Great Spirit, while slowly exhaling the sacred smoke into the night air. Returning the ceremonial pipe to the Wicasa, and greatly relieved, he quickly took his place within the circle of the chiefs. He had successfully passed the first step in his initiation. For once, even his father, Thunder Eyes, who was standing with the other braves, was finally proud of Short Bear.

Standing Elk, having returned second, was the next to be invited into the circle by his chief. Stepping forward, much more confidently than Short Bear, he drank the potion offered by White Wolf. Taking a deep breath and relaxing, he started his story.

"The first thing I can clearly relate is the feeling of confusion and disorientation I experienced during the early days of being alone." He paused, looking down at the floor.

Raising his head, he went on to recount the instant when he first refocused…just prior to his initial encounter with the bear. He tried desperately to describe the thoughts going through his mind as he made the decision to attack the gigantic beast. The chief was unable to hide his smile as the crowd broke out in laughter, envisioning the sight of the boy and the bear facing each other.

Undaunted, he continued, "I considered trying to outrun him, but I was sure he would win. Then, I remembered the words of White Wolf, who told us: *'There is only one thing a brave can do when he is outflanked…attack!'*"

He described his assault on the huge dangerous beast, and how, after charging past the bear, he ran straight to the stand of trees that he had spotted earlier. He recounted the specific details of how he successfully managed to lure the bear up into the tree after him. The image of a very angry bear, foolishly pawing at the branches and leaves of the trees, managed to bring a smile even to Standing Elk, himself. This was the first time he was able to appreciate the humor of his own story.

Feeling even more confident, he continued by describing his taunting of the enraged animal. When he reached the part of the story where he escaped, while leaving the bear still up the tree, crazily tearing at the boughs, the council members could not stop themselves from roaring with laughter. Standing Elk felt a big grin spreading across his face as the elders emphatically nodded their approval.

Taking the council's acceptance as a cue, White Wolf ceremoniously handed him the medicine pipe. The boy drew deeply from the pipe, holding the smoke, as he had been taught, before releasing it to the night air, to be carried to the Great Spirit. When he finished, he carefully returned the pipe to his Wicasa. His part of the ceremony completed, Standing Elk proudly took his seat in the circle next to Short Bear. He let out a deep sigh of relief, hoping no one heard him.

Lone Feather was the next to be ushered into the center of the ceremonial circle. He took the potion, as the two boys before him

The Quest

had done, slowly drinking the liquid. Having done so, he returned the container to White Wolf. Running Fox signaled the boy to relate his story. Lone Feather complied with the direction of his chief, and began his tale. As it is true with most travels, a majority of the days are rather empty and uneventful. The third boy's journey was not any different. Reaching the place in his story where he was attacked by the large bird, he captured the attention of the entire group. It was an omen, a sign from the spirit world. However, it was only White Wolf who truly understood the secret of it's meaning. The boy himself was at a loss as to how it should be interpreted.

Lone Feather finished his story, knowing it would fall to White Wolf to interpret it's meaning at a later time. For now, the story served its purpose, having validated him as worthy. Receiving the chiefs' approval, the boy was now much more at ease. Smoking the pipe, he offered up his prayers to the Grand Father on the warm summer breeze. Then he quickly took his place beside his brother and Short Bear.

At last, it was Flaming Sky's turn to stand before his father, and his father's cousin, relating his adventures. Flaming Sky had donned his best buckskin shirt and pants in honour of the occasion. In addition, he wore a brand new headband, a belt and wristbands made from the skin of the snake he killed. There he stood, gazing past the chief, seeing only his mother, Spotted Deer and Morning Star standing together. Morning Star was wearing a brand new snakeskin headband, a mate to the one Flaming Sky was wearing. The young couples' eyes met fleetingly, interrupted when White Wolf offered the potion to Flaming Sky. After taking a generous swallow, he passed the cup back to his Wicasa.

Taking a deep breath, the boy commenced relating the story of his journey. He told them of fashioning his weapons from materials he found along the way, and how he was able to nourish himself with small game, fresh fish and a variety of fresh, edible roots and plants. Humbly, he spoke of his encounter with the snake, relating his thanks to the Great Spirit for the gift of the viper, which provided food for his journey and its skin for his future use. He expressed his gratefulness for finding the cacti with an abundance of sacred buttons, waiting for him to harvest, as he had promised White Wolf he would.

The intensity of the crowd's interest steadily increased as he started narrating the events of his encounter with the Pawnee hunting party. Recounting in great detail his long night of hiding from them in the tree, he breathlessly described his quiet invasion of their camp, and counting coup by taking an object from each one of the four warriors. The entire village had seen the captured pony, which he named Pawnee, in celebration of his victory over the enemy.

"The scalp was given to White Wolf for proper disposal," he explained reverently, "and our shaman has buried the Cheyenne warrior's scalp in the sky with full honours."

Flaming Sky concluded this part of his story by offering up the notched eagle feather and the decorated Pawnee arrow to Chief Running Fox, the final trophies of his bravery. After receiving the verbal approval of the council, he continued with the account of how he led the sleeping warriors' ponies away, thus leaving the hunting party on foot. White Wolf and Running Fox were already familiar with this part of the story; however, Flaming Sky was about to unveil a part of the adventure that, until now, remained untold. It had been spoken of neither to his father, Running Fox, nor to his father's cousin, White Wolf.

"After liberating one pony for myself, and scattering the other three, I decided to travel even further south in search of the bloom of an extremely rare flower described to me by White Wolf. It is a plant found growing only deep inside the borders of the land of the savages. Now that I owned a horse, I could travel much farther and faster than by walking. I enjoyed the freedom of riding south in search of the flowering plant. With luck, I would have enough time to harvest the plant and return to the village on schedule.

The Quest

"I knew the blossoms harvested from this plant would greatly please my shaman," Flaming Sky declared. "These plants are rare and, because of the danger involved, he only gathers as many of them as he can every third or fourth quest into the southern desert. Due to it's scarcity, White Wolf uses it very sparingly, and only on the most important occasions. The red flower is strong medicine, and well worth the risk involved in gathering it."

White Wolf had given him a very complete, detailed description of the plant, which he described by memory. "The stalk is thick and tubular. The average height is approximately four hands. The stem bears three leaves, similar in size and shape to those found on a corn stalk. The weight of the blossoms is such that the plants are often bent over, even to the point of touching the ground. A large, thick bud grows at the top of the stem, and it is slow in blooming. Once it blooms, its time of power is short lived. The pod slowly separates into two tightly wrapped, twin, red cocoons. Eventually they change from a V formation into a horizontal position. Quite often there is a third bud, only one-fourth the size of the others. It is this bud that possesses the strongest medicine.

"The blossoms must be picked just as they are on the verge of blooming," he explained. "If picked too soon, or too late, the power of the flowers is lessened. The larger blooms are to be harvested first, and kept separate from the smaller, more potent ones. Once picked, the petals must be carefully peeled away and immediately dried in the warm sun. After being properly preserved, they are to be stored in the small herb pouches and carried home."

The boy, who had been well schooled by the old man, was pleased that this was the season of blooming. "I was confident in my ability to locate and preserve several flowers. He prepared me well, and I was anxious to begin my search. My plans were laid, and I turned Pawnee southward, heading straight toward the borders of the land of the savages. Once I reached the boundaries of their territory, I altered my tactics. If my memory of what White Wolf told me was correct, I would be deep in the southern desert in no more than two suns."

He explained that it was far too dangerous for him to continue riding by day. "The possibility of an encounter with the desert devils, as Chief Running Fox calls them, increased with every step my pony took. I realized it would be a great deal safer to travel at night, while sleeping during the daylight. The moon, which was entering its full phase, provided more than adequate light to make night riding possible. In the early morning hours of the new day, I looked for a likely place to rest. Later, I hunted for small game. I chose campsites that were neither inviting, nor hospitable, thereby decreasing the chances of meeting any hostile hunting parties. Traveling south, I constantly searched the terrain for signs of the blooming plant, until, eventually, my vigilance bore fruit.

"In the dawn light of the third sun," he said, grinning, "I spotted one of the rare plants I had been patiently seeking. Gazing about, I saw at least six or seven of them scattered over the expanse of my visual range. The nearest plant was in full bloom, proudly displaying it's blood-red blossoms. From what I observed, the others were still budding. It appeared my timing was perfect; but, to guarantee their full potency, I had to harvest them while they were at the peak of their power, which only lasts four sunsets."

It was very late by the time he finished gathering all of the flowers he was able to find. Completing his harvesting, he searched for a place to make his night camp. He had been so intent on his task that, up until this instant, he did not see the small wisps of smoke drifting skyward from a nearby campfire. He quickly hid his pony in a thicket and quietly proceeded on foot in the direction of the smoke.

"Approaching the campfire," he told them, "I heard the sound of voices speaking in a strange dialect. Had I accidentally stumbled across a campsite of the savages? Taking very slow, deliberate steps, I silently worked my way through the underbrush, maneuvering myself into a position where I was hidden, but with an excellent

The Quest

view of the desert devils. There were six of them, whose faces were coloured with war paint. They were gathered around a naked Comanche, whom they had captured and staked over an anthill. He was stretched out, spread eagle, over a mound of fire ants. His wrists and ankles, bound with rawhide, were attached to wooden stakes driven solidly into the desert floor.

"What I saw next," he grimaced, "was something so inhumane, I will never forget it. Never…not for the rest of my life! I was on the verge of learning how the people of this tribe earned the title of savages. Watching the laughing savages as they rubbed the juice of the juniper in a thick layer over their nude prisoner's body, one of them applied the juice to the man's face, squeezing the liquid into his eyes, nose, mouth, and ears. The Comanche tried pulling away, but was unable to do so, as his head was securely held in place by another one of the painted desert devils.

"A look of terror crossed the man's face as the ants, attracted to the sweet juice, began swarming over his bare flesh. The biting must have felt like stinging drops of acid piercing his skin. Small droplets of blood were appearing on his body as the ants went about ripping their way into his exposed skin. Screaming in agonizing pain, he desperately tried shaking the insects off of his face, but his efforts were to no avail. Countless numbers of fire ants, with thousands of tiny little feet, were tracking through the syrupy substance on his face. The hoard of devouring death was growing thicker and more aggressive, vigorously eating its way into his eyes."

He paused, looking down with grief. "Repeatedly, the man screamed in agony, his pain constantly growing more unbearable. I watched in shock as the brave's body wrenched and twisted in a valiant but fruitless effort to break free of his bindings. By this time, the carnivorous ants were already crawling up his nose and into his mouth. Coughing and gagging. he uselessly tried sneezing the ants out of his bleeding nostrils The insects, eating their way into his sinuses, were making it impossible for him to breath. Shaking his head violently, he screamed with terror as they chewed their way into his brain. He tried spitting them out of his mouth, but his attempts were useless, as the ants were already feasting on the lining of his throat. Invading his ears, they quickly worked their way through the delicate membrane, into the inner ear. His screaming increased until it became one endless cry of pain beyond belief," he related solemnly, fighting his feeling of nausea.

"I remember watching the brave biting down on the crawling invaders. No doubt he was sickened by the sharp, bitter, burning taste of the ants," he commented. He related how the Comanche brave fought valiantly, without success. "His body continued convulsing as the insects ate their way through his eyelids, stealing the last of his sight. He let out another tormented scream, which turned my body into a mass of quivering shivers," which he experienced again, telling this horrible tale. "It did not take as long for the voracious ants to totally engulf the unfortunate brave's unprotected body as it does for me to tell about it, but it seemed like an eternity to me as I watched. The brave's breathing became increasingly weaker and laboured as the tiny creatures invaded his lungs. His screaming grew weaker, as his entire body was being consumed by thousands and thousands of vicious, hungry, biting ants. The blood seeping out through the tiny wounds only served to draw more ants to the free meal.

"Up to this point in time, it was the most horrifying thing I had ever seen," he said numbly. "It was nothing compared to the horror which I was about to witness."

The boy took a deep breath, calming himself before continuing. "With his energy almost completely spent, the staked warrior was convulsing, and thrashing helplessly about. I watched one of the savages, with a sinister smirk on his lips, menacingly approaching the dying man. Kneeling down next to the Comanche, he grabbed him by the hair with one hand, producing a knife in the other one. While the victim was still alive, the savage cut into his scalp at the hairline, ripping the skin back while slicing into the victim's head.

The Quest

The savage continued with the ghastly ordeal until he removed the entire scalp from the bound victim. The captured warrior let out one final, muffled cry of anguish as the savage waved the Comanche's own bloody scalp over his expiring body," the boy said, almost retching at his own memories.

He paused for a while, and everyone remained silent. "I have great sorrow in my heart and respect for this valiant brave," he said solemnly "watching the desert devils laughing at the tortured warrior's pain and disgrace, showing no respect for the sacrifice he was making for their pleasure. The leader of the group arrogantly tied the fresh scalp to his lance, proudly displaying his new trophy.

"Having observed their brutality first hand," he said in a hushed tone, "I truly understand the meaning of savagery. Despite my outrage, I held my silence, even though my blood was flowing like lava through my veins. I never imagined that any people could be this cruel. I struggled successfully with my raging urges for revenge, overcoming them by remembering my first duty. I was to return with the harvest, unharmed."

The elders looked at Flaming Sky in a state of stunned disbelief at his tale. "I stayed in hiding, waiting for the savages to return to their hunt, remaining hidden until after they broke camp and were safely out of sight. I deeply regretted there was nothing I could do to avenge the dead warrior, as I carefully made my way to where the tortured body lay. It was impossible for me to retrieve the body without being attacked by the raging insects, so I did what little I could. Digging up chunks of dirt with my fishing spear, I spread earth over the dead warrior's body. The ants, still feeding on the carcass, were also covered with the dirt, thereby becoming part of the funeral mound.

"After finishing my responsibility to the dead brave, I returned to where Pawnee was waiting for me. Seeking the shelter of a nearby thicket, I remained in hiding, retreating into a restless sleep throughout the heat of the day. At nightfall, I cautiously turned northward, heading toward home and the Sacred Hills of our ancestors. I rode only at night, until I was well beyond the northern border of the savages." Here his story ended.

The council remained sitting silently in shock for some time, trying to comprehend the extremes of his experience. Finally, Running Fox and White Wolf remembered to signal Flaming Sky to take his place within the center of the circle. He had told his story well. Receiving the ceremonial pipe from White Wolf, the young brave drew the smoke slowly from the bowl, just like the others before him. After releasing the smoke to the Grand Father, he respectfully returned the ceremonial pipe into his father's cousin's hands.

Having completed his part of the ceremony on such a solemn note, Flaming Sky went to where the other three boys were sitting, silently joining them. Together the four young braves sat awaiting the end of the ritual The ceremonial pipe was passed around the council once more. After all the elders smoked, Running Fox declared the ceremony officially concluded.

The boys walked around the circle, paying their respects to the chiefs, before rushing off to be greeted by their families. All of them had succeeded in earning the right to proceed to the next step of their initiation. Tomorrow they will fast and meditate for four risings and settings of the sun, but tonight is a time for celebration and feasting…and so they did.

Chapter 2

LEGENDS

During this time of cleansing, the boys were constantly together, preparing themselves for the next step of their initiation through continuous meditation and prayer. From this time forward, they would have no further contact with their families until the rituals were completed, other than the part their fathers were to play in the remaining preparations and testing. The fasting was intended to help in the purification of their bodies; therefore, the boys were encouraged to drink as much fresh water as possible.

"Water," explained the Wicasa, "being a flushing agent, will help purge your bodies of impurities, while allowing you to maintain your strength in anticipation of the warmer days at hand."

A majority of their final instruction would come under the guidance of their Wicasa, White Wolf. His was the responsibility of teaching them the prayers and magical chants they will be required to recite. Only with his assistance will they be capable of navigating through the gateway leading to the next level in their rite of passage, along their way to achieving the status of adulthood. Although

White Wolf was solely charged with the obligation of preparing them spiritually for the challenges awaiting them, each of their fathers shared the responsibility of instructing them in the ways of the people.

White Wolf often reminded them, "You are taught the history, traditions, and the rules governing our tribe. Never forget the most important rule of all: '*No matter how large or how small the number, the tribe is always one family.*' Survival, of the family is dependent upon the people thinking, acting and living as a single, unified being."

Each morning of the cleansing phase, their activities began with the rising of the sun. First they went to the river, where they filled skin containers with fresh drinking water. Once the containers were full, they bathed themselves in the cold stream, after which they presented themselves to their shaman for the start of the day's lessons. Their first activity of the new day was the repeating of chants they were to use while dancing their pledge to the sun. They also studied the prayers to be recited during their purification in the sweat lodge. They completed each day's lessons by meditating, after which the boys returned to the river, bathing themselves in preparation for the evening's meeting in the lodge house. It was here they learned the history of the people.

They had heard bits and pieces of the tribe's story throughout most of their young lives; however, from this time forward, they were to be receptacles and narrators of that knowledge. In time, it would be their responsibility to pass on this verbal record to the next generation. So it had always been done, father to son, from the very beginning of time. It was on the fourth and final night that White Wolf told the legend of the coming of the sacred dogs.

"We have always been nomads," he told them, "living off the abundance provided by the land. We have long dwelled in harmony and peace with the earth. Living this way is a most difficult existence. We follow the game for our food. The deer, elk, and bear provide us with meat and clothing; however, it is the buffalo which has always

The Quest

been our greatest gift from the Grand Father. Tatanka is the main source of our food, clothing, blankets, and a majority of our weapons and tools. Every spring we trail the buffalo north. Every autumn we follow the herds south. We depend upon their bounty for the tribe's survival. We not only count upon them to supply us with fresh meat for the season of the sun, but also to provide us with the dried meat needed to sustain us through the long, cold nights of darkness.

"In the time before the coming of the sacred dogs, our grandfathers searched for the buffalo on foot, wandering across the prairie until they located a herd, thereby necessitating the need to set up their camp as near to the grazing animals as possible. In the predawn light, the braves quietly ventured on foot into the milling buffalo, constantly trying their best to remain on the outer edges of the herd. However, the instant the animals smelled the scent of blood from the hunt, they would panic and begin running wildly, spreading themselves out in all directions. It was not unusual for our ancestors to have two or three braves killed on any given day. Many others were seriously wounded during the ensuing hunt, but the tribe survived. They would have the food they needed to sustain themselves…but at a price.

"Some of the women skinned and gutted the animals, while others went about the chore of cooking the fresh meat over open fires. After everyone ate their fill, they continued working until the hunt was finished. Then the women returned to their sewing, the men to mending old weapons, and making new ones. Many arrows were always lost during the hunt and needed to be replenished as quickly as possible.

"The tribe could only live comfortably in one place for short periods of time. As the buffalo migrated, the tribe moved with them. Without any beasts of burden, save their dogs, the journey was extremely slow and enormously difficult. The dogs could only pull a limited amount of weight on the litters; therefore, much of the burden was carried on the backs of the people." White Wolf nodded before continuing his speech.

"The people were always on the move, constantly following the brown stream of life from place to place, until the weather forced them to make winter camp. If the hunt was good, the moons of the winter snow passed more comfortably. Unfortunately, they were unable to carry sufficient supplies to ensure having enough food stored to feed them all until the time of the spring thaw. All too frequently, the very old, as well as the very young, were lost to the icy breath of the unceasing winter winds sweeping through the plains of our land. And so they lived from season to season, from generation to generation," he paused, "until the coming of, Tashunca, the sacred dogs.

"For many changes of the seasons, our people had been hearing rumors of the existence of such animals, but none of them had ever seen one. The stories about the sacred dogs traveled north from the great deserts beyond the farthest edge of the southern plains. These tales included descriptions of the beasts. Although they were similar to large dogs in appearance, each was strong enough to carry a man on its back without slowing down its speed. There were rumors they were capable of carrying very heavy burdens over long distances without tiring. It was said they were swift, light on their hoofs, and were easily trained for domestic purposes. The only problem involved was catching one," he said, raising his eyebrows.

"Reportedly, they were so fast that a warrior on foot was completely out-matched by them. The people thought, 'If they really do exist, they will not be easily captured.'

The people prayed, continuously hoping the stories told of these beasts were true. They often thought of how much easier their lives would be with such animals in their possession. So they waited, and they watched. Moon after moon, winter after winter, they waited until, finally, one day, their patience was rewarded.

The Quest

"The incident occurred during the time of my father's grandfather's grandfather. He was a great warrior who became known as Dream Catcher, as there was no dream of his people he was not courageous enough to pursue. He was a young brave at the time, when one of the scouts brought word of having seen several herds of these wondrous creatures, these sacred dogs. The nearest ones were located approximately a two-day walk from their camp. This was the news Dream Catcher had been waiting forever to hear. The plan was already conceived in his mind, and five of his comrades were ready to follow his lead. The young warrior and the other five braves were given permission by their chief, as well as the blessing of the medicine man, prior to undertaking this mission.

"Eagerly, the six of them gathered up the equipment needed once they actually found these beautiful animals, which the people would come to call Tashunca: ponies, or horses. The young men ate well that night, sleeping long and deep in preparation for their perilous journey. They were up, dressed, and on their way at first light. Loaded down with as much rawhide and hemp as they could carry, they started on the quest that would guarantee their place in the history of the tribe. These six were determined to change the life of the people forever; and, change it they did.

"Midway through the third day of their search, they finally got a distant glimpse of the ponies. One of the young braves initially spotted them grazing close to where the valley narrowed at the mouth of the gully, and near the entrance to a small box canyon.

Taking their blankets with them, and being very careful to make sure they remained down wind, the braves approached the grazing herd. In all, they counted four young mares and two male colts. If the stories they heard were true, the absence of a stallion leading the herd greatly increased the probability of the hunters' success.

"Quietly approaching the ponies," he continued, "the six braves spread out, silently surrounding them on three sides, thus leaving the animals only one exit, and that was to the north, leading them into the trap. Dream Catcher and one of the other braves positioned themselves behind the ponies; meanwhile, the other four men formed a line on either side of the grouping of animals. At Dream Catcher's signal, he and his companions advanced, wildly waving their blankets at the horses.

"Bolting, the sacred dogs dashed around frantically, searching for an escape. The four braves running along side the herd now joined in by waving their blankets, making it impossible for the out-flanked horses to veer to the left or right. Thus, they were left with no other option than to run due north, allowing themselves to be driven into the box canyon. Once the ponies were inside the canyon, three of the men remained at the entrance, guarding against the risk of losing any of the precious animals. Dream Catcher and the other two braves gathered branches to construct a barricade at the canyon's entrance.

"It took the braves several days; but, eventually, they were able to break the horses. At first, the animals were very wild and skittish. Dream Catcher, with the help of three braves, worked the mares. In the meantime, the remaining two men took on the task of taming the two colts. The colts, like many young animals, were fairly trusting, even of humans. The older ponies, however, were not of the same mind. Each man chose one animal to tame. From that time forward, the men and horses remained matched together, to build a sense of trust and safety between them.

"The process used has remained unchanged to this day. Each brave starts by slowly and calmly approaching a horse, stopping whenever it becomes agitated. Once the animal settles down, the brave cautiously advances, stopping and restarting as often as necessary. The technique takes a great deal of time and patience before reaching the point where man and horse are able to stand quietly, looking into each other's eyes.

"The man gently strokes the horse's muzzle and neck, while simultaneously speaking softly to it. Gradually, the stroking of the pony is extended until, eventually, the brave is gently rubbing the

The Quest

horse's entire body. In time, each grows used to the sound of its warrior's voice and accepting of his touch. Once the sacred dogs are more at ease with the brave, the next step of the process begins. The man first slips a loop of rope around the horse's muzzle, allowing it to gradually get used to the feel of it. Next, he gently lays a blanket across the horse's back, while continuously soothing the animal with the stroking of his hands, and the softness of his words. It does not take long for the pony to accept the feel of the blanket.

"The major task the men had to accomplish was training the animals to become comfortable with the sensation of the warriors' weight on their backs. In order to mount the horse, the brave grabbed the mane while hoisting himself up so that he was lying on his stomach, across its back. If it became spooked, or started to buck, the brave simply let go of the mane, safely sliding off onto the ground. The process was repeated until the pony was willing to tolerate the weight of the man. When it appeared at ease with the situation, the brave mounted, hoping it would accept having the man astride it's back. Occasionally the horses showed streaks of resistance, but nothing that was not easily handled by the riders. It took about eight days to complete the chore, forming a bond of brave and beast.

"The five braves, with one pair riding double, rode northward toward their village on the mares, leading the colts behind them. Dream Catcher, who remained behind on foot, was determined to travel farther south in hopes of finding more of these wondrous beasts for his people. The scout reported seeing many more ponies than just the six they had located so far; thus, he decided to continue his search. At first light the following morning, he set about his quest, heading into the southern plains in his pursuit of more sacred dogs. "On the evening of the third day of his solitary travels, he came across his elusive quarry. It started when he smelled smoke carried on the late evening breeze. Instead of looking for a place to set up his own campsite, he cautiously headed toward the scent. It was long after dark before he neared the camp and was able to see the light of the fire. He used the light cutting through the darkness as a homing beacon.

"Carefully and quietly, he followed the flickering flames, leading him directly to the campsite. Here he spotted seven sacred dogs tied to the brush downwind of the camp. By the time he arrived at the site, the encamped hunters had finished eating their evening meal and were preparing to sleep. He patiently waited, watching them from the darkness and listening to them talking, as they bedded down for the night. He learned enough of the language from his elders to recognize the speech he was hearing was that of the savages. He accidentally stumbled across an entire nest of them.

"Maintaining his vigilance from the darkness until he was sure all seven of them were asleep, he cautiously made his way to the edge of the camp where the ponies were tied. Softly and speedily, he went from pony to pony, untying them. The instant he finished, he took the reins in his hand and quietly led the horses away from the camp, heading toward the northern sky. Once he was a safe distance from the savages, he tied the reins of six of the animals together, attaching them to the end of a long rope. Mounting the seventh, a young healthy sorrel, he rode stealthily into the dark with the six horses securely in tow behind him.

"He kept the horses moving at a nice even pace until the sun came up. The instant it became light, he started riding as fast as he could, guiding the trailing horses. Shortly past high sun of the following day, Dream Catcher, riding the sorrel, and leading the other six ponies, proudly paraded into the center of the village. This is the story of how Dream Catcher earned his name. Because of his bravery, the dream of our people came to be, and Tashunca, the sacred dogs, were introduced into the life of the tribe." Having finished his story, White Wolf fell silent, patiently waiting for the questions, which were always asked following the telling of this tale.

"Did the savages ever know who took them?" asked Short Bear.

The Quest

"No," replied White Wolf. "The owners of the horses never discovered who had taken them."

"What happened to all of the ponies?" inquired Lone Feather.

"Except for the sorrel, which he kept, Dream Catcher gave the stolen horses to the chief, who became his father-in-law," explained White Wolf.

"What about the first six ponies they trapped and tamed?" questioned Standing Elk.

"The first six were kept by the braves who captured them. By the passing of the four seasons, the size of the herd had almost doubled. Within the completion of five winters, they were able to raise, capture and steal enough horses to allow every brave in the camp to possess at least one."

White Wolf continued with his concise answers to their questions: "Yes, it was because of the horses that their nomadic life became less strenuous." "No, our people never went to war over the theft of the seven horses Dream Catcher brought home." "Yes, eventually Dream Catcher did become a chief and a wise leader of the people." "Yes, this is why ponies are still used as a part of the asking price of a wife,"… and so on. Soon, all of the questions were asked and answered, and the night's lesson drew to an end.

The only remaining business was for the boys to receive their final instructions for the next day's event: the spiritual cleansing ritual of the sweat lodge. White Wolf reminded them to continue fasting until after the completion of the ceremonial sweat. Once more, he reviewed the chants and prayers they were to offer up to Wakan Tanka. They concluded by repeating the prayers they were to recite the first time around the circle.

"On the next three rotations," added White Wolf, "you may each freely express your own thoughts, wishes, or desires to the Great Spirit. It is customary. The ritual will require a total of four complete turns around the circle.

"At the conclusion of the fourth round, we will remain silent, awaiting any response to our individual prayers. The answers are most commonly revealed in the form of a vision. Remember," he admonished them, "you must allow yourselves to completely surrender to the experience. Become one with it. Allow yourselves to totally embrace it. You will be safe. I shall be there, should you have need of me.

"Once you have completed the ceremonial sweat, you may wish to plunge your bodies into the river to cool yourselves. When requested to do so, you will describe your visions to your shaman and to your chief. Afterwards, upon our having thoroughly discussed your vision, it is customary for you to offer a small token of appreciation to each of them. Sage or tobacco are acceptable gifts to be given on such occasions. After you have recounted your visions, and they have been satisfactorily evaluated, we will conclude the ceremony and retire to the feast."

The boys dragged their aching bodies back to their lodge for the night, their minds swimming in the mire of all they had to remember. They were exhausted, and they were hungry. A good night's sleep would relieve the weariness, but only food, which they were still denied, could curb their hunger. They bedded down for the night, their thoughts taking them off in different directions. Flaming Sky dwelled on thoughts of his betrothed, Morning Star, who was going through her own training, preparing for her final testing.

Morning Star's challenges lay in different areas than his. She was fine-tuning her skills in the arts of home and hearth: cooking, sewing and childrearing. Her tests will evaluate her mastery of the concepts of being a wife and a mother. She will first demonstrate her sewing abilities by mending old clothes, and by fashioning new ones. Then comes the evaluation of her talents in attending to the proper upbringing of the children. She will display her cooking techniques by using the proper herbs and roots to prepare a meal to be served

The Quest

with or without meat. It is her responsibility to ensure the health of her family, just as it is her mate's obligation to provide food while keeping them safely protected. Tomorrow, she, too, will engage in her own purification rite, along with the other girls who are coming of age. White Wolf, as the most captivating teller of tales, has the honour of teaching the history of the people to these young maidens, emphasizing the contributions made by the women of the tribe.

"There is only one true story to be told," he began. "However, it is a legend, which comes attached with a variety of conflicting details. Some versions of the tale are always more difficult to comprehend than others."

The old man paused momentarily, studying the eyes of his listeners. Content he was successfully capturing the complete attention of Morning Star and the other verging maidens, White Wolf started spinning his story.

"She came to us on a white cloud, sent by the Great Spirit who lives in the sky, arriving here in the same state in which she was originally born. Arriving as a young maiden, with all the innocence of a wondrous child, she truly was a Wankan, a Sacred One. The Grand Father created this young woman, Himself, and sent her on His breath. Although often called Running Moon, she is most generally referred to as the White Buffalo Woman. She entered the land of the warring tribes with only two possessions in her keeping: a prayer pipe, and the Sacred Bundle."

Pausing, the old man displayed the Sacred Bundle. "It has been handed down from Holy One to Holy One. There have been many generations in which it was not claimed by any man or woman. It is possessed of strong medicine, and has the power to recognize its true caretaker and protector. The Sacred Bundle can never be possessed by one who has shed the blood of one of his own people. When my time comes, I will pass it down to the next Wicasa."

Replacing the Sacred Bundle in its proper location, he returned his attention to the story of the Holy Woman. "She was very pleasing to the eye, with skin as soft as a newborn. Her medium-length hair was the colour of a shining raven wing, with a light-brown tone to her oval-shaped face. Her eyes, which were perfectly spaced, possessed the power to look through a person to the truth. The lines of her mouth were straight, with lips that were not as full as many. Although her rounded nose was slightly smaller than average, it was nonetheless beautiful. All of her physical attributes were intoxicating, including her well-proportioned breasts. Despite her delicate frame, she was fierce of spirit." White Wolf spoke of her in a loving, but solemn tone.

"For four full-cycles of the seasons, she walked without clothing from village to village, from camp to camp. Appearing almost out of nowhere, she spoke to the chiefs and to the councils, advocating peace and harmony among all of the Sioux, constantly encouraging an end to the petty wars continuously ravaging the people. From her, they received the prayer pipe with which to offer up words of gratitude to the Great Spirit for the abundance of His great gift of Tatanka, and to pray for unity, strength, and guidance. By the end of the fourth autumn, the wise ones were finally understanding and accepting her message. Once the Sioux people stopped making war upon themselves, she abandoned her nudity in favor of wearing fulllength deerskin dresses, remaining with the people four more complete revolutions of the seasons. During her time, the streams of migrating buffalo were abundant, meeting the needs of all the tribes.

"The first shaman was chosen by her, and with the help of the power of the Sacred Bundle, she identified the peoples' first Wicasa, chosen by the Great Spirit. It was to him that she entrusted the Sacred Bundle. Although the contents are objects of great power, they are never to be discussed with anyone…ever!" White Wolf paused, his words hanging in the still air. "Its medicine is to be used sparingly, only when the need of the people is so great that it is beyond human endurance.

The Quest

"In the ninth winter, she disappeared, just as mysteriously as she originally manifested among them. Running Moon began her mission speaking to small groups of independent, warring tribes. She ended it addressing a united Sioux nation, a people with a common destiny. This is the legend of Running Moon, the Sacred One, the White Buffalo Woman, the emissary of Wakan Tanka." With the telling of his tale completed, White Wolf allowed Morning Star and the other girls to ponder the story before speaking again.

"I told you there were other versions of this legend. Our brothers, the Cheyenne, tell a similar story of White Buffalo Woman, and are the first to refer to her as Running Moon. They say, while she was requesting our ancestors to make peace, she was also appearing among the separate Cheyenne tribes with the same petition.

"It was during her four winters of instruction to our separate peoples that the hostilities between the Sioux and Cheyenne finally came to an end. Through her intercession, we awakened to the fact that we are brothers…two sons of one father and two mothers. Since that time, both of our peoples have flourished.

"You have seen the Sacred Bundle, which, in time, will be passed on to our next Wicasa, if and when the Great Spirit so chooses. We have remained fortunate. The prayer pipe she gave us, as well as the Sacred Bundle, have remained safely with us ever since that time. The pipe will be given to the shaman who replaces me.

"Our Cheyenne brothers did not fare as well. Generations ago, their Sacred Bundle was lost to them when its keeper and his tribe were annihilated by the treacherous Blackfoot. No one knows for sure the ultimate fate of the Bundle. Cheyenne legend says he who is of three tongues, the son of a Blackfoot who is not of Blackfoot blood, will someday retrieve the lost Sacred Bundle and place it into the hands of a great chief who is not Cheyenne. Armed with the powers of the Sacred Bundles of the Sioux and Cheyenne, and with the blessing of the Grand Father, he will unite our great nations against the final assault aimed at our ultimate destruction."

Having finished this version of the story, White Wolf again remained silent, allowing Morning Star and the other girls to contemplate its meaning. There were no questions for him to answer, so he dismissed them to their sewing lessons.

Flaming Sky missed her. They had not seen each other for well over a quarter of the changing moon. He remembered how especially pretty Morning Star looked the first time she wore the new snakeskin headband, which he presented her upon his return from his survival quest. Contemplating their impending future together, he wondered, "What will it be like? Will we have a family? If so, how many children will we have? What will it feel like to take on the roles of husband and father?" The thoughts in his head continued along this vein until, finally, he drifted into sleep.

He was hoping they would marry in less than another full cycle of the seasons. The ceremony was anticipated to take place shortly after the autumn buffalo hunt; but, the choice of the exact time belonged to her parents. He had not yet presented the purchasing gifts to her father. There would be time enough after completing the hunt. Her father's asking price was four ponies, two new bows, thirty arrows, and one buffalo robe. The young warrior was already crafting the bows and arrows. His father and White Wolf promised to acquire the necessary ponies for him, but it was up to him to procure the buffalo robe. The robe was to be made from the hide of an animal that he himself killed, single-handedly.

"There is plenty of time left," he thought. "The autumn hunt is at least two or…maybe three moons away."

Thus the thoughts flowed through his mind, as he drifted peacefully into sleep. It was a very deep and restful sleep. It was a sleep where he dreamed not of Morning Star, but of Sleeping Possum, the girl from the stream, who often visited him in his nightly visions.

Chapter 3

THE SWEAT LODGE

White Wolf's spirit helpers were engaged in their tasks long before sundown on the last day of the history telling. They started by carefully inspecting the sweat lodge for any signs of holes or tears, while one examined the lodge flap, ensuring it would remain sealed tightly, holding the heat and steam inside the buffalo-skin structure throughout the ceremony. Satisfied the sweat lodge was in good repair, the women turned their attention to constructing the pit, digging it in close proximity to the lodge.

The finished hole was a rectangular depression, approximately one-and-a-half paces by two paces, and one pace in depth. They prepared the pit by lining the bottom with several long pieces of hard, slow-burning, thick wood. Across the top of the hard wood were six large rocks in two groupings of three. Confident the rocks were properly positioned, the four women added kindling. Sitting next to the fire, patiently waiting, they continuously fed the base of the fire with dry tinder. Once the faster-burning twigs and smaller sticks were engulfed in flames, they added larger pieces of hard firewood, stacking them in an upright position against the rocks in the center of the fiery pit.

The fire spreading across the lower layer of the hard wood, working its way up the standing logs, caused the flames to shoot upward into the night sky. From the sky to the earth came a response in the form of a deep layer of black velvet, displaying brilliant, shimmering, night fires of its own. The four spirit helpers meticulously fed the flames throughout the long night, ensuring the temperature of the rocks would be perfect by early morning, when they were to be used.

The ceremony, itself, was to include the fathers of all four boys. This was the first time since the boys' formal initiation started that all seven of them were to be involved in the ritual. The four men arrived shortly after sunrise. Sitting quietly around the fire, they waited for the boys to make their appearance. Raven Wing, the father of Standing Elk and Lone Feather, was very tall, with a hard, lean body. He very seldom spoke, but he usually had a slight smile at the corners of his mouth. Thunder Eyes, although he was close in age to the other fathers, appeared to be much older, having far less tone to his body than either Running Fox or Raven Wing. His face was worn beyond his age, and his eyes were dim from his constant struggle with the demons attempting to escape from behind them.

The day was in perfect harmony with their purpose. The sun was barely up, but already the chill of the night air was dissipating into another warm summer's day. Today, the constant prairie breeze was light. It was winding it's way gently through the camp, like a lazy stream, casually trickling along on its journey to the great waters.

Just as the sun was clearing the final mountain peak, the four, fasting boys arrived at the sweat lodge. After paying their respects to their chief, their Wicasa and their fathers, they took their places next to their own fathers around the fire, sitting together, silently watching the four helpers finishing the preparations.

The women, squatting across from each other, formed two pairs. Placing a medium thick tree branch on either side of one of the

The Quest

glowing rocks, the women lifted it out of the fire they had so carefully tended during the night. White Wolf rose and opened the flap of the tipi for them, watching them carefully place the rock in the center of the sweat lodge. While one pair of the women adjusted the last rock into its proper position, the other two took this opportunity to visit the nearby stream and fill several containers with water. The contents of the water skins were very important ingredients for White Wolf in performing the purification rite. The women, placing two of the water containers inside the lodge, positioned the remaining water skins outside, next to the flap, well within easy reach for White Wolf. Completing their chores, the spirit helpers sat down with their backs to the men.

White Wolf and the other three men stood up and disrobed, and the four boys followed the example of their elders. Laying their clothes and moccasins aside, they entered the sweat lodge one at a time.. After the three men and their sons seated themselves inside, White Wolf entered, taking his place within the circle of naked bodies. He sat directly in front of the lodge flap, with Flaming Sky sitting to his right, and Running Fox sitting on the other side of his son. To the left of White Wolf were Standing Elk, Raven Wing and Lone Feather. Next to Lone Feather was Thunder Eyes. Sitting between Thunder Eyes and Running Fox, was Short Bear.

The boys' eyes darted anxiously around the circle, coming to rest on White Wolf. The old man took one of the containers and, as he poured the cold water over the searing hot rocks, he softly chanted. A sharp, sizzling sound sliced through the silent air, followed by hissing, billowing clouds of dense steam. The old shaman repeated the process several times, until the lodge was filled with steam thick enough to blot out everything. They could barely see the outlines of each others' bodies.

Initially, Flaming Sky felt as if he were being engulfed by a heavy cloud, saturated with minute droplets of water, suffocating him. He forced himself to take long, deep breaths through his mouth, trying to increase the amount of air flowing into his lungs. Feeling somewhat fearful at first, he persisted in his efforts, eventually establishing a deep, regular pattern. Gradually, as his breathing became more relaxed, his fearfulness faded. Soon he found his mind becoming filled with the sounds of the chanting prayers offered up by White Wolf to the Great Spirit. No longer preoccupied with his own uneasy thoughts, Flaming Sky was aware of a lightness surging across his shoulders, as if being relieved of a heavy, troublesome burden. Again exhaling deeply, he felt his entire body become calmer and at ease.

With his emotions under control, he was free to concentrate his attention on White Wolf's words of power. A slight smile of relief crossed his lips as he felt himself surrendering to the experience of the ceremony. Comfortably breathing in the steam, he was no longer feeling separate from it. Instead, he was feeling as though he was connected, inseparable from the steam, and strongly bound to the other seven souls who were sharing the experience with him. For the first time in his young life, he was unfettered and completely free. He was an eagle, gliding through endless thick layers of billowing clouds. Upon completing the chanting of the opening prayers, White Wolf offered up his personal prayer to Wakan Tanka.

The lodge remained silent for several heartbeats before White Wolf passed around the sacred desert blood. Each of them consumed one of the dried, red petals from the flowers in White Wolf's dwindling supply. Flaming Sky, having been taught the correct way of properly ingesting the dried bud, deliberately crushed it four times between his teeth, before grinding it into a semi-solid form. Then, gathering it together as best he could, he swallowed it. On an empty stomach, it did not take long for the herb to have an effect on him. Its purpose was to intensify and to clarify the visions the ceremony was designed to induce. He felt results of the enhancer before completing the first circle.

For a brief instant, he seemed to be existing outside of his physical body. Simultaneously, he was aware of never feeling more physically

The Quest

alive than at this moment. He was experiencing peacefulness beyond anything he had ever known. It must be the feeling of bliss often spoken of by the older braves, something he had never before encountered. His body was vibrating. His mind, looking inward, revealed all of his hopes and dreams, while exposing all of his deepest fears and nightmares. It was as if he were being turned inside out, and then back in again, arriving in the end with a clearer perception of himself and his path.

Continuing, White Wolf offered up a prayer of thanksgiving to the Grand Father for the gift of the young warriors in their midst, who were still under his protection and guardianship. He recited a prayer on behalf of the boys' future. Waiting a respectful length of time after White Wolf finished praying, Running Fox was the next to declare his thoughts to the Great Spirit. Then, starting with Short Bear and ending with Flaming Sky, each of the remaining six, in turn, offered up their thoughts to Wakan Tanka. The boys, searching deep within themselves, were hoping to find the right words to express what they were experiencing. Thus engaged, they completed the first round of the circle.

After completing the circle for the second time, White Wolf opened the flap of the lodge. The four women entered, and with their carrying sticks, quickly exchanged the old rocks for the heated ones directly from the fire. They replaced the old water with fresh containers of cool spring water. With their chores completed, they exited the tipi, closing the flap behind them. The cool rocks were returned to the fire to reheat, in case they were needed later in the ceremony.

The old man again secured the lodge flap from the inside before pouring fresh water over the new, heated rocks. Once more, a sharp hissing sound filled the tipi, accompanied by new, thicker clouds of swirling, spinning steam. As the heat intensified, the sweat poured down the drenched bodies of the boys. The salty water streaming down their faces stung their eyes. The men, through years of experience, were used to the intense heat and humidity of the sweat lodge; the boys, however, were not.

The recitation of the prayers and wishes expressed in dreams rotated around the circle two more times before reaching its completion. When it was time for Flaming Sky's last turn to offer up his voice to the Great Protective Spirit of his ancestors, he had journeyed far into his vision. He remained mute, consumed by what he was seeing.

He was suspended above a huge fire built within a large circle of dancing braves. It was obviously a Wacipi, but it was unlike any powwow he had ever witnessed. He recognized the words of his own language being chanted, even though the chant, itself, was one he never heard until this very moment. There was sadness echoing in the words, yet simultaneously, there was a spirit of hopefulness in the dance they were performing. Never before had he seen this dance executed, nor did he recognize any of the people he was envisioning. Transfixed, he watched the dance growing in intensity, rhythm, and emotion.

A strong feeling of despair swept through his entire physical body. It was a deeper sense of loss than he had ever experienced. It was even more painful than the loss he still felt over the disappearance of

Sleeping Possum. The heaviness of the vision hung forebodingly in the choking steam, as ominous as the blackest clouds of the darkest winter. Fascinated, he watched the dance proceeding to an even higher pitch. In the mist surrounding the circle of dancers, new images were taking form in the swirling night vapors.

Initially, he was unable to recognize any of these new faces. They were strangers to him. Gazing into the mist, he watched the new images continuously evolving into complete visions of Sioux warriors in full battle gear, wearing war paint. As these new braves danced closer to the circle, more painted warriors emerged from the swirling darkness, advancing on the circle of dancers, while drawing ever closer to the fire.

Some of the braves were emerging into a clearer focus. Flaming Sky was seeing recognizable faces as the newer dancers made their appearances.

The Quest

He was stunned by the images he was seeing, as he found that he was even gazing upon his own face. Soon he was recognizing the faces of every member of his tribe, their staring eyes appearing to be looking straight through him and into a distance beyond. Next came the figures of braves known to him, but who were no longer alive. The deceased warriors from generations past were now entering the dancing circle.

The young warrior redirected his attention onto a group of people from his own generation. He was pleased to see himself wearing the trappings of a medicine man. His father, Running Fox, was wearing the headdress of the Chief of Chiefs. Proudly standing next to Running Fox was his father's cousin, White Wolf, looking much older than his present age. The others were all there: Raven Wing, Standing Elk, Lone Feather, Short Bear, Thunder Eyes and Morning Star.

"Strange," he thought, "she does not look as if she has aged very much at all. In fact, she appears to be completely unchanged. Curiously enough, so does Short Bear."

Indeed, Morning Star's appearance was young and beautiful, very similar to what it had been the last time he saw her. The only difference in her appearance was she was wearing her snakeskin headband and a single feather in her hair, an outward sign that she was a married woman. He smiled to himself.

Fascinated, he watched as the energy of the spirits of the dead warriors of the distant past was being absorbed by the braves dancing around the fire. He was amazed watching the circle of Sioux warriors dancing, unharmed, in the flames of the bonfire. Not only were they unscathed, but they were actually growing stronger in body and in spirit, each time they braved the purification of what he could only assume were sacred flames. Having run it's course, the vision gently faded into the mist, eventually drifting out of his mind.

The other three boys were each preoccupied with their own mystical dreams and visions. *Short Bear was observing a huge herd of peacefully grazing buffalo, stretching endlessly in all directions. The bison, calm and docile, were lazily chewing the prairie grasses. All of a sudden, something unseen spooked them. Aimlessly milling around, their confusion growing, the animals were slowly working themselves into a frenzy. Without warning, they blindly charged. The thick dust rising from their pounding hoofs obscured the animals from his sight. When the dust and the flying dirt eventually settled, he saw an empty prairie, once again tranquil.*

The vision shifted into one of Thunder Eyes, standing alone in the middle of the now deserted prairie. Short Bear watched his father howling like a wild coyote, railing uncontrollably. His distraught father was screaming like a woman in labor, his arms flailing and shaking as he cursed the Grand Father. Suddenly, without any warning, the shouting man fell silent. Short Bear was mystified by this strange image, unable to unlock its true meaning.

Lone Feather's vision, by contrast, was only slightly softer in nature. *He was a large bird, circling high above the foothills, effortlessly riding the warm air currents. He was a hawk, sailing over the endless expanse of the prairie, gliding peacefully until he was suddenly overcome with an urge to fly higher. Locating an updraft to speed him on his way, he launched himself skyward. Like an arrow in flight, he sped upward into the deep, blue canopy covering the land. Flying higher than he had ever imagined it was possible to fly, he spread his wings and soared through the endless sky.*

Then he saw it…a dark ominous image, lurking high overhead. Initially, he was unable to identify the silhouette outlined against a blinding sun. The object was menacingly diving directly toward him. A golden-orange light shimmered brilliantly behind the giant bird that Lone Feather now recognized as a huge eagle. Screaming, the eagle increased its speed, continuing it's descent toward him. The colours of the setting sun reflecting off of the bird's profile made it appear as though the eagle's wings were trailing flames.

The Quest

Lone Feather, attempting to avoid the attacking eagle, descended to a lower, safer height; but, still, he was diving for his life. The attacking eagle with the fiery wings continued pursuing him, even as he fled to a more protected level. It was here that the sun in his vision first contracted; then expanding until it exploded, scattering the images into the nothingness of the mist within the tipi.

In Standing Elk's vision, *he saw an image of a warrior on horseback at the top of a hill, looking down and across a large valley. He was in ceremonial war paint, and wearing the headdress of a war chief. Looking closely at the image, underneath the coloured paint on his face, he saw a much older man who bore a strong resemblance to himself and his brother, Lone Feather. The future warrior looked strong and healthy, but it was obvious he had seen many winters. In his hand he held a long, strange-looking stick. Watching, he saw the brave who he realized was his descendant pointing the stick at an object in the valley. Standing Elk was startled when the stick spat out fire and smoke, while speaking with a voice of little thunder. In the distance, he heard the sound of hundreds of such thunder sticks. The roaring reverberated all the way across the valley and back again, echoing repeatedly before fading away into the mist, as did Standing Elk's vision.*

How long they sat in silence, lost in their visions, Flaming Sky did not know. After what seemed to be an eternity, he returned to the present, realizing his vision had run it's course, and he was now back in the sweat lodge. His moment of timelessness ended with
White Wolf opening the flap of the sweat lodge. He watched the sunlight reflecting off the mist, creating hundreds of droplets of multicoloured flashing lights. As the mist of purification dissipated, the sparkling explosions faded into the disappearing steam which had created them.
One by one, the occupants of the sweat lodge exited into the cool prairie breeze. The four boys immediately raced down to the stream,

where they threw themselves into the chilly water, cooling off their overheated, sweaty bodies. The older men smiled at the sight of the boys hurling themselves into the icy stream. Although the men were also headed for the brook, they approached the flowing water with an air of dignity. In truth, they appreciated the cooling water every bit as much as did the boys, but they were not about to show it.

Once they were all cooled down, they dressed, and returned to the meeting lodge, where they completed the day's ceremonies with the offering of gifts in appreciation to their Wicasa and their chief for guiding them through the purification rite. Surrounded by the council of elders, the boys nervously took their assigned positions in front of Running Fox and White Wolf.

Smiling, the old man gave a nod, signaling the boys to begin. One at a time, the young braves offered their gifts and described their visions to the tribe's chief and shaman. The usual gifts consisted of tobacco, sage and other similar items. Short Bear was the first to pay his respects to the two older men, offering each the gift of tobacco, which they graciously accepted. Having presented the gifts, he related his vision in great detail. After listening very intently and carefully, White Wolf found himself unclear as to the complete message contained within the image and was unable to offer an acceptable interpretation.

"I will meditate upon your vision, and will share any insights I might glean from it," promised White Wolf. Pleased, Short Bear returned to his place.

Lone Feather was next to approach the chief and the Wicasa. He offered them his gifts of sage. The young man completed recounting his experience, and waited quietly for White Wolf to interpret his vision.

"This vision is a statement that you, Lone Feather, will rise to great heights within the tribe," the old man said proudly. "However, there will be one who will outshine you. You will earn a place of honour among the people, and you will be held in high esteem as

THE QUEST

a warrior and a hunter. You have seen the spirit of the next Wicasa, the flaming eagle. It is he that you will serve." Pleased to know he would be of service to his people, Lone Feather returned to his place between Short Bear and Standing Elk.

Now it was Standing Elk's turn to offer his gifts of tobacco to Running Fox and White Wolf. After making his offering, he described the strange sights he had seen in his vision. He was eager to know White Wolf's interpretation.

"The image, itself, is straightforward," White Wolf confirmed. "It is true you will grow up to become a great war chief and protector of the people. You shall father a line of great warriors. Someday, in the far distant future, one of your sons will rise up to fight alongside the great one, Tashunca Uitco. Under his direction, one of your descendants will lead his braves into battle against an unknown future enemy for the survival of our people, a combat in which both sides will use the smoking sticks of fire."

Flaming Sky's vision was the only one left to be interpreted. He approached his father and his father's cousin with a profound sense of confusion. As was his right to do, he chose to postpone the gift giving. Instead, the young brave chose to describe the image of the spirits of the dead as they were called forth to engage in the strange new dance.

"But what is the purpose of calling upon the dead warriors?" he asked the elders. "What is it that they are being entreated to accomplish?" No one answered.

"Go on," encouraged Running Fox.

White Wolf listened very attentively to the boy's words. Unfortunately, the old man did not possess a clear interpretation of the true meaning of this vision. Both Running Fox and White Wolf were extremely pleased as Flaming Sky spoke of seeing himself wearing the robes and the headdress of a medicine man. However, White Wolf remained concerned, not having received any clue of the identity of his successor as a Holy Man.

"It appears the young Flaming Sky will someday become a shaman," he thought to himself, thankful for this confirmation. "But who is destined to become the new Wicasa?"

Before returning to his place with the other boys, Flaming Sky offered his gifts. To his chief he gave the rattle from the snake he killed. It would make a good addition to his father's medicine bag, and Running Fox was very proud to accept his gift. To White Wolf, the young man presented two full pouches of desert blood, the dried petals of the rare, red blossoms he gathered on his quest. White Wolf was overjoyed as he accepted this precious gift to add to his depleted supply. The boy was deeply gratified by White Wolf's gracious acceptance. Flaming Sky returned to his seat next to Standing Elk.

With the ceremony concluded, four very tired boys dragged themselves off to their lodge for a well deserved and desperately needed sleep. For the remainder of this day, and the entire day following, the boys were allowed to rest. They were permitted to eat, but only roots, plants, herbs, and fruit. They were still in a state of purification and, therefore, were not allowed meat. The fresh vegetation would be sufficient to replenish and strengthen their bodies for the remaining ordeal. The final ritual was to take place two days hence. Meanwhile, they will use this time to rebuild their physical energies, and to strengthen their spirits.

On the second rising of the sun they will offer themselves up as protectors of the people by taking part in the ancient practice of the Sun Dance, the final doorway through which they must pass on their way to manhood. The older braves were acutely aware of the dangers involved, and the level of pain the boys will have to endure. If the four boys are capable of withstanding the suffering, they will prove themselves worthy warriors of the tribe. It will be a day of rejoicing for them…and the entire village.

Chapter 4

DANCE TO THE SUN

For the boys, the next days were a time of resting and recuperating. They ate lightly, drank large amounts of fresh spring water, and completely avoided the consumption of meat, which was forbidden during their time of purification. Only easily digestible foods were allowed, such as fruits and plants. This diet was sufficient for rebuilding their strength, which was returning rapidly. The last full moon cycle had been long, stressful and extremely exhausting for them. During this time of rest, they allowed themselves to lavish in the simple pleasures, such as lying on the grass in the warm rays of the sun, staring into forever through the endless sky. Often, they spoke of their future, sharing dreams and fears. They had come a very long way together, and were appreciative of the support of their friends throughout this strenuous time of limit testing, each learning more about himself and each other than ever anticipated.

This process was forging an unbreakable link between them that would remain forever. Each one was aware that, very soon, the bond being sealed between them and their people would be sanctified by the shedding of blood…their blood…in the dance to the sun. Soon they will be called upon to voluntarily spill their blood as a symbol of commitment to protect the tribe, signifying their willingness to endure suffering and, when necessary, bleed…or even die for the good of the people. The thought of this ritualistic act was creating an almost overwhelming sense of anxiety. Like everything else achieved up to this point, each one will have to endure this ordeal alone.

While the young initiates were resting and trying their best to successfully handle personal demons, White Wolf was fasting, smoking his pipe and meditating. He remained diligent in attempting to gain insight into the visions seen by Short Bear and Flaming Sky.

By contrast, the images seen by the brothers, Standing Elk and Lone Feather, appeared straightforward and were more easily understood.

"The fact that the brothers are both to become important members of the tribe and will provide great service to the people is simply being reaffirmed by the contents of their visions. And, in the twilight of his life, a descendant of Standing Elk's will lead our people against a heretofore unknown enemy. Yes," nodded White Wolf, completely comfortable with his interpretation.

However, the meaning of the visions of the other two boys was an elusive secret, remaining hidden from him. Pondering the visions more deeply, he thought aloud, "All of the boys, with the exception of Short Bear, were active participants within their visions. Only Short Bear was unaware of seeing himself within the images he was shown. What, if anything, does this mean?" White Wolf pondered endlessly to himself, but despite all of his efforts, the question concerning the absence of Short Bear continuously mystified him. Discouraged, having the answer avoid him time and again, he finally gave up, and concentrated his attention on solving the enigmatic vision experienced by Flaming Sky.

The old man was extremely pleased with the message within Flaming Sky's image, foretelling the boy will become a medicine man.

The Quest

"But who will he become the Wicasa for my people?" he queried himself. "Where is the Holy Man I have been praying for? Is it the flaming eagle's destiny to learn the sacred secrets from another?" White Wolf wondered, having not received a clear answer.

"There is also the necessity of taking into account the strange dancing and the mournful chanting Flaming Sky saw and heard. What does it mean? Why were our dead ancestors joining this dance? What is the purpose of this ceremony?" He turned these thoughts over slowly in his mind, like rotating a rabbit on a spit.

Returning his attention to the fiery eagle in Lone Feather's vision, he noted, "The image certainly bears a strong resemblance to my own vision of the eagle I witnessed walking unharmed through fire. Who does the eagle symbolize?" he asked, hoping an answer would come to him, but it did not.

From past experience, he knew the true, complete meaning of these images would be revealed to him in time. To say the old man was waiting patiently for these revelations would not be entirely true. The reality was he was greatly concerned. "The people will need a Wicasa to take my place when my time comes," he worried. "Who will it be? Will I have enough time left to adequately train his mind, and guide his spirit, or will that responsibility be left to another?" He listened, but all he heard was the still, dark silence of the night.

On the day of their pledge to the sun, the morning light came early for the boys. It was a day they had always looked forward to with both pride and trepidation. They were aroused from their sleep before sunrise by the spirit helpers, who led them to the pole anchored into the ground near the lodge house, where the ceremony was to take place. White Wolf, in full regalia, waited in silence as they respectfully and timidly approached him. The boys had been instructed on the physical process of the ritual, as well as the truth behind its symbolic meaning. In addition, they had witnessed the dance performed by young aspirants many times during their lifetimes. They were well prepared by their shaman for what was to follow.

Even so, White Wolf caught them stealing a quick glance at the pole, and at the four ropes of rawhide hanging from it. The pole, itself, was about six arm spans high, and the ropes were each about seven arm spans long, with the last few hands at the free end of the rawhide split into a two-piece prong. At the very end, the pieces of rawhide were divided a second time into a span the length of a finger. Reality was stimulating their anxiety.

As they dared, each of the four boys turned his eyes to White Wolf, fixating on the owl's claw in the old man's hand. Flaming Sky was aware, as part of the ritual, his chest was to be cut; however, only now did he truly understand what that actually entailed. A knife cut is quick and clean, but an incision made by a bird's claw rips into the flesh, tearing it apart. The cutting into his skin was to be more painful than he originally anticipated.

Although they were equally qualified, in deference to his age, Standing Elk was the first chosen to participate in the ceremony. Flaming Sky did his best not to watch White Wolf taking the owl's claw and, very deliberately, making four small vertical incisions in Standing Elk's chest, but, try as he might, could not stop watching, even as the blood streamed down his friend's upper body. He wanted to avoid watching what was to happen next; however, he found himself hopelessly transfixed upon what he was seeing. Unable to look away, he stared at the excruciating pain on Standing Elk's face as White Wolf inserted small, sharp pieces of wood into the bleeding, fresh wounds. A little wobbly at first, the boy finally staggered to his feet, almost fainting as the shaman tied the looped ends of the rawhide to the sticks piercing his chest.

Flaming Sky winced as Standing Elk clutched his medicine bag tightly in one hand and the sacred sage in the other, while blowing his whistle furiously in response to the pain he was experiencing. Seeing the look on Standing Elk's face, he felt his own muscles tightening.

The Quest

He experienced an emptiness inside him, as though he had been struck a blow to the solar plexus. Knowing he was to be next, he stared down at the ground, attempting to avoid looking at White Wolf's bloody hands. Flaming Sky was not sure if he was praying out loud or just quietly screaming to himself; however, before he could resolve the question, he was being signaled to take his turn. Breathing deeply, trying to relax, he started the long walk to where White Wolf stood awaiting him.

Lying on the grass, tightly clenching his whistle between his teeth, he felt his body tensing as White Wolf took the skin approximately a hands width beneath his collarbone and pinched it between his fingers. The boy grimaced, as the owl's claw tore into his flesh on one side of the pinched skin, trying his best not to look down at his blood now streaming out of the wound. Before adjusting to the pain, he felt the claw ripping into his flesh a second time, parallel to the first cut. The two small incisions were less than a finger-length apart. The shaman was careful to make the incisions deep enough to penetrate the skin, but shallow enough to avoid damaging the underlying muscle. Flaming Sky tried breathing, discovering it was a task not easily accomplished. Just as he was thinking he could not tolerate any further pain, White Wolf began repeating the procedure on the other side of his chest.

Experiencing the agony of the incision and the trickling sensation of the blood as two distinctive events, Flaming Sky's whole body was shivering as he realized the pain was on the verge of increasing. He heard the loud, shrill sound of his whistle as he bit down on it, blowing as loud as possible, trying not to think about the two small, sharpened splints being inserted into his open wounds. The pieces of smooth wood were polished until the edges were as sharp as a knife blade. White Wolf tied a strand of rawhide to each of the indented ends carved into the implanted slivers of oak, pulling the knots tightly, thus ensuring they would remain fastened throughout the entire ceremony. Standing up, the light-headed Flaming Sky felt his chest burning like a raging prairie fire. There was only one way to quench the flames ...dance to the sun.

The pain shot through his body anew, forcing him into an upright position. His head was swirling, and his eyes were glazed, as he fought against the urge to vomit. Shuffling forward toward the sun pole, as instructed, he attempted to get in step with the rhythm of the beating drums. Without any conscious effort on his part, his body was moving automatically. He tried focusing on the movement of his feet, in a vain effort to keep his mind from fixating on the searing torment in his chest. The technique only worked intermittently, his awareness inevitably returning to the burning, throbbing sensation he was experiencing. Growing weak, he felt tributaries of blood flowing downward, seeping into his waistband.

Blowing the whistle even louder, he started dancing backward, away from the blurry pole. Just as he was sure, beyond a doubt, that the suffering could not get any worse, it did. Reaching the full extension of the rope, and exerting his weight against the cords, he felt the sharp edges of the wood cutting into his flesh. The heightened tension caused his skin to stretch, bringing with it a glorious new level of agony. Each time he retreated away from the pole, increasing the tautness of the rope with his body's weight, the pain exploded in intensity.

"How is it possible to endure this until sunset?" he questioned himself.

Flaming Sky was so preoccupied with his own suffering, he failed to realize the other two boys had joined the dance. The four whistles were constantly blowing. In one hand, each held their medicine bag, while clutching a small Bundle of sacred sage in the other. Within a short period, the four boys became attuned to each other and, as if they had been given a signal, they were all moving in unison, chanting as they danced. They repeated the chants White Wolf taught them, interspersed with the sounds of their whistles. Over and over, they moved in rhythm, continuing their constant approach to and retreat from the sun pole, chanting. Each time they leaned backward, away

The Quest

from the pole, they blew their whistles louder, and the shrillness lasted longer. As the boys danced, the cutting pain increased in intensity and severity, spreading like a raging fire throughout their bodies.

Flaming Sky was breathing heavily by the time the sun reached its mid-point in the sky. He felt small trickles of sweat stinging his eyes and inflaming the four open wounds on his chest. Increasingly distracting was the fact that the throbbing in his head was louder than the resounding drums. His lower back was tight and aching, his neck and shoulder muscles were pulsating with sharp, searing pain. His legs were heavy and felt immoveable. Hot, piercing flames sliced through his hip joints, sending flowing rivers of fire shooting down his thighs and flooding into his knees.

In spite of the agony, he danced and chanted, as did the others. With the muscles in his legs cramping, he felt as if he could no longer continue moving. Through the anguish, somehow or another, he persisted, as did his three companions. The sun drifted leisurely on its journey across the sky. The beating of the drums grew louder and louder as the pain intensified, and still the boys danced. They heard the words of White Wolf in their minds: *"You must never, ever, give up."*

By late in the day, nearing sunset, all four boys were moving very slowly. The tiredness of their bodies was extremely evident. Every fiber of Flaming Sky's being was aching. His suffering steadily increased as the day crept along; yet, he endured, valiantly dancing and chanting through the pain. He had long since passed beyond the time when he was able to identify the source or, more accurately, the sources of his physical anguish. With his body exhausted and completely spent, his only desire was to be free…free of the ritual, free of the dance, and, most importantly, free of the pain. However, instead of quitting, he danced on, his body growing heavier with the journey of the sun, until he was positive he could not take one more step without crumbling to the ground.

The battle raged on, as the struggle within him increased. The temptation to stop, to end the pain, was unceasingly combated by his determination to endure the ritual. He must complete his commitment and honour his word. However, he was unsure as to how much longer he could hold out against the pain without giving into the temptation of surrender. Unable to take one more step, he was on the verge of quitting when, suddenly, it happened. The pain was gone…or maybe the pain was still there, and it was Flaming Sky who was gone, having vacated his body.

It made little difference to him which it was. In either case, he was finally free from the constant aching of his body and the heaviness of his legs. Before, his breathing had been difficult and laboured; now, by contrast, he was totally unaware of breathing. He had arrived in that time of being out of space, and in the space of being out of time. White Wolf had done his best to prepare him for this effect, but, until now, he could not have anticipated the impact of this miraculous event. Prior to this occurrence, Flaming Sky had no idea of what the old shaman was trying to teach him. Now, experiencing it for himself, he understood. He was truly free.

It was impossible for Flaming Sky to gauge the exact length of time that passed since he transcended the torture. He observed the sun starting to nestle into the mountaintops. Directing his attention to his three companions, he saw by the look in their eyes that they had each reached their place of peace, relatively free from physical suffering. His eyes were drawn to White Wolf. The old man was giving them a sign: *as soon as the sun leaves the sky, you are at liberty to break yourselves free from your restraints.*

It took Flaming Sky a while to build up the courage to even think about attempting it, as he refocused upon the excruciating pain that was his chest. Taking several deep breaths, he summoned all of his strength; and, blowing his whistle with ferocity, he attempted the final movement backward. Pulling as hard as he could, he stretched the rawhide to its maximum extension. Attempting to pull away from

The Quest

the pole, he felt the sharpened pieces of wood cutting into his tautly stretched skin, as the wood fought desperately to free itself from the confinement of his chest. He exhaled, relaxing himself as best he could before attempting a second time to free himself from the sun pole. Stepping in place to the rhythm of the drums, and blowing his whistle, he stretched backward to the full length of the rawhide. Pausing, gathering all of his strength and courage, he leaned back as far as he could. Thrusting his body backward, he felt the small pieces of wood slicing their way out through his skin. There was a sharp, fiery pain as he broke free of the ropes. Falling backward, he landed unceremoniously on his rear end, realizing he was listening to the loudest sound he ever heard in his entire life. The deafening noise was coming from his own whistle. Releasing the whistle, he gently collapsed onto the grass, unable to move.

In the meantime, Standing Elk had successfully released himself from the pole. Lone Feather and Short Bear were trying their best to free themselves, but so far they remained attached. With one last effort, Lone Feather threw himself backward with all the force at his command. The wooden pieces came ripping out of his chest, like arrows shot from a bow. This left Short Bear dancing, alone. The three boys remained where they had fallen, too exhausted to move. Concentrating their attention on the dancing Short Bear, they watched as he continuously struggled to end his agony. Repeatedly, he attempted to break free and, repeatedly, he failed.

Thunder Eyes, who had been quietly pacing, chose this time to commence screaming at his son. He shouted profanities at the boy, ridiculing him for being the last one still connected to the pole. Short Bear felt his father's angry words slicing through his soul.

"Coward! Weakling!" shouted Thunder Eyes. "You of no courage, how could you be a child of my loins!" he continued. "I am ashamed to call you son. Surely the Great Spirit was playing an evil trick on me when he sent you through your mother's womb to me." He went on most vilely berating his son. No doubt he would have said even more to the humiliated Short Bear, had not Running Fox commanded him to silence.

Trying to pretend he was not crying, Short Bear once more strained against the rawhide. The agony in his heart was stronger than the pain in his chest. This time, his flesh gave way to the sharply honed pieces of wood, allowing him to fall backward to the ground in painful exhaustion. He was having difficultly breathing and regaining his sense of awareness. Completely spent, he lay there with his three friends, hurting too much to laugh, and feeling too proud to cry. It was finished. They had completed their blood sacrifice and were now men, warriors, courageous protectors of the Lakota people.

White Wolf picked up the ointment prepared for them prior to the start of the ceremony. Walking over to the boys, who were still lying on their backs in a daze, staring into the night sky, the old man attended to their wounds. First he cleaned them. Once the cuts were properly cleansed, he carefully applied the ointment to their bloody, torn flesh. Returning the ripped flesh to its proper position before bandaging their chests, he wrapped their torn skin as tightly as possible, allowing only enough slack for his patients to breathe. His goal was to keep the flesh immoveable, thereby allowing the ritualistic wounds to heal correctly.

Upon his completion of administering to the young men, White Wolf offered up a prayer to the Great Spirit, an invocation thanking Him for giving the people more braves to strengthen their tribe. "Oh, Wakan Tanka, Pilamaya, we thank You for Your gracious gifts of four new Sioux warriors…warriors who have shown their willingness to bleed and to die in the performance of their duties to Your people. Grand Father, watch over them. Protect them. Favor them and Your people. Provide us with many new children." Due to their weakened condition, it was customary for the boys' fathers to assist the new initiates back to their lodge. However, as there were only three fathers, White Wolf happily

THE QUEST

accepted the honour of helping Lone Feather back to the tipi of the unmarried men, where the tired braves spent a sleepless night.

Even with the shaman's medicine, Flaming Sky remained in great pain. It was difficult to breathe, as it antagonized the wounds. The tightly wrapped bandages severely restricted his ability to expand his lungs. It was impossible for him to become comfortable. Every breath, every movement was torturous. The only way to ease his pain was by lying flat on his back, while breathing as lightly as possible.

It was in this position that White Wolf found the young men when he returned to their lodge. He carried a wooden bowl, containing a very strong and pungent potion. one by one, he managed to make each of them take four large sips of the liquid. The taste was repulsive, making it very difficult to swallow. They gagged, choked, sputtered and grimaced, but, eventually, with the old man's persistent encouragement, they successfully forced it down. By the time he finished attending to the young warriors and left the lodge, the initiates were already drifting into sleep…something none of them believed possible a short time ago. They slept deeply that night.

For the next three days, they rested, as White Wolf continued caring for them. The spirit helpers brought the boys fresh water and food. Their meals now included small portions of buffalo and deer meat, several times a day. The young braves spent a majority of the next several days sleeping, allowing their bodies to heal. Of course, medicine man and the four women made daily reports to the boys' families as well as to Morning Star. "Within the passing of five or six suns, they will be up and going about their new activities as men of the tribe," he proudly reported.

The young warriors were well healed within six days. thanks to White Wolf's potions and salves Their bodies started rebuilding energy almost immediately; however, complete physical recovery took a little longer. The four will henceforth bear the scars left on their chests by dancing to the sun. Proudly, they will wear these marks with honour, to the very last days of life…and, maybe, even beyond. Indeed, they had earned the right to be called warriors. Only one test remained before passing into adulthood.

Killing a buffalo was a chore they were anticipating with great pleasure. In less than two full moons, it will be time for the autumn hunt. All hunts are important to the tribe's survival, but the autumn hunt carries the extra burden of being the last major hunt until the return of the warm days. It's purpose is not only to provide the food presently needed by the tribe, but to supply the food necessary to sustain them during the long, unforgiving, winter snows ahead. For the very first time, the newly anointed warriors will be allowed to participate in this event.

The hunt awaited their future. For the present, there was more than enough to occupy them. They worked diligently on honing their skills, from weapon making, to hand-to-hand combat. No longer were the young warriors engaged in these activities only among themselves, as they were now allowed to compete with the older braves. Competition was much greater, as were the rewards of their success. Constantly they practiced improving their abilities with the bow and arrow, as well as the knife and tomahawk.

Often they took time away from tuning their warrior skills to fulfill one of their most important functions as braves: *providing food for the people*. At first light, in small groups of two braves each, the hunters departed from the camp, heading in eight different directions, spreading out like the spokes of the medicine wheel. They set forth as quietly as possible, so as not to scare their quarry. After waiting until the advanced hunters had enough time to form an outer perimeter, encircling the area between them and the camp, the remaining hunters ventured forth in small groups of three to five. Noisily, they spread outward, hoping to drive prey toward the advanced group of waiting hunters. They engaged in this process throughout the day, until the sun was preparing to set. Gathering up the day's kill, they made their way back to the camp under a twilight canopy.

The Quest

Their days passed as if they were living a dream, which was exactly what they were doing. Evenings were usually spent with their families, or in the company of the other young men. At night, they studied the dark sky, in hopes of solving the mysteries of the stars. They listened attentively to older braves, recounting tales of great deeds accomplished by renown warriors of the past. In addition, they heard stories of noble and honourable acts performed by the newer generations, including the present one. The tales told by their fathers of the ancient warriors on horseback performing heroic feats inspired the young men to work extraordinarily hard at becoming expert horsemen. They learned to ride on the bare back of a pony running at a full gallop, simultaneously practicing to shoot a bow and arrow, or to hurl a lance into a moving target with their free hand.

Except for the completion of the first buffalo hunt, their initiation was at an end. However, the intensity of their training steadily increased. They were learning what it means to be a Lakota brave. Not only were they responsible for feeding the people, but they were charged with the obligation of protecting the tribe from all enemies, no matter the source, be it man, beast or demon.

The young warriors were always welcome at the campfire of their families for meals; however, now they came as invited guests. As such, it was customary for them to bring something to the meal as a gesture of respect and appreciation. It was with great pride filling their chests that the four experienced giving back to their families.

While the young men were actively engaged in perfecting their skills, Morning Star, was polishing her own crafts. With her mother's help, she went about the first task of building a tipi for her and Flaming Sky to occupy as husband and wife. She completed fashioning her wedding dress, and was near to putting the finishing touches on the shirt and pants Flaming Sky was to wear at the ceremony. She concentrated a majority of her time and effort on improving her cooking skills. It was important for her to be able to make a tasty, filling meal out of whatever he brought in from a hunt, no matter how meager it happened to be. She was mastering the art of blending herbs and plants with small amounts of meat, creating savory, satisfying, nutritious meals.

Morning Star was proficient with a hunting knife, and an excellent skinner of animals and cleaner of fish. She was taught not only how to prepare food, but how to procure it. She was an exceptional spear fisher. When there was nothing available to harvest, she and the other women often fished while the men were away hunting. By the time of the autumn hunt, when it came time for skinning and butchering the buffalo, her skills would be more than a match for any of the other women.

It was not always just work and study for the young couple. Every now and again, Flaming Sky was invited to take meals with her at her parents' lodge. Usually they were meals she prepared completely on her own. Often, after eating, they were allowed some time together. Subject to her parent's constant watchful eye, they held hands while strolling around the camp, gazing at the stars and contemplating life's mysteries. What secrets did the future hold for them? What would their lives together be like? They talked of having children, in addition to other topics of concern to any young couple in their circumstances.

They shared their dreams, enthusiastically discussing things they were daily learning. Morning Star loved to hear Flaming Sky recount the story of his counting coup on the Pawnee. She beamed with pride as he told of taking a feather, a scalp, an arrow and the pony he named Pawnee in remembrance of his brave deed. Time was passing pleasantly for them, but, unfortunately, not so for everyone.

White Wolf remained concerned as to who the Great Spirit will choose to be the new Wicasa. Having received no sign, he reexamined the visions of the boys, hoping to find a heretofore missed clue hidden within one of their images. "Standing Elk's is very concise, clearly showing what his place within the tribe will be.

The Quest

He is destined to become a warrior, and eventually, a great war chief, whose descendents will fight the last great battle using the mysterious sticks of fire. No. Standing Elk, has a different destiny awaiting him. His visions confirm he is not destined to be a Holy One," concluded the Wicasa.

"Short Bear, on the other hand, is the least likely of the four. He has the potential of becoming a decent medicine man. In time, he could become a good shaman…not a great one, but adequate.

However, despite this potential, it is obvious he is lacking the traits necessary for him to evolve into a Holy Man," he mused. 'And then, there is the possibility that Short Bear, like his father, might prove untrustworthy as a medicine man when it comes to handling the sacred herbs without giving in to the temptation of misusing them." He would only consider Short Bear as the very last choice as shaman, but could never imagine the Great Spirit choosing him Wicasa. As always, he was once more left with Lone Feather, and Flaming Sky. It was clear to him that either one would be a good choice of the Grand Father, but he found himself leaning toward one.

"In Lone Feather's vision," he recalled, "he was the hawk, not the fiery eagle diving out of the sun. The hawk was subservient to the flaming eagle, which is similar to the eagle of my vision. He who is the flaming eagle is to be served by the hawk. No. His vision makes it clear. Lone Feather is not the one for whom I wait. He is a better choice for shaman than Short Bear, but neither will be the Grand Father's gift to my people."

"And then there is Flaming Sky," he thought out loud, taking a deep breath. "His vision cast him in the role of a shaman and, indeed, I favor him as such. But it does not necessarily mean the young man will become a Wicasa. Many Holy Men throughout the history of the tribe have been warriors…some even war chiefs," he continued. "If Flaming Sky is destined to follow the path of a Holy Man, when will he do so? Now," he questioned, impatiently, "or later in life, after he has grown in wisdom?"

The old man received no confirmation, and there was no validation clarifying White Wolf's vision of the fiery eagle. Although his cousin's son remained the best prospect of the four, he was beginning to face the possibility that maybe none of them was destined to be chosen Wicasa. "Maybe the bird of prey of my image has not yet made his way to the people. It is possible I will be gone long before he is revealed." After he completed turning it over in his mind, the answer always remained the same. "Only the Great Spirit knows who will replace me, and when. I have no choice. I must await the Grand Father's Will."

The time was approaching when he must inform the counsel of his choice for shaman. It needed to be accomplished before moving to winter quarters. Meditating, while smoking his pipe and praying to the Great Spirit, asking if he was making the right choice by selecting Flaming Sky as medicine man, he received no confirmation, indicating the decision was his to make. Thus, the days and nights passed for the old man.

He knew Raven Wing, the father of Lone Feather and Standing Elk, would not take offense if neither of his sons was chosen to be the next shaman. They each have a path of proud service to the people laying ahead of them. Thunder Eyes, on the other hand, was much less likely to be as accepting of White Wolf's decision, as he never recovered from his own failure of many winters ago. "To him, bypassing Short Bear will, no doubt, reopen old wounds," worried the old man, "possibly releasing the demons dwelling within him."

White Wolf prayed and meditated over the details of all possible outcomes, as was his way. 'It is time," he declared to himself. "The choice is mine, and mine alone. My selection is made, and I will stand by it, no matter what the consequences. Only time will confirm or rebuke the wisdom of my choice." He resolved to call a counsel meeting for the announcement of his decision.

The Quest

When the counsel was comfortably seated, White Wolf carefully unwrapped the ceremonial pipe and gently set it down in front of him. Taking the prepared blend from his pouch, he deliberately packed the bowl with the mixture. Once it was full, he took a small flaming stick from the fire and respectfully lit the sacred blend, drawing slowly and deeply from the pipe, releasing his prayer on the smoke as he exhaled. He passed the pipe to his chief, Running Fox, who also drew from the pipe, before passing it to his right. The pipe slowly made its way around the circle, passing from elder to elder, from chief to chief, until it made its way safely back to White Wolf.

The four young warriors were seated immediately behind the counsel members. They, like everyone else, understood the importance of what was unfolding before them. Tonight the shaman was to name his successor. White Wolf stood facing the four young men, summarizing the process he had been going through before arriving at his decision. He acknowledged each of them as honorable students.

Speaking to the counsel, he softened the truth of his reasons for rejecting Short Bear as his replacement. The reasoning behind his decision to bypass Standing Elk and Lone Feather met with the approval of the counsel, as did his choice of Flaming Sky as the tribe's new medicine man. The young warrior graciously accepted the honour, and the council was dismissed. From that point forward, he was destined to follow a different path than that of his three friends. Although remaining a warrior, he was to undergo intensive training with White Wolf, in preparation for assuming his new responsibilities to the people

Flaming Sky completed making the bows and arrows he was to present as part of the marriage price. True to their promise, his father and White Wolf procured the six horses. Everything that could be done in preparation for their marriage was completed. Now, all they could do was wait for her father to choose a time after the hunt.

There was nothing he and Morning Star could do to speed up the process. The decision was Two Claw's.

With the autumn hunt in the future, the new apprentice had ample time in the present for his studies with White Wolf. Even though he was excited, and feeling honoured to be chosen as the tribe's new medicine man, a part of him was feeling unworthy. There was no doubt concerning his bravery, and knew he was destined to become a great warrior; however, this new role was placing an enormous responsibility on his young shoulders. He already possessed a very good knowledge of the healing properties of many plants and herbs, but now he was to assume responsibility for their acquisition and proper application. After learning to recite the ancient chants, he will be entrusted with the words of power, the key to releasing their mysteries.

The fact that White Wolf was not only their shaman, but their Holy Man, was a rare combination. Flaming Sky was confident he would develop the skills necessary to function as shaman, but was secretly praying not to be chosen as a Holy One. Following in the footsteps of the shaman would be difficult, and more than enough to fully occupy him through several cycles of his life.

His three friends were happy with their apparent destinies within the structure of the tribe. Standing Elk was content knowing which path his feet would walk, as was his brother, Lone Feather. Short Bear, on the other hand, was greatly relieved not to be inheriting the responsibilities of the medicine man. He never shared his fear of this possibility with anyone…not even his closest friends. Under the present circumstances, Short Bear was glad to be living in the lodge of the unmarried men, and not in the tipi of his father.

As White Wolf had foreseen, Thunder Eyes was irate at the fact his son was passed over for this great honour. During times of stress and anger, Thunder Eyes customarily reverted to his old habits of misusing the sacred herbs. Aimlessly, he went wandering throughout the camp, ranting and raving incoherently, cursing the Great Spirit

THE QUEST

and damning His Universe. After several days of this erratic behavior, he gradually returned to a calmer emotional state. "It is this rage smoldering deep inside of him which will ultimately be the cause of his destruction," thought White Wolf. "It is simply a matter of time."

The young men went about their daily training, preparing themselves to fulfill the duties they had sworn to take on as warriors. The four of them remained close, even though Flaming Sky was often missing from their activities. At day's conclusion came their time for talking, and for dreaming. In the evening, after the camp quietly settled into sleep, they talked long into the summer's night. Naturally, their favorite topic was the upcoming autumn hunt. It was a crucial step, confirming their permanent status as tribal warriors, by proving their ability as providers . Only after a young warrior kills a buffalo with his own hands can he claim the right to take a wife. The hunt is his final passage into manhood. The hide of the buffalo is highly prized among the gifts usually presented to the girl's parents. Horses are also a standard offering. Whenever a warrior has a special talent, such as Flaming Sky's skill as a maker of weapons, the product of his art is received as a cherished gift by the father of his intended.

Thoughts of young women of the tribe were consistently on their minds, and were a common topic of their nightly talks. At present, only Flaming Sky was betrothed. It was also true, however, that each of the other young warriors carried the reflection of a special young maiden in his eyes. If any of them were to choose a wife in the near future, they would already be the proud possessors of a valuable buffalo hide to offer as partial payment. They were young, and the blood was pulsating through their bodies like fiery, white water.

Whatever time he had away from his studies, Flaming Sky spent with Morning Star. White Wolf, understanding their need to be together, knew she was good for him, helping him to overcome selfdoubt in many areas of his life. He was very aware of the young man's fearful resistances to his new responsibilities, which were a natural counterpart to his enthusiasm and zest to achieve. Although

Flaming Sky never said a word, the old man understood his fear of the expectations others had of him. Yet, he remained confident the young man would become an excellent shaman. The old Wicasa did his best not to increase the pressure on the novice with his own desire for a new Holy Man. He understood the burdens of the new medicine man, knowing full well only time and the young man, himself, could resolve them. "It might take him winters to do so," White Wolf thought, "or a lifetime, if ever at all."

In the meantime, the young man went about the business of memorizing the chants, while slowly comprehending the mysteries of their magic. He was learning the secrets of the spoken word, as well as the power of the breath of life itself. Not only was he starting to understand the true potency of their medicine, but he was recognizing the power within the spirit of White Wolf. It was obvious the old man was truly touched by the Great Spirit.

"Will I ever be favored by the Great Spirit and become a Wicasa like my father's cousin is hoping?" he continued asking himself. The answer, evading him, was replaced with the lurking uncertainty of youth. The following days came and went as gently as a lazy stream flowing through a lush green meadow. Flaming Sky studied, memorized and learned, dreaming of the future which was about to unfold for him and Morning Star.

Chapter 5

THE HUNT

The season of migration was upon them. This was the time for the great buffalo herds to make their way to winter pastures. The days were not as long, nor were the nights as warm. Soon the herds will be on the move, and Running Fox had already sent out runners. Most of the braves waited patiently for word from the scouts. Most, that is, but not all.

The four young men were understandably excited and anxious for the chase to be underway. While waiting, they finished their final preparations for the hunt, arrows and lances were sharpened and honed to perfection. Each painted special signs on his arrows in order to identify his individual kills. If they are to earn the full rights of adulthood, including the right to take a wife, they must prove the skin offered to the girl's father is theirs, by right, to give.

While the men were making their preparations, so were the women. Some sharpened their knives for the skinning, while others constructed litters to transport the hides and meat. Once the pursuit was underway, two of White Wolf's spirit helpers were to remain behind in camp to help care for the old ones and the children. Except for those left in camp, this hunt, as always, was to include every able member of the tribe, each aware that success was imperative for their survival.

It was just prior to sundown of the third day when word of the herd arrived at the camp. About a three day's ride away, the first signals were being relayed from the farthest outlying scouting party. The smoking clouds spoke of a very large group slowly meandering toward the scout's location. A short while later, a second smoke signal was seen drifting upward on the prairie breeze, followed soon after by a third and, eventually, a fourth signal, reinforcing the messages of the other scouts. The massive herd stretched from beyond the vision of the first scout, all the way past the last scout, who was at least a full day's ride away.

The camp was a beehive of frantic activity as the news instantly spread among the people. "The words in the smoke proclaim Tatanka has returned! The size of the herd is tremendous! It will be a plentiful hunt."

The people were excited, relieved, and extremely thankful for the return of the buffalo. Tatanka's arrival confirmed their survival was ongoing, assuring them of fresh meat now, as well as dried meat to nourish, and new skins to protect them through the lean days of greyness ahead of them. They were grateful to the Great Spirit for His gift of survival for the people.

The four new warriors were too excited to sleep. Wrapped in their blankets by a small fire, they chattered and laughed late into the darkness. It was as if each of them possessed seven tongues. They teased each other, boasting as to which of them will kill the first buffalo, who will bring down the biggest and who will slay the most. Despite their playful antics, which helped release the excitement exploding within them, they remained mindful of the importance of the hunt. For them, it was more than just a new contest. It was now necessary to prove themselves as worthy providers for the tribe. In addition, to be accepted into adulthood with the privileges of men,

THE QUEST

they must prove themselves worthy of meeting the responsibilities for taking on a wife and a family.

No one was more aware of this than Flaming Sky. If he is to claim Morning Star as his wife, he will have to prove his worth to Two Claws, her father. "This is the way it is. This is the way it always has been. This is the way it will always be," he reminded himself, feeling pressured within. The thought lumbered heavily through his mind, followed by numbness, and finally a restful sleep with dreams…and, eventually, the deep nothingness, where the aware mind is at last free of its constant vigilance.

The entire camp was up early the next morning. The villagers were anxious to start their journey across the prairie, where the countless buffalo awaited. The hunters, riding at a trot, led the way. A majority of the women traveled on foot; however, the older women were mounted on the horses rigged to carry the litters of meat and skins. Running Fox, in his customary position, riding at the head of his people, was followed by the war chiefs and White Wolf, who decided to join the hunt at least one more time. Behind them came the older and more experienced warriors, holding themselves in respectful restraint, followed by the young warriors, eager to improve themselves worthy in their first hunt.

The four friends stayed close together in their own little group, having been instructed to first observe the older warriors as they hunted. Once a young brave felt ready, he was free to join in. They had been cautioned repeatedly to remain on the very outskirts of the beasts, never allowing themselves to be caught inside the perimeter, where they could easily become trapped. The hunt is a serious and extremely dangerous activity, as the young men were about to learn.

The hunting party meandered leisurely across the softly rolling hills and lush green prairie grasses. Running Fox wanted everyone, including the horses, to be well rested when they arrived at the herd. The activity customarily lasted several days, continuing until the chief decided enough meat and hides had been taken to assure the tribe's survival against the inevitable cold and icy winds raging from the north. At their present pace, Running Fox estimated arriving before the sun was directly overhead, providing sufficient time for a good day's hunt, long before the sun is ready for its nightly nap.

The seasoned hunters were pleased, as there would be fresh meat for the hunters and skinners, as well as the people left behind at the village. After the first kill, the runners will begin their work, loading the horses that will pull the litters laden with meat and hides back to the village. The people waiting there will have their share of the day's bounty, and help in its preparation.

The late morning breeze was losing its chill by the time the hunting party arrived at the crest of the butte. Looking out across the plains, they saw the herd stretching farther than they could see. Flaming Sky and the other young braves were stunned, doubting their own eyes. They were immobilized, gazing upon an endless sea of brown life flowing across the infinite prairie. As children, they heard stories of great numbers of buffalo migrating through their lands since the beginning of the people's history. Now they were witnesses to Tatanka, flooding the plains in all directions.

The Great Spirit created the animals to be extremely strong and fast. However, He gave them one weakness, one tiny flaw. They were the recipients of extremely poor eyesight. Unfortunately, the pitiful beasts could barely see twenty paces in front of themselves. Beyond that distance, everything appeared to them in blurry shades of grey and flickering light. When they stampede, they raise so much dust and dirt, they are almost without any sight whatsoever. Thus blinded, they become increasingly disoriented, eventually running headlong into each other, thereby compounding the confusion and chaos. That is always the plan: *attack, stampede and confuse the animals.* Once the beasts are in complete disarray, the hunters move in for the kill. Ever since the people acquired horses, this is the way it has always been done. Today was not to be any different.

The Quest

Flaming Sky and his three companions sat upon their ponies, observing the tactics and admiring the skillfulness of the older hunters riding straight at the herd. Whooping and hollering as loudly as they could, they freely expressed their anxiety and their joy, emotions suppressed for a very long time. They had been waiting for an excuse to release these feelings, and release them they certainly did. The buffalo lazily gathered speed as the hunters rode directly at the right flank of the herd. Dust, dirt and large chunks of earth were tossed up into the air, creating a fog-like shroud, engulfing the disoriented beasts.

Some of the animals started to stampede, but the herd was not yet reacting as one. As the awkward behavior of the buffalo became more confused and erratic, the hunters attacked. The men stayed on the outside of the frantically running animals, picking them off, one by one. As the massive beasts came crashing to the ground, the smell of blood in the air further terrified the already panicky animals into a greater frenzy. They were in complete pandemonium, charging each other aimlessly, completely out of control. Sightless and helpless, they were caught in a snare of their own making. Their fate had just become inevitable.

As to which of them was the first to charge, no one will ever really know. Flaming Sky and Standing Elk were not sure but, almost as a single action, they prodded their ponies with a sharp nudge to their flanks. Attacking at a full gallop, they were joined by the other two as they engaged in the hunt. Despite forewarnings of the noise, Flaming Sky still found himself astonished and deafened by the roaring of Tatanka's thundering hoof-beats. He felt the shaking ground quivering under the pressure of the animals' weight, as their hooves gouged into the dry earth. The terrain, itself, was rolling like waves of the great lake of salt.

The earth was violently trembling as Flaming Sky arrived at the outer edge of the frenzied herd. The air was so thick and cloudy that it was almost impossible for him to breathe. The denseness of the dust, mixed with the smell of the buffalo blending with the strong stench of fresh buffalo chips, was suffocating the air completely out of him. In spite of coughing and choking, he continued the chase. With his bow already in his hand, and an arrow clinched between his teeth, he dug his knees into Pawnee's sides to steady himself. With his free hand, he removed the arrow and readied his bow.

Pacing his gait with a large bull, he let loose an arrow, which went sailing two full hands above the animal's hump. Flaming Sky reloaded his bow and let loose a second arrow, landing in the buffalo's right shoulder. His third shot entered the animal's rib cage, puncturing one of its lungs. The beast was struggling for its very breath. His fourth arrow entered the soft tissue of the neck between its hump and head, severing the spinal cord. The beast's legs gave way as it came stumbling to the ground. It slid forward on its front knees and muzzle, until it eventually stopped, crumpling into a lifeless pile at the edge of the herd.

Flaming Sky let out a war whoop that rang out even above the thundering buffalo. Shaking his bow in the air, and looking back over his shoulder, he saw Morning Star and her mother running to the place where the slain buffalo had fallen. He watched as they went to work, gutting and skinning the beast. With a renewed confidence, the young man eagerly rejoined the hunt.

Meanwhile, Standing Elk made his first kill, having used only two arrows. Both of his shots found their way into the soft, vulnerable area at the front of the hump. The stunned animal paused momentarily before collapsing to the ground. Standing Elk let out a war cry, as he and Flaming Sky waved at each other through the thick, dust-filled air. Then, off Standing Elk galloped, chasing another buffalo. His aim remained true, and by the day's end he downed another four of the huge animals. It was a good day's hunt for him. He had just cause to be proud of his skill as a hunter. He was an accomplished hunter of great ability, which would be of lasting benefit to his tribe. Both he and Flaming Sky passed the final test of their manhood.

The Quest

Lone Feather's aim and luck were not as good as that of his brother's, nor even his friend's. It was necessary for Lone Feather to replenish his arrows after having only two kills to his credit. He discovered that riding a pony at full gallop while shooting an arrow at a moving target was proving to be much more difficult than when he was practicing back at camp. The endless layers of dust made it difficult for him to breathe, and virtually impossible for him to see clearly. Several times he left the hunt, searching for fresh air to breathe, and an opportunity to get the dust and dirt out of his throat and eyes.

By the setting sun, Lone Feather was completely exhausted and covered with streams of mud from layers of dirt mixed in with sweat running down his body. He resembled a desert flood, with dozens of rivers cascading down his chest and limbs. His eyes burned and his body ached from the arduous hunt, but the young man did not seem to notice. He was too caught up in the excitement of his day's work to pay any attention to it. Lone Feather also proved himself a worthy warrior, earning the title of Lakota brave.

Short Bear's first hunt, although successful, was unspectacular. By nightfall, he had used all of his available arrows, while having only one kill to show for his day's efforts. It took him six arrows to finally bring down his first large bull, but down it came, its blood seeping into the thirsty earth of the prairie. Glancing back, Short Bear was filled with great pride as he watched his mother and his younger sister running to the fallen animal, where they commenced skinning the beast.

Turning his pony away from the herd, Short Bear rode in the direction of his mother and sister. It was customary for the wives to carry extra weapons for the hunters. As Short Bear was unmarried, this chore was the responsibility of his sister, who was barely thirteen moons younger than he. Since Short bear was even less skilled with the lance than a bow, she only carried a supply of extra arrows. She came running up to him, as he approached her at a full gallop.

Without dismounting, he traded his empty quivers for full ones. Off he rode, grinning widely, looking back at them one last time before losing sight of them as the clouds of dirt closed in behind him, eventually obscuring them from his vision. On he galloped, struggling to remain astride his pony while simultaneously trying to control his bow and arrow. The constant vibration of the earth was creating a continuous challenge, adding to his difficulties.

Running Fox, on the other hand, was having a great hunt. His horse was swift and his aim was true. Riding at top speed alongside the stampeding herd, he sought out his prey. Once having selected a prime bull, he charged it. Riding as close to the animal as possible, he took his shot, usually bringing the buffalo down with one arrow. His bow created a challenging amount of work for the women who were skinning and butchering. By the time the sun was approaching the horizon, Running Fox, feeling enough animals had been killed for the time being, called an end to the day's hunt. Tired men and exhausted horses wearily made their way to the temporary campsite, set up by a handful of women who were not involved in the hunt.

At the beginning of each day's hunt, a few women stayed behind to straighten up the camp and build cooking fires. A majority of the women followed the men who were trailing the herd, working in small groups of twos and fours, with the strongest, most agile women running behind the hunters. As soon as an animal was killed, they rushed to it, immediately gutting and skinning it. Once the main butchering was finished, some of the women carved the carcass into smaller, more manageable pieces. One or two of them remained to finish butchering and loading the fresh kill onto the litters before moving on. In the meantime, the faster women in the group ran ahead to the next slain buffalo, starting the process again. Usually, by the time the bodies were dismembered, women with litters were there to help with the final butchering and loading.

The work of the women was arduous, specialized, and as finely tuned as the working of a beehive. The dangers were acute. Nimbleness

The Quest

and speed were imperative. They stacked as much meat on the litter as it would hold and the horse was capable of pulling, without spilling any of it. Once the loaded litters were secured for travel, the women led the horses from the hunting field to the temporary campground. Once the litter was unloaded, the group of running women returned with the litter to the hunt, butchering and preparing another load of meat and hides.

The women in the camp were cooking large slabs of buffalo meat over open flames. Once they were sure there was enough meat on the fire to feed everyone in the hunting party, some of the camp women turned their attention to a more thorough cleaning of the hides, while others continued tending the fires. Each specialized group of helpers performed with great skill, according to their ability and training.

The majority of the day's kill was tightly packed on litters, covered with the hides, and secured with ropes of rawhide. After the cargo was stabilized, it was ready to transport. Traveling in small groups, each woman led two of the horses back across the plains to the village. It took half the night for the group to complete its journey. The moon, entering its time of fullness, provided them with enough reflecting light to easily and safely complete the trip.

When they arrived at the village, the elders and children helped the travelers unpack the litters, while others fed and watered the horses. The older village women immediately began cooking the fresh buffalo meat. Generous portions were served to the ones who had stayed behind in the village; however, the vast majority was destined to be smoked, dried and set aside as provisions for the grey days and the freezing nights that lay ahead.

The traveling women rested whenever possible, using the opportunity to visit with their friends. Once the meat was cooked, they feasted with the remaining villagers and shared news of the hunt. Afterward, they slept until awakening in the pre-dawn. First tending to their morning needs, they ate a light, warm meal before embarking on their journey to rejoin the hunting party. On the way back to the hunting camp, the women rode one horse while leading the second one, thus assuring their swift return, shortly after first light.

The hunters returned to the temporary camp, tired and hungry. First they fed and watered their horses. When the ponies were properly attended to and hobbled, the men collapsed around the campfires. Resting for a while before eating their fill of freshly cooked buffalo meat, each loudly recounted his part in the day's activities. They laughed contentedly, knowing it had been a profitable day. Within another day or two, they would have all of the meat needed to sustain the people throughout the empty months that were to come.

Eventually, the women skinning and packing the meat and hides made their way to the campfires. They sat together, chattering among themselves, eating their fill of the feast. Yes, the hunt had been successful. The people were happy, and feeling safe about the frigid winds awaiting them in only a little more than a moon. Tonight, the people of Running Fox were content and secure about their future. The feasting was short lived, as they needed to rest. It was time for gazing at the stars with gratitude. Soon they would retire for the night, sleeping deeply and peacefully, dreaming of another day of bountiful hunting.

Morning came early for everyone in the hunting party. The four young men were no exception. Eagerly they made their way to one of the fires that had been maintained throughout the night. An early morning chill was hanging in the air, but they seemed unaffected by the temperature. Their blood was liquid fire, running hot and furious through their veins. It would take more than one cold night to quench the flaming excitement of their first hunt. In fact, they had spent a large part of the night exchanging stories of the day's adventures. If they were tired, their bodies certainly seemed unaware of it. Their spirits were soaring, and life was full of promise.

The Quest

They replenished their quivers with a fresh supply of arrows. After consuming some freshly cooked buffalo strips, they were ready for the day's activity. They felt the vibrating earth underneath their feet. The constant quaking of the ground, and the roaring echoes of their pounding hooves were casting a strange, seductive allure. Hearing the resounding thunder of hoof beats, it was as if the animals were calling to them, enticing the hunters. *"Come and run with the herd… if you dare."*

Morning Star and Flaming Sky spent very little time together the night before. She was kept busy helping the other women with the skinning, butchering, and cooking. They were only able to sneak off by themselves for a few precious moments before returning to their separate preparations for the following day. It would continue this way until after the people migrated to their winter campsite. She would remain extremely busy, even after the actual hunting was completed. Preserving the bounty of the hunt was the responsibility of the women. In her new status as a woman, Morning Star now had an important role to play.

Additionally, she had a very special buffalo skin needing her attention and preparation, in order to be offered as part of Flaming Sky's payment to her father. Usually Flaming Sky's mother or a sister would have completed this task; however, Morning Star decided to do it herself, which was her right. There was much needing her attention, which would keep her mind and body occupied. She remained patient, as she had waited her entire life to become united with Flaming Sky. She prayed the time left before moving to winter quarters would go by quickly. In the meantime, she worked, she waited, and she dreamed of their future.

After eating their fill of warm food, the hunters gathered their weapons, rounded up their ponies and prepared to ride. White Wolf, who was again joining the hunt, decided to switch from a bow and arrow to the lance, having found it was not as easy as it used to be for him to ride a pony at full speed, while shooting arrows at buffalo.

No. The lance was his weapon of choice for today. He still enjoyed the excitement of the hunt, even though he was slowing down.

If the truth were known, White Wolf was more than a little anxious to redeem himself for what he considered a poor day's hunt. Yesterday, with his eyes filled with dust from the stampeding herd, blinding his already weakening eyes, it had taken too many shots to bring down his prey. Using the lance would enable him to guide his horse with one hand, allowing him better control of his pony while racing alongside the swiftly moving herd. The old man's only desire was to enjoy this hunt, uncertain if it was his last one. Every autumn he grew older and slower, while the buffalo, by contrast, grew younger and faster. With his heart light, and his lance at the ready, he joined Running Fox at the head of the riders, beginning what might very well be his final hunt.

Starting the second day of the hunt, Short Bear was desperate to improve on his ability as a provider. Late last night, before retiring, his father, Thunder Eyes, went out of his way to publicly berate his son for his apparent lack of hunting skill. More than anything else, Short Bear wanted to please his father. He wanted to receive Thunder Eyes' approval at least once in his young life. Unfortunately, he still heard his father's angry words slicing through his heart: "I asked for a son and, instead, I got you....you, who rides like a squaw and hunts with the skill of a warrior three days dead! Your youngest sister is a better warrior than you could ever hope to be!"

Short Bear did fairly well during the early morning hunt; however, he was still having trouble adjusting to the noise and seeing through the thick clouds of muck. Not known as one of the tribes' better horsemen, he found it difficult to cut a bull out of the group and separate it from the herd. On the positive side, he already doubled his kill from the previous day. His confidence level was slowly rising and he was determined to impress his father. Thus,

The Quest

with his mind preoccupied with such thoughts, he went charging into the outer edge of the herd.

As he attacked, a large group of trailing animals split off to the far right of the main body. Before he realized what was happening, Short Bear and his pony were trapped, caught in the open space between two rapidly moving streams of crazed beasts. Still unaware of what was occurring with the splinter group, the young warrior tried closing in on a lame bull at the edge of the main herd. Short Bear was concentrating so hard on maneuvering the animal into position for the kill, he remained totally unaware of what was occurring behind him and to his right. Suddenly, for some unknown reason, the stream of stragglers abruptly veered sharply to the left, rejoining the main herd. While some were cutting in front of Short Bear, the rest of the group surrounded him, ensnaring him in a mass of thundering flesh. Glancing to his right, he saw the splintered herd tightly closing in on him. Unfortunate for him, by the time he realized his situation, it was already too late. He was completely enclosed by the frenzied animals. Escape was impossible.

Encircling Short Bear, the animals re-formed one mass, with him caught in the middle of a torrid sea of flesh and bones, pressing against his pony. It was then that one of the randomly slashing horns ripped into his pony's shoulder. The smell of freshly spilled blood added to the chaos of the group. In pain, the horse reared up on its hind legs, frantically pawing at the empty air. As the horse recoiled, Short Bear dropped his weapons. Grabbing the horse's mane with both hands, he held on with all of the strength at his command. The horse tried valiantly, but unsuccessfully, to regain its balance. Bringing its front legs down, the pony became hopelessly entangled with the stampeding herd. The thundering sounds of the hoofbeats prevented the young warrior from hearing the sound of the horse's legs shattering. The weight of the horse gave way, causing it to stumble headlong in front of the charging animals.

The collapsing pony catapulted Short Bear into the middle of the surging chaos. Bouncing off the back of a large bull, he landed on his side with a thud, directly in the path of the oncoming hooves. He felt a sharp pain in his head as he went crashing to the ground. All he could see was a mass of brown flowing over him, feeling the cutting hooves tearing deep into his flesh, his own warm blood, thick and sticky on his skin. Aware of an enormous weight crushing his bones, he winced with pain as a burning sensation filled his chest. Desperately trying to breathe, he was unable to, as his lungs had already collapsed. The last thing he experienced was the piercing pain filling his head…then he felt nothing. In a heartbeat it was over. The raging buffalo went on trampling his body deep into the earth, endlessly scattering the small bits and pieces of his remains across the prairie.

Flaming Sky, seeing Short Bear disappear into the midst of the herd, rode as fast as he could to try to help his friend; however, even before starting, it was obvious he would never make it in time to save him. He saw Short Bear being flung to the ground. Try as he might, it was impossible for him to breach the barrier and reach his comrade. After several failed attempts, he retreated to a safer distance. Sitting astride Pawnee, he watched the stampeding beasts continue their crazed running, unable to see Short Bear's pony. All that remained for him was to assume his friend and the pony had both been trampled to death…and to cope with his own sudden feelings of emptiness and helplessness. He was stunned, and frozen.

The herd moved on, unabashed by the minor inconvenience of the young warrior and his horse under hoof. Flaming Sky's eyes fixed on the spot where Short Bear disappeared into the dust and the pulsating mass of bodies. Finally, turning his pony away from the scene, he looked around, searching for Thunder Eyes. "Finding Thunder Eyes will be the easy part. But telling him," he sighed, "will be much more difficult."

The Quest

It did not take him long to locate Short Bear's father. Thunder Eyes was hunting with Running Fox, near the front of the hunters. Approaching the two men, he signaled them to move farther away from the herd, as the noise was much too loud to allow the three of them to hear each other without shouting. The young man was aware this was not the kind of news meant to be delivered that way. No. They had to move far enough away from the din so his words could be clearly heard and understood.

Riding to the top of a knoll more than a hundred strides away, he nervously waited for the two men to join him. From this vantage point he watched the endless herd stretching out in all directions. Off in the distance were the hills directly west of him. To the east was the endless sea of brown flesh flooding the prairie. Even from here, there appeared to be neither a beginning nor an ending to the southward flowing stream of buffalo. "Several days will pass before the animals finish migrating through the hunting grounds. We will have to wait until the herd finishes passing before we can even think about looking for any remains of Short Bear." But in his heart, Flaming Sky knew they would never find any sign of his friend.

The young brave took a deep breath, holding it for a while before heavily releasing it. At this moment, his fear of Thunder Eyes was blocking out his grief over the loss of his friend. He did not know how he was going to find a way to tell Thunder Eyes what had happened to Short Bear. Breathing deeply, he anxiously watched the two older men approaching him, with a look of concern on their faces. They were sure he would not have interrupted the hunt unless it was a matter of great importance.

Flaming Sky was very glad there was someone else with Thunder Eyes. He was especially happy that the someone was Running Fox. From past experience, he was certain Thunder Eyes' reaction would be one of anger and blame, with the man's rage directed at him. Right now, his mind was spinning with reasons as to why Thunder Eyes reacted this way. He was trying very hard to understand the man's underlying frame of mind.

"It always seemed Thunder Eyes resented me for being born during the night of the raining fire. Short Bear was born three days after the flaming sky, a fact he bitterly holds against me." Flaming Sky tried to explain to himself, "This must be the reason why I was especially singled out as the target of his fury on so many occasions. Thunder Eyes' anger toward Short Bear was fueled by his disappointment in his son's abilities, but also by his ire toward me…which must be at least partially triggered by the timing of our births." Although he was trying desperately to understand, this explanation did not help his present situation.

When the riders were close enough to hear him, Running Fox gave Flaming Sky permission to speak. Taking another deep breath and releasing it very slowly, the young man began the story at the time he first realized Short Bear was in trouble. He pointed out the exact spot where the young brave had fallen. "I saw him through the dust, completely surrounded by the buffalo. I rode as fast as I could, but he had already disappeared into the herd. There was nothing I could do. No one could have helped him. It was too late."

All the while, he was carefully watching Thunder Eyes' reaction to his words. The older man's fists tightened as his arms and shoulders tensed. Clinching his teeth, a look of pure hatred shot out of his eyes, pouring over Flaming Sky like boiling water. By the time he reached the stage in his story where Short Bear had been lost in the dust, disappearing into the herd itself, Thunder Eyes, unable to contain himself any longer, began shouting profanities at him.

"You!" he howled at the top of his voice, "It should have been you! Not Short Bear, but you!" He continued ranting, "You always thought you were so much better than everyone…that you are so special. You are too good to have to put up with us. Well, Chief Running Fox may be your father, but I say you were sired by a weasel, and incubated in buffalo dung!"

The Quest

"Enough!" interjected Running Fox. "That is more than enough! You know Flaming Sky never wished any harm to your son. They were like brothers. Everyone knows this. Now, be silent!"

At this point, Flaming Sky lowered his eyes and turned Pawnee away from the older men. He sadly rode off, unable to bear the verbal tirade against him, still trying to understand the anger of his friend's father. He could hear Running Fox and Thunder Eyes arguing in fearsome voices. Thankfully, he was now too far away to understand what they were saying. He never did learn the content of their exchange. Running Fox did not tell him and, for his part, he thought it wise not to ask. The topic remained forever un-broached.

Before the day's end, word of Short Bear's death made its way throughout the entire hunting party. Running Fox was not the only one who observed Thunder Eyes' outburst at Flaming Sky. Although the noise of the herd obscured his words, the other hunters clearly understood the language of his body and the sounds of his raging hatred. Even through the dusty air, they clearly saw his fury, and witnessed the futile attempts by their chief to calm Thunder Eyes, as they watched Flaming Sky riding dejectedly away.

There was a great sadness in the camp that night due to the death of the young warrior. One could sense a thick fear hanging in the air…a fear of what Thunder Eyes might do. The story was already spreading that, as usual, he immediately sought refuge by misusing the sacred herbs and ceremonial plants. The people were saying Thunder Eyes had stolen some dried petals of the rare desert blood that had been presented by Flaming Sky as a gift to his Wicasa. No one other than White Wolf truly understood their secret power, nor comprehended the sacred magic within the red flowers. The rarity of these plants serves as a clear sign that they are truly blessed by the Great Spirit. Indeed, a Wicasa is fortunate to have them in his possession; however, he who misuses their medicine might well become lost in the darkness, possibly never to return.

There was little time for mourning Short Bear, as it was imperative that the hunt be finished. The meat needed to be prepared and stored for it's future use during the winter ahead. A majority of the people, caught up in performing their tasks, tended to forget all about Thunder Eyes. No one recalled having seen him during the last days of the hunt. Although Short Bear's mother and sisters went on working side-by-side with the other women, his father was nowhere to be found. No one bothered taking the time to look for him. The hunt progressed as it had to…on schedule.

During the next two days, two more braves and three women were lost to the relentless herd. Several more hunters were seriously wounded. There were multitudes of cuts, bruises, blisters, and broken bones among the hunters and the skinners, requiring White Wolf's attention. Three more ponies were lost during the ensuing pursuit. However, for a hunt of this magnitude, the total number of casualties was extremely light, and well within the limits of acceptability.

White Wolf gave up hunting on the last two days, returning instead to his duties as shaman and healer. His spirit helpers cared for the more lightly wounded hunters and skinners, allowing the old man to direct his skills toward serving the ones who were more severely injured, whose wounds required his time and attention. He went about his healing, working his cures with the magic of his herbs and the power of his prayers.

Eventually the hunt ended, but the work did not. The women were intently involved in preserving the food needed for the cold, gray days ahead. The members of Short Bear's family had been given very little opportunity to properly grieve their loss. Now, with the hunt ended, his mother and sisters possessed the time to personally lament his passing. A public ceremony would have to wait until after the hunt was concluded. They concerned themselves with Thunder Eyes' disappearance from the camp on that fateful day, as he had not been seen by anyone since then. He had disappeared many times in the past

The Quest

and, on more than one occasion, remained absent for a full moon. So, although his family was concerned, they were not yet fearful for him.

In the meantime, the workers went about their tasks, rigging new litters to attach to the hunters' horses. In addition to carrying its rider, each pony would drag a litter filled with meat and hides. The days were growing shorter, and the nights were becoming colder. It was imperative for the meat to be moved as quickly as possible to the main camp.

Due to the plentiful bounty of the hunt, a large portion of the meat and hides could not be taken to the main camp in one trip. A second trip would have to be made the following day. Several of the women and hunters stayed behind to protect the stored meat from night marauders. The women, taking turns sleeping, constantly fed the fires as they attended to the task of preserving the buffalo meat and hides. The men alternated standing guard and sleeping in shifts. So it was the hunt ended and the night began its passage toward the dawn.

The men and women of the hunting party who had journeyed to the main camp arrived back at the hunting camp shortly after sun-up. Everyone was tired. It had been an extremely exhausting four days and nights. The work continued but, thankfully, the pace was slightly slower than previously. By mid-day, the horses were packed and the camp struck. The last of the weary hunting party was ready to embark upon its homeward trek.

Despite being fatigued, their spirits were high. All, that is, except the families of the fallen...including the family of Short Bear. Hopefully they would have time to openly grieve and put him to rest once they reached the main camp. This was the only plan they could cling to, as they had nothing of Short Bear, himself, to bury in the sky. A majority of their remaining work, once they returned home, could be completed as a small group, working away from the main body of workers, allowing them some semblance of privacy.

After the herd completed its trek past the hunting camp, Flaming Sky and his two friends returned to the place where Short Bear was last seen. The ground was soft and mushy. The hooves of the animals had churned the soil like a field plowed in preparation for spring planting. The three braves were unable to locate anything identifiable as a part of Short Bear's body or clothing. His remains were sliced, ground, and spread over the endless southern trail, becoming forever a part of the perpetual prairie, feeding the grass which, in turn, feeds the buffalo. Short Bear had contributed his life to this ongoing cycle. With nothing of him left to bury, his family could only set aside some of his possessions in the burial grounds, hoping his wandering spirit would find them on its way to the afterlife.

The villagers worked very hard during the next several days, storing meat and preparing the campsite for its move to winter quarters. It was decided by Morning Star's father, Two Claws, that the marriage ceremony would be postponed until after the tribe's return to the summer campsite. His decision did not please the young lovers, Morning Star and Flaming Sky, who were hoping to spend winter camp together as husband and wife. However, Two Claws' decision was final. Not even Running Fox had the right to overturn her father's decision. They must wait until after the spring thaw.

In the meantime, they will pass the days watching the children play in the snow on sleds made of buffalo ribs and hides. They will watch the women gathering close together by the cooking fires, exchanging gossip. They will listen as the men talk of great deeds, which become grander with each retelling. During the long nights, they will yearn for each other. Morning Star continued perfecting her domestic arts, and Flaming Sky intensified his training with White Wolf in earnest. From time-to-time, they were able to steal a few moments together in the evenings; however, privacy was not easy for them to come by. Whenever an opportunity presented itself, the two of them held hands, while gazing into each other's eyes, and dreaming of the future they assumed was awaiting them.

Chapter 6

MORNING STAR AND THUNDER EYES

By the time of the spring thaw, White Wolf's apprentice, Flaming Sky, was well on his way to mastering the art of sanctifying the herbs and plants. He memorized numerous chants and prayers to be recited during their preparation, and spent several long periods a day in quiet reflection, hoping light might be shed upon his path. When not with his teacher, the young man occupied his time in solitude, concentrating on his studies, thus allowing him to retreat into the cave within his own mind. He quietly, patiently waited for the Great Spirit to enlighten him, and guide him along the correct path.

White Wolf was extremely pleased with the progress Flaming Sky was making. However, he often asked himself questions regarding the sign that had been shown to him, which continued to burn in his soul: *A flaming eagle who walks in an inferno, unharmed. An eagle purified by fire and strengthened by the consuming flames.*

"The boy is well chosen as a shaman." he affirmed to himself. "He has the favor of The Great Spirit. But I have not seen a sign nor any confirmation acknowledging a new Holy One. Maybe my people will have to wait another generation or so before the Grand Father sends the flaming eagle."

The old man pondered on whether or not there would ever be a new Wicasa for his tribe. Not every tribe has one. His concerns, as always, were for his people. He was aware he would not live forever, and this preoccupied his private thoughts. He was yet to be given a sign linking Flaming Sky or anyone else, for that matter, to the image. He prayed for clarification, and while patiently awaiting an answer; he continued teaching the young medicine man the skills of a shaman. "Old man," he admonished himself, "the Great Spirit will appoint a new Wicasa if and when He chooses. It is not for you to concern yourself with His unfolding. It is your responsibility to train Flaming Sky…not to worry about that which is beyond your control."

Being a Holy Man, White Wolf was responsible for the spiritual well being of his people. As such, he knew eventually he would have to confront the destructive behavior of Thunder Eyes. The reprobate had sneaked into camp slightly less than a moon cycle after the establishment of winter camp. Up until now, the coward was managing to remain hidden from the gaze of White Wolf. If nothing else, the old man was patient, knowing, in time, he and Thunder Eyes would stand in each other's eyes. He did not know when nor how, but when the opportunity presented itself, White Wolf would be ready for his encounter with Thunder Eyes.

Despite his grief for Short Bear, Flaming Sky was called upon by his Wicasa to assist in offering the prayers of thanksgiving to the Great Spirit. There was always a price to pay during each buffalo hunt, and this one had been costly, indeed. After the meat was prepared

The Quest

and stored for the winter, the entire village met at the council fire. They gathered, with the chief and elders sitting in the center of the lodge, surrounded by the warriors, the older boys, and finally, the women. Although his heart was heavy, Flaming Sky was prepared to recite the chants and prayers. It was his honour and responsibility. As usual, the ceremony opened with the smoking of the sacred pipe. However, this time, the pipe was passed by White Wolf to Flaming Sky, who, after smoking, handed it to his father and chief, Running Fox. Upon completion of the ceremony, the tribe danced the dance of the bountiful hunt. He was confident that all had gone well with the ritual. White Wolf was well pleased with his apprentice.

For the impatient Flaming Sky, the cold, gray days in winter camp were a time of endless waiting. He longed for his promised one, Morning Star. The first ceremony to be conducted upon their return to summer camp will be the one binding them together for a lifetime. Often he fantasized, dreaming of the life they would share, and the children she would bear. These thoughts filled his heart with joyful expectation.

However, despite his anticipated happiness, there was an overwhelming sadness dwelling in Flaming Sky's heart. He deeply missed his friend, Short Bear. The burial ceremony, without Short Bear's remains, felt empty to him. The two boys had been more like brothers than friends. Their families had known each other prior to the birth of their sons. Their fathers trained together as young braves, even as their mothers learned the skills of a Lakota woman. Their tipis were always in close proximity.

Reminiscing, he recalled his earliest memories involving Short Bear's family. He was unclear as to his exact age at the time, but aware he was walking. *He saw himself stopping, standing a safe distance away from the family, watching them enjoying their evening meal. Two things were clear in his mind while pausing there in silence, staring at them. First, he was certain he knew these people, and, second, he was terrified of Thunder Eyes There was something about the man that was evil. Although unsure as to the source of these feelings toward Thunder Eyes, he was certain these emotions were as true as they were strong.*

Short Bear was sitting across from his mother, Snow Bird, and his two younger sisters. The older girl was on the verge of walking, while the younger girl was still a toothless breast feeder. Snow Bird was encouraging Flaming Sky to come to her, offering him a piece of meat; but, remaining leery of Thunder Eyes, he would not approach. He remained motionless as she walked over and gently handed him the precious morsel of food. Grabbing it, he ran quickly away.

After that, his only memory of the story was from his mother's retelling. Much laughter was usually evoked when she told of how her son of two winters took the meat between his teeth, like a young wolf, running home as if pursued by evil spirits. Taking refuge behind his mother, he closed his eyes very tightly, refusing to budge until his father took him by the hand and led him to his place at the campfire. There the brave lad sat triumphantly devouring his hard won prize.

From then on, except when one or the other was being punished, Flaming Sky could not remember a day when he and Short Bear were not together. He possessed a variety of images, picturing himself and his mother sharing morning meals with Snow Bird and her three children. Short Bear had been a good friend. He was a nervous boy who was easily influenced. If the truth were known, the only real trouble Short Bear ever got into was when he followed the lead of his friend, Flaming Sky. Neither boy was really bad; however, Flaming Sky was very curious, high spirited and extremely impatient. His drifting images returned him to the time when the two of them went fishing by themselves.

After a morning of diligent fishing, the boys managed to catch three rather small fish. To them, the catch was huge. Of course, having caught the fish, they were now determined to cook them. Gathering small, dry branches, they stacked the firewood behind the tipi of Short Bear's grandfather, Yellow Coyote. Once there was ample fuel, Flaming Sky borrowed a flaming twig from a nearby campfire. Proudly returning

The Quest

with the fire, he promptly applied the burning stick to the stack of wood. After a few failed attempts, Flaming Sky finally managed to light their campfire...as well as Yellow Coyote's tipi. When the excitement was over, and no one was injured, they discovered grandpa's tipi had burned all the way to the ground. Their parents ensured it was many winters before either of the boys tried his hand at cooking again.

And, of course, there was the time Flaming Sky decided to take it upon himself to teach Short Bear the subtle art of flying. *Flaming Sky was engaging in one of his favorite pastimes, gazing at an eagle sailing effortlessly in a cloudless sky. He watched the bird streaking across the sky like an arrow in flight. Diving toward the ground, as if it was going to crash, the eagle then flapped its wings, soaring upward.*

After laboring for two days fashioning a pair of wings out of pieces of animal hides and small saplings, Flaming Sky concluded it was now time to test them. With Short Bear in tow, Flaming Sky made his way to the outskirts of the camp. Crossing to the other side of the river flowing past the village, they climbed up a small knoll onto a flat ledge, approximately four paces above the ground. With a clear run of forty strides and favorable winds, the conditions were perfect for their virgin flight.

As expected, Flaming Sky was eager to try his plan, attempting to release himself from the restraints of the earth. Short Bear helped him attach the wings to his arms with pieces of rawhide. Clutching the tips of the wings with his hands, off he went, charging toward the end of the ledge. Then, jumping as high as he could, with his arms beating wildly, off he soared...straight down to the ground. He tried hitting the ground running, but was unsuccessful as he went crashing onto the solid earth, skinning his knees as he landed. Undaunted, he repeated his attempt to fly several more times. The results, unfortunately, were always the same.

Finally, he decided it was time for Short Bear to take his maiden flight. Flaming Sky helped him strap on the homemade wings; then, walking carefully to the edge of the small cliff, they paused. Short Bear was much more resistant to the honour of flight than was his friend. His head was emphatically shaking, "No," as Flaming Sky encouraged, "Yes."

They debated back and forth until Short Bear, as he always did, gave in to his friend's persistence. Holding out his wings, he backed up as far as possible, awaiting Flaming Sky's command. At his signal, Short Bear ran as fast as he could to the very end of the ledge, where he frantically tried to stop…but it was too late. Having passed the point of no return, off he went, sailing into empty space, his arms helplessly flaying the air as he came plunging to the ground in a rolling mass. There he lay in a heap, both wings broken…as was Short Bear's leg.

Flaming Sky, fearing the worst, immediately ran back to the camp looking for White Wolf. Short Bear was in pain, truly a good reason for summoning aid. But Flaming Sky's uppermost concern was his fear of Thunder Eyes' reaction to the accident, and he wanted a person of authority with him. True to form, Thunder Eyes threw all of the blame on Flaming Sky. The broken leg gave him one more excuse to berate him. Understandably, his own father, Running Fox, was not overjoyed with his son's behavior either. The boys were forbidden to have any contact with each other for one full cycle of the moon. Short Bear did his recovering under the caring hands of his mother, Snow Bird, while Flaming Sky did his repenting under the watchful eye of his mother, Skipping Bird.

Flaming Sky grinned softly to himself, remembering these childhood antics. He even admitted to himself that he may have actually contributed to Thunder Eyes 'blaming attitude toward him. However, he suddenly became somber as the next memory came rushing in on him. It was a dark memory shared by the two boys. Although they often discussed it with each other, neither one of them ever comprehended exactly what transpired. Their memories of the incident were similar. Flaming Sky knew he was very young when the event occurred.

He recalled sitting in his parents lodge, lost in his own world, playing with one of his toys. His mother was attending the small fire while mending the family's clothing. Without warning, Running Fox came staggering into the tipi, his clothes drenched in blood. His face bore the expression of a man in shock. Skipping Bird became hysterical the instant she saw him.

The Quest

She was so upset that, at first, she failed to realize the blood covering him was not his own. Flaming Sky remembered squatting in stunned silence, watching them argue, his mother remaining extremely agitated. She appeared to be angry with Running Fox. He never understood why his mother was so distraught. After all, his father was alive, and unharmed.

Flaming Sky, mulling this over, remembered that Short Bear's version of what happened in his lodge was nearly the same. The main exception was the fact that Thunder Eyes raged wildly, like an animal which had lost its mind. Whenever their parents did talk about this incident, it was always in hushed tones of secrecy. The topic was never discussed openly in front of the boys. It was obvious someone had been killed. Even after all of these many passings of the seasons, there were still unanswered questions remaining.

Later, they learned the deceased warrior was one of their fathers' hunting companions. The boys did not recall ever hearing the man's name spoken. They managed to overhear enough bits and pieces of scattered conversations to realize, not only were Running Fox and Thunder Eyes present, but Thunder Eyes, somehow or another, was responsible for the death. The rumors of his involvement were always spoken in low tones and hushed whispers. If the elders became aware the boys were listening, they immediately changed the topic of their conversations. On one occasion, Flaming Sky overheard enough to realize Thunder Eyes had indeed been misusing the sacred herbs. Apparently, he was under their influence when the fatal accident occurred.

So it was that Flaming Sky spent the quiet time of the gray days and black nights of winter camp, remembering his life-long friend, and grieving his death. Even after the winter came and went, and the days grew longer and warmer, his memory of the fallen Short Bear remained a festering wound. The turning of the season did not temper his sense of loss.

The return trip to summer camp carried the promise of warm sun and an abundance of food available to the tribe for hunting and harvesting. The move was welcomed with great enthusiasm by all. Flaming Sky and Morning Star were especially joyful for the return. True to their word, Running Fox and White Wolf delivered the six gift horses to Two Claws, as promised. The weapons crafted by the young brave were finished and ready to present to the young maiden's father as partial payment for the honour of receiving her as his mate. The buffalo hide had been meticulously cleaned and fashioned expertly into a fine robe by Morning Star. The gifts were ready for presentation to her parents.

The marriage ceremony was to occur after the tribe settled into summer camp at the foot of the Black Hills. Morning Star's first priority was to put up the tipi she made for her and Flaming Sky to share. With the help of her mother, Spotted Deer, it was erected far away from the heart of the camp, near the extreme edge of the settlement, close enough to the village to share in the safety of the group, yet far enough away to enjoy their long-awaited privacy.

When the day finally arrived, it was Running Fox who spoke to Morning Star's father. The chief bargained with Two Claws, as was the custom. When an agreement was finally reached, Two Claws turned to his daughter, asking her if she was willing to accept Flaming Sky as her mate. After waiting a modest amount of time, she happily agreed to the union.

Standing in reverent silence in front of White Wolf, the promised ones watched him slowly removing the ceremonial knife from his waistband. Taking the blade, he very carefully made a small incision in the palm of each of their right hands. Placing Morning Star's palm in Flaming Sky's, their blood blending, he wrapped a small piece of ribbon around their wrists. Holding their hands together with his own, White Wolf recited the ancient words of the ancestors, declaring to all present that Flaming Sky and Morning Star were now bound

THE QUEST

together for their lifetime as husband and wife, in accordance with the traditions and the laws of the people.

There was great rejoicing among the people as the young couple rode the ceremonial white horses to their new tipi. Here they were to privately spend the next full cycle of the moon together. It was a time of getting to know one another on a more intimate level. During this interlude, they were left completely undisturbed. Morning Star's mother prepared food for them daily, leaving it outside their tipi, next to the sealed flap. They used this uninterrupted interval to freely explore and learn the art of pleasuring each other. Making good use of this opportunity, they learned about each other physically, emotionally and spiritually.

The next several moons passed swiftly and uneventfully. Flaming Sky resumed his studies with White Wolf, who prayed, meditated, and took several short trips to gather fresh, local herbs and plants. He returned from his last journey well supplied, making it unnecessary for him to make the long, dangerous, trek into the southern deserts.

In the tipi of the newlyweds, Morning Star was busy sewing clothes for their first child, who was due to make its entrance during the moons of the sunless sky. The arrival time of their baby would be perfect. When the tribe was ready to return to summer camp, the child would be old enough and strong enough to make the journey safely.

As it had been during the last several summers, the game was plentiful, and the harvest bountiful. The people were happy, and grateful to the Grand Father for His generous gifts. The warm days of summer were quickly becoming shorter, and it was clear that the time of the autumn hunt was drawing nearer with each dawn. Even now, the loss of Short Bear remained heavy within Flaming Sky's heart; however, his new life with Morning Star was going a long way toward easing his pain. While enjoying his present role as a young married brave, he was looking forward to his future as a father with mixed emotions.

White Wolf spent the peaceful days of summer contemplating the mysteries still perplexing him, as he struggled with many important, un-clarified issues. Only now, in retrospect, did he fully understand the meaning of the vision Short Bear described upon his return from his survival trip. The message was painfully accurate. "The buffalo will return the boy to the earth from which he had come."

There were, however, three unresolved visions continuously plaguing the old man. First, and foremost, was his vision of the flaming eagle. The second vision vexing him was the image his cousin's son described of seeing the mountains of buffalo bones. The third unresolved riddle was Flaming Sky's vision of endless generations of deceased Sioux, solemnly chanting while dancing as one entity around an enormous campfire. Since this image was seen by a young one, the old man was aware his old eyes were never to witness such a dance, no matter what the significance, nor was it for him to decipher its meaning.

Concerning his own vision, the old shaman trusted he would eventually receive the answer to its meaning. He took comfort in the fact that he chose the new tribal medicine man wisely. "The vision of the eagle is not connected to the new shaman," he concluded. "Its revelation will be the signal ending my yearning for a Holy Man, if, in fact, the Great Spirit is to bless us with one. My work here is done," he resolved. "It is for the Grand Father to appoint a Holy One, if He chooses, as it is for me to await His Will," he reminded himself. "Often the future is obscured from an old man's eyes and it is seen only by the eyes of the young. Understanding it is best left to the ones who will live it. It is in the Hands of the Grand Father, as it should be, not in mine," he reiterated, again attempting to release his fruitless pondering. This acceptance granted him some peace of mind. White Wolf prayed to live long enough to see the Great Spirit

The Quest

choose the Wicasa; however, he was content that the Great Spirit would reveal the mysteries of his images at the proper moment. "When He does, it may be to the young one rather than me," he reasoned, with a slight wisp of sadness.

Satisfied with the harmony of the situation, the old man rededicated his time and energy solely to the advancement of his cousin's son's training. Flaming Sky was learning much faster than originally anticipated. By the end of the summer, he would be ready to learn the secrets of the sacred mixture of cacota, sage, pompotote, and tobacco for use in the ceremonial pipe. The teacher and his student often spent consecutive days and evenings together, practicing the healing rituals, and administering to the sick and injured.

It was at this time in his training that the young medicine man first understood the true value of White Wolf's spirit helpers. They chopped the wood, tended the fire, and cooked the old man's food. When White Wolf was too involved with his duties to hunt, the women collected food from the villagers for their meals. His duties often required him to be gone from the camp, and during these times they were called upon to use their knowledge of healing to administer to the people. In times of his absence, they maintained his lodge as well as their own, and mutually shared the responsibility of making his clothes. They were, indeed, the old man's extra eyes and hands. By serving White Wolf, they were serving their people and the Great Spirit.

Although Flaming Sky had the good fortune of having Morning Star, his beloved mate, to care for his domestic and personal needs, as shaman, he will have need of these talented women to help him in his duties. The four women understood the powers of herbs and plants, and were excellent tutors for the young man, thus freeing White Wolf to engage in other pursuits of his craft. Each spirit helper was a specific receptacle of specialized knowledge, which they shared willingly with the new medicine man.

While the sweetness of life abounded for the people, Snow Bird was not having nearly as pleasant a time as were her friends. Thunder Eyes continued disappearing for days, and often for even longer periods of time. Eventually, when he did return, he was always in an ugly mood. During his long absences, with no man to provide food for her and her two daughters, they were forced to rely on the generosity of their neighbors, as well as upon their own fishing skills. The three of them worked hard, gathering and preserving their share of the summer fruits. Snow Bird's father, Yellow Coyote, and Running Fox always brought the family some of whatever they shot…usually rabbits, deer, elk, birds, and an occasional forest buffalo.

Snow Bird went about maintaining her family as best she could on her own. Whenever Thunder Eyes returned, he immediately disrupted what little stability they had forged in their lives. It was rumored that, when he was in one of his rages, he often beat his wife and daughters. On more than one occasion, Snow Bird had taken her daughters and retreated to the safety of her father's tipi. In the course of time, she always ended up forgiving Thunder Eyes, and returned home with him. After recurring intervals of absence, each decreasing in duration, the situation always disintegrated, and the pattern repeated. As the time of the autumn hunt and the anniversary of Short Bear's death was drawing nearer, Thunder Eyes' mood was growing darker. The bowstring of his rage was tightening, and was just about to snap.

White Wolf and Flaming Sky left camp the same day that the scouts were sent in search of the herds. The old man needed to take his apprentice to a quiet place, away from the distractions of village life and marital bliss. It was time for Flaming Sky to learn the secret magic of blending the sacred herbs. This was the most mystical and powerful of all of the shaman's medicine. In all of the young man's training in using the ceremonial plants, this was the single most important lesson. Blended correctly, with a purity of purpose, the

The Quest

smoke serves to clarify the visions sought by the user. When the mix is properly altered, the smoke becomes worthy of carrying prayers to the Great Spirit. If the combination of herbs is used in a profane way, the user might well find himself deprived of his wits, as Thunder Eyes often did.

Whether Flaming Sky was to be a shaman only, or was destined to the eventuality of becoming the tribe's Holy Man, only the Grand Father knew. In either circumstance, it was necessary for him to finetune the powers of his mind. As the medicine man, it was to be Flaming Sky's responsibility to serve as the interpreter of dreams and visions, starting with his own. He will serve the tribe in this capacity until one with a clearer vision steps forward, relieving him of that responsibility.

The two men set up their camp a day's ride from the settlement, carefully ensuring they would remain within visual range of the scouting party's smoke signals. Their sign could be easily seen, allowing sufficient time to gather their weapons and join the hunt. From their position, after nightfall, they gazed upon the lights from the campfires of the scouts, which, from a distance, resembled fireflies hovering in the air on a warm summer's night. The men sat close to their own fire, as White Wolf initiated a lesson on the unique powers of each plant and herb. Taking his time, he led his cousin's son slowly through the maze, revealing to him their hidden magic.

Flaming Sky was learning the proper procedure for gathering and storing herbs, memorizing the chants to be repeated during their harvesting. He was taught the correct technique of drying the harvest, thus preserving it at maximum potency. Then, there was the mixture, itself, which was always best blended just prior to using. When necessary, it was acceptable to pre-mix the herbs until it was time to smoke them. White Wolf meticulously guided him through the chants and prayers spoken at each step of the process, from the gathering, drying and blending to the actual offering carried aloft by the winds to the Great Spirit. They worked late into the first night, and White Wolf was justifiably pleased with how quickly the young man was comprehending, integrating, and applying his lessons. So far, his training was going extremely well.

The men awakened with the rising sun, and the lessons began anew, the young man eagerly absorbing the wisdom of the old one. They took occasional short breaks, renewing themselves with drink and food, while clearing their minds and relaxing their bodies. Watching him work diligently throughout the day, White Wolf decided now was the time to deliver the gift.

"Tonight Flaming Sky will demonstrate his knowledge by mixing the herbs while repeating the prayers, totally on his own. Afterwards, he will smoke the special mixture in the pipe…his own pipe…the one which I made for him," he thought to himself with a slight smile on his lips. The pipe was carefully carved from a buffalo bone. This was a project the old man methodically worked on during the long, cold, grey nights, patiently shaping it, and boring out the stem. He had hidden it well, until now.

As was their custom, after finishing their evening meal, they sat wrapped in blankets, huddling close to the warm fire. Flaming Sky waited, expecting the old man to continue his nightly instructions. Instead, White Wolf set the pipe, which was protectively wrapped, down in front of his cousin's son. Smiling, he gestured for the young man to fold back the covering. The instant he saw the gift, Flaming Sky's eyes lit up like two blazing flames. Grinning broadly, he excitedly picked up his pipe. He knew it was his, as White Wolf had etched the young man's sign on the bowl of the pipe. The bowl was made of clay specifically shaped to fit into the opening of the hollowed-out bone. The pipe was decorated with a single eagle feather, with good medicine symbols carved into it, similar to the ones on White Wolf's prayer pipe.

"It is appropriate for every medicine man to possess an everyday prayer pipe, in addition to the ceremonial one," White Wolf said

The Quest

fondly to the young man. "I have crafted it with time, patience, and strong medicine."

"Truly, it is a gift that I will treasure forever," said Flaming Sky with appreciation. He knew that, when it was his turn, he, like White Wolf, would take his pipe with him on his final journey into the after life. "But, tonight," he smiled happily, "I will smoke it for the very first time."

White Wolf listened as Flaming Sky expertly chanted the prayers, while preparing the herbs to be smoked. The young man carefully crumbled them, blending and chanting as masterfully as if he had been doing it his entire life. His recitation of the prayers was accurate; however, he was still too young and inexperienced to truly comprehend the power of the words he was speaking. Meticulously, he poked several small pinches of the mixture into the receptacle, packing the blend down firmly enough for the herbs to burn evenly, while loosely enough to draw the smoke effortlessly up through the stem. He was confident the bowl was properly packed for smoking. However, instead of lighting it himself, he handed it to White Wolf, requesting that the old man offer up the first breath of prayer from his new pipe to Wakan Tanka.

White Wolf, exceedingly pleased, smiled approvingly, graciously accepting the honour being offered. He was impressed with Flaming Sky's gesture of respect, which displayed a great deal of wisdom for such a young shaman. Taking a smoldering stick from the fire, the old man lit the pipe, offering up the first breath. After finishing his devotion, he passed the pipe to his successor. They took turns smoking and offering up prayers to the Grand Father. The ceremony completed, they sat waiting in silence.

Closing his eyes, Flaming Sky directed his attention inward, into his true self, resuming his plea for guidance. Following the instructions given him by White Wolf, he envisioned himself as a bear, hibernating peacefully in a cave of soft, blue light. He did not have a long wait, once his mind found the silence.

Charles Richard Latona

He saw an image of himself as he appears now, and watched himself slowly growing older. Observing his evolvement into an old man, he observed more eagle feathers added to his war bonnet. From the appearance of the image of himself, he estimated he was at least another forty winters older, bearing a very striking physical resemblance to his father's cousin. In his vision, he was the same age as White Wolf is now. He was taken aback, noticing for the first time that, not only was he wearing the trappings of a medicine man, he was also wearing the white-buffalo-skull headdress of a Holy Man. Gazing deeply into his own old eyes, he saw the look of sorrow, and signs of suffering in the lines etched into his face. The vision slowly faded into swirling smoke, which silently drifted away.

Once they were sufficiently refocused following their meditations, Flaming Sky described his vision to the Wicasa. The image was clear in terms of its meaning. Flaming Sky was to become the new Wicasa, which was most pleasing to White Wolf. However, there were still questions troubling the old man.

He was anxious to know when his cousin's son would assume this role, and how the vision of the flaming eagle relates to this. "Is the flaming eagle the one for whom I have been waiting?" he wondered, silently. "Have I been so focused upon wanting a Holy One that I have misinterpreted the message of the vision? Maybe," he thought, "the flaming eagle is to be the one who will teach and guide Running Fox's son along the path of the Wicasa after I am gone."

The two men discussed the vision and its possibilities well into the night. The moon was high and full by the time they drifted off to sleep. However, for Flaming Sky, his sleep was not peaceful. He dreamed a familiar dream of when he was very young. *He was sitting in a shallow stream next to a small summer campfire. On a warm night like this, the fire's main purpose was to provide light, not heat. Seeing himself playing in a wide spot in the narrow stream, he remembered the cooling sensation of the flowing water. His parents had brought him to this quiet stream with another family, who remained unseen in the shadows.*

The Quest

It started with the full moon gradually growing dark, until, bit-by-bit, its light was completely extinguished from the sky. They were attempting to explain the phenomenon to him; but, before he could even hope to comprehend what they were saying, they stopped talking, extremely unsettled by what was now occurring. At first they attempted to remain calm, behaving as if this was not an unusual event. The face of the moon was turning a brownish-red colour. The blood-red hue completely painted the moon's surface as, slowly, the sphere began spinning like a toy top. By the reaction of his parents, he was certain this was an evil omen.

This reoccurring dream revisited him a handful of times throughout his life. Each time it occurred, some catastrophe always followed soon afterward. The last time was a full turn of the seasons ago. He remembered having the *blood moon* dream only days prior to Short Bear's death. In the morning, after eating, Flaming Sky recounted his dream to the old man, even though they had discussed it on previous occasions.

"I concur," said White Wolf, "it is the foretelling of some evil about to befall the people."

"The autumn hunt is about to begin," offered Flaming Sky. "Perhaps something bad will occur during the hunt. Maybe something unforeseen will happen to the herd."

"No," cautioned White Wolf. "I feel it will be much closer, and more intimate. The people will suffer a loss, right enough, but the loss will also be personal."

Flaming Sky struggled with his memory of the dream, searching for clarity as to the disaster which was on its way, but found no clues. All he could do in the present was what he had always done in the past: wait for the dreaded event to occur and prepare himself to suffer another loss. In the past, after one of these dreams, Flaming Sky remembered someone always becoming seriously ill or mortally wounded.

"Maybe White Wolf is wrong," he mused to himself with wishful thinking. "No, he is most accurate in his interpretations," he finally resolved. "There appears to be no reason to expect anything less this time."

The two medicine men agreed it was time for them to return to the camp. Even as they talked, they continuously scanned the east, looking for a signal from the scouts indicating the herd had been located. It was not until White Wolf stood up that he finally paid any attention to the morning sky.

"Look! The signal of smoke comes from the opposite horizon!" he shouted to Flaming Sky. "It is in the west. It comes from the village!"

It was a pressing message, instructing them to immediately return to camp. They realized the seriousness of the message, as the smoke spoke of urgency. The sender did not elaborate as to the reason why they were being recalled. Just knowing they were needed was reason enough for them to strike their temporary camp and prepare to depart as quickly as possible. However, they first smothered their campfire with green grass, and responded to the communication before extinguishing it completely. It was an easy day's ride back to the village and, by pushing their ponies to the maximum, they could arrive at their destination by late afternoon, before sunset. Riding their horses as if they were being pursued by demons, they headed home.

They were riding much too fast to allow for any conversation. Arriving at the top of a grassy knoll, they paused. From here they could see the camp with the river winding next to it. The village looked peaceful enough, and yet they had been recalled. Breaking into full stride, the two medicine men galloped at top speed into the camp, where Running Fox was waiting for them.

A dark expression lay upon his face. They knew by the look of his countenance something was seriously wrong...not that either of them ever doubted it. There was a look of deep sadness in Running Fox's eyes. It was a look Flaming Sky had never before seen on his father's

The Quest

face. Dismounting, the two men approached their chief in silence, as he motioned them to follow him into his lodge. Once inside, the three men sat motionless by the small fire without speaking. It was extremely difficult for Running Fox to talk. However, he was finally able to compose himself well enough to tell the tale of what had occurred.

"The incident took place shortly after sunset last night," he began solemnly. "Following their evening meal, Morning Star and Skipping Bird went to visit Snow Bird and her two daughters. The three women were busily sewing, discussing the preparations Morning Star was making in anticipation of the arrival of her first child. They talked of her giving birth several moons before our move back to summer camp, a good time for a child to arrive. Sitting there, happily chatting, working, and watching the two younger girls, they went about doing their chores.

"Suddenly, without warning, their tranquility was shattered by the staggering entrance of Thunder Eyes, who was strongly under the influence of ceremonial herbs. Incoherently slurring his words, ranting and raving against his wife and their two remaining children, he rambled on, shouting profanities at the top of his voice. Without warning, he lunged angrily at Snow Bird, striking her in the face, leaving a small cut on the bridge of her nose." Running Fox paused momentarily to compose himself.

"It was at this point Morning Star interceded," he continued. "She stepped between Thunder Eyes and his woman, quietly trying to talk him back into this reality. In a fit of rage, he grabbed the pregnant girl, flinging her aside as hard as he could. Stumbling, she landed, stomach first, on the top of the hot stones surrounding the fire. Rolling over in an attempt to escape the flames, she weakly struggled, trying to get to her feet. Before she could, Thunder Eyes, taking a step forward, kicked her directly in her mid-section. Sprawling to the ground, she curled up in pain, clutching her stomach and groaning. She let out a hysterical cry as she felt the warm blood oozing down the inside of her thighs. There she lay, holding her stomach and sobbing.

"Upon seeing this, Thunder Eyes backed out of his lodge, uneasily making his way to where his horse was tethered. After several unsuccessful attempts, he finally mounted his pony. Snow Bird went chasing after him, shaking her fist and cursing him. She stopped long enough to gather some stones, which she hurled at him as he rode away. He did not even look back. Fleeing, he disappeared into the darkness enshrouding the camp."

Running Fox breathed deeply before continuing his story. "Snow Bird ran back into her tipi to check on the condition of Morning Star. She stopped just inside the lodge, her eyes fixed upon the young woman in the arms of Skipping Bird. The pregnant woman was holding her stomach and writhing in pain. Snow Bird watched as Skipping Bird lifted her new daughter's skirt above her knees and, placing her hands between the young women's legs, waited. Morning Star was screaming in agony while clutching desperately at her midsection." His voice faded momentarily. "Snow Bird watched your mother remove a small bloody mass from under your wife's skirt. Morning Star did not need to be told. It was obvious the small bundle of bloody flesh cradled in Skipping Bird's hands was without life. She had lost her unborn child. My new daughter, your wife, miscarried." He paused, looking into his son's eyes, waiting for his words to have an effect. Flaming Sky was motionless, unable to comprehend the magnitude of his loss.

"By this time," Running Fox continued, regaining his chieftain tone, "Two Claws, and I came running into the tipi, while several braves stood hovering around outside. The instant he became aware of what had happened to his daughter and grandchild, he and the gathering of warriors were in favor of immediately pursuing Thunder Eyes. However, I was eventually able to convince them it would be prudent to wait until dawn. It was too dark to successfully follow

The Quest

Thunder Eyes' trail. Furthermore, they were unsure as to which direction he had ridden.

"Snow Bird's eye was blackened, again. It was a sight her father, Yellow Coyote, had seen much too often. He was tired of seeing his daughter bruised and beaten. In spite of their righteous rage, Two Claws and Yellow Coyote allowed themselves to be guided by my counsel and to await your return.

"At my urging, Yellow Coyote was eventually persuaded to find the spirit helpers, and bring them to minister to the two women. There was little they could do for Morning Star, except prepare a tea of herbs for the pain, and make her comfortable. The child was dead. There was nothing they could do for him."

At this point, Running Fox stopped relating the story, allowing his son time to absorb what he had thus far been told. Flaming Sky's first impulse was to run to his tipi in order to console Morning Star. Before he could, Running Fox stopped him. The rest of the story was even more difficult for his father to tell. Solemnly, he continued.

"Morning Star cried the entire night through, groaning in pain and in sorrow for her loss. As soon as she was capable of being moved, Skipping Bird had some braves carry her to your lodge, where she could rest. Your mother and Spotted Deer attended her throughout the long night. At first light, I ordered the signals to be sent to you. In the meantime, the two women left an exhausted Morning Star quietly asleep in your lodge, as they went about attending to their morning chores. There was wood to gather, and fresh water to fetch from the stream. Spotted Deer chopped some dried buffalo meat from which to make a broth for her daughter when she awakened. By the time they returned to your tipi, they discovered Morning Star was gone. They spread the word among the people and, immediately, the entire village set about looking for her. Aware of her fragile condition, we assumed she could not have gone very far.

"Soon after we first signaled you to return, we heard Yellow Coyote crying out in anguish. He found Morning Star's body, lying face-down in the river, several hundred paces downstream from the edge of camp. There was a large gash on her forehead, and she was not breathing. Yellow Coyote did his best to revive her, but it was to no avail." Running Fox choked, "She was already dead." With a heavy sigh, he paused; then, regaining his objectivity, he continued. "Whether she drowned accidentally or by her own intent, there is no way of knowing. The question is unimportant and unanswerable."

Flaming Sky was immobilized. Slowly shaking his head in shocked disbelief, he whispered, "This is not possible. How could I lose my wife and my son in less than a day?" Looking away from his father, he felt rage burning like a fever within his veins. His instinctual desire was to chase down Thunder Eyes and exact his revenge.

Running Fox and his cousin talked long and hard before convincing the young brave that his first duty was to properly care for the remains of his wife and child. They understood the need of both Flaming Sky and Two Claws, wanting to exact their just retribution upon Thunder Eyes; but, the cousins knew it should wait until after Morning Star and her unborn child were properly buried in the sky. "I have convinced Two Claws to wait until he puts his daughter and grandson to rest. Later, you and he can pursue your revenge on Thunder Eyes," he reminded him.

The spirit helpers cleansed and prepared the bodies of Morning Star and her stillborn son. Dressing her in her wedding dress, they tied her snakeskin headband around her forehead, covering the wound at her temple. Her tools for cutting and sewing were laid on either side of her. Next, they wrapped the unborn baby and placed him so she was cradling him in her arms. Flaming Sky, Two Claws, and Spotted Deer gently covered the mother and child with the buffalo robe that had been a part of Morning Star's marriage price.

White Wolf chanted the prayers, thus allowing Flaming Sky to mourn with the rest of his family over the loss of a wife and child, a daughter and grandson.. They prayed and chanted until long after nightfall, concluding the formal ceremony by leaving the mother and

The Quest

child in their new resting place at the entrance to the spirit world. The mourners returned home, grieving privately throughout the night and into the dawn.

With the light of day, the mourning time was suspended. Justice was the first and the only order of business on the agenda of Flaming Sky and Morning Star's father. "The hunt can now begin"

Chapter 7

THE GAUNTLET

Once their morning needs were cared for, the council met, with all of the braves in attendance. As was customary, Running Fox and White Wolf sat next to each other at the head of the circle. Two Claws was seated to the left of Running Fox. Flaming Sky sat on the right-hand side of his Wicasa. Not only was Flaming Sky the husband, but he was also the tribe's new medicine man. As such, he was required to sit next to White Wolf, rather than beside his father, Running Fox. The young man would be required to play out both of his new roles today. There was only one topic before the council and everyone shared that concern. It was utmost in all of their minds.

"What is to be done about Thunder Eyes?" was the common cry of the warriors, who were all more than willing to track him down and return him to the village for his just punishment.

Reminding them that the autumn hunt was to start as soon as the herd was located, Running Fox declared this to be a two-man excursion. The choice of the two men who were to undertake this assignment was obvious and unanimous. The council fully supported

THE QUEST

their chief's choice of Flaming Sky and Two Claws. They had been the ones most injured by the loss, and it was only appropriate they should be the ones undertaking the task. Had it not been for the impending hunt, Running Fox would have certainly accompanied them. Their final instruction from their chief was clear. "Return the coward alive. Allow our people to dispense his punishment according to our tribal law."

The two warriors gathered their weapons and procured a week's supply of provisions in preparation for their pursuit. With no time to hunt fresh game along the way, they supplied themselves with ample dried meat and fresh water, giving them the advantage. Thunder Eyes must search for food and water in order to sustain himself, thus slowing down his escape. They, on the other hand, were free to concentrate on their sole objective: capture the fugitive. Flaming Sky threw an extra blanket over Pawnee in anticipation of the chilling late night air. They would be making cold camps until they caught their prey.

No matter how much the two wanted to punish Thunder Eyes themselves, they were honour-bound, and could not. They were entrusted with the responsibility of capturing and returning him, allowing the tribe to mete out his justice. Riding the ponies in a slow, circular pattern, they searched until locating Thunder Eye's tracks, leading north. On the verge of initiating the pursuit, their attention was suddenly drawn to the eastern sky, alive with smoke signals. "The herd has returned!" Now, two very different hunts were underway, both honouring the life and spirit of the people.

Two Claws and Flaming Sky set out in a northerly direction at a leisurely pace, knowing Thunder Eyes will not stray too far away from the village. Like a wounded animal, he will seek a safe refuge in which to hide from his pursuers. They discussed several different plans and variations that might be necessary in order to apprehend their quarry. Two Claws, who was close to White Wolf in age, had known Thunder Eyes his entire life, and clearly comprehended the renegade's mind. He was confident the wretch would attempt to conceal himself among the thickets of the nearby forest.

After two nights of cold camp, and two days without any sign of Thunder Eyes, they decided they might not be approaching the problem correctly. "Thunder Eyes is a coward. He will never face either of us, let alone both of us," Flaming Sky observed aloud. "No. He will avoid a confrontation. Therefore, in order to ensnare him, it will be necessary to entice him to come to us."

It was late afternoon of the third day when they laid the foundation of their trap.

Bringing the horses to a halt, they began talking loudly. As they did, their raised voices grew harsher, sounding very angry as they exchanged words. "So, I was right about you," yelled Two Claws. "You are not Running Fox's son. You were sired by a snake, and birthed by a cowardly coyote! I should have insisted on having a real warrior ride with me."

"Old man," retorted Flaming Sky, "you should never have left your campfire. You are too feeble to be of any use to me. Your bones creak, and I can hear the death rattle in your breathing."

"Stay or go!" Two Claws spit back at him. "I do not care what you do, as long as I am free of you."

With these words hanging in the air, Flaming Sky turned Pawnee southward, as though he was returning to the village. As the young warrior rode away, Two Claws shook his fist at him, screaming insults against the young brave's manhood. Stopping, Flaming Sky took a long menacing look back over his shoulder at his taunter. Then, turning his head without speaking, he urged Pawnee forward into the woods. The older warrior watched as his young companion disappeared into the shadowy thickets of the forest. Once Flaming Sky became a part of the woods, Two Claws continued following the faint trail left by the fleeing Thunder Eyes.

When the sun set, Two Claws did not make a cold camp. With the nights bitter cold and the winds icy, he allowed himself to be

The Quest

warmed by a small, cozy campfire. After eating some dried buffalo meat, he added more wood to the low flame before curling up next to it in the warmth of his blankets. He was soon asleep, breathing in a deep, regular pattern, typical of someone in a restful state of dreams. Except for the sounds of the old warrior sleeping, the camp was completely silent.

Out of the darkness came the sharp snapping sound of small twigs crackling under the weight of human footsteps. The sounds grew louder as Thunder Eyes approached the campsite. He stood motionless for a moment, carefully surveying the camp. Believing Two Claws to be alone and deep asleep next to the fire, the coward drew his knife from his belt and quietly resumed creeping toward him. Reaching the campfire, he stopped, carefully inspecting the area, ensuring that it was still safe for him to approach Two Claws. Raising his knife straight above his head, he stopped, looking down at the man sleeping next to the fire, verifying he was still asleep.

Just as he was about to plunge the knife into Two Claws 'chest, he heard the sound of the arrow imbedding itself into the trunk of a tree just in front of his face. It came so close, he felt the wind on his cheek as it passed him. Instinctively, he turned his attention toward the direction of the arrow's source, panicking when he was unable to see the bowman. His eyes were anxiously darting back and forth in an effort to find the one who had taken a shot at him.

Flaming Sky came jumping out of the shadows and into the light of the campfire, screaming a horrific battle cry as he did. This was the signal for which Two Claws was waiting. Thunder Eyes, shocked by the sudden appearance of the second warrior, was caught completely off guard as the sleeping man sprang from his bed role, yelling and lunging at him. Grabbing the renegade around the neck with his right arm, he used his left hand as leverage to tighten his hold. Growing weaker, the captive dropped his knife, as his body became limp from the constant pressure exerted on his windpipe, cutting off the breath of life.

In all likelihood, had Flaming Sky not interceded, Two Claws would have surely squeezed the life completely out of Thunder Eyes. "Stop! Stop now!" he yelled, grabbing the shoulder of Morning Star's father. "We must return him unharmed to our people! They are to decide his fate, not you! Running Fox has commanded us to bring him back alive!"

His words did not have any effect on the wrathful warrior, who persisted with his strangle hold on Thunder Eyes. "I hate this vile excuse of a man every bit as much as you do," hollered Flaming Sky, trying to convince him. "Maybe even more. I, too, have suffered a great loss at his hands and am eager for his death but …we…must not be the ones who kill him!" he screamed. "Not here! Not now! He must be returned to the village for his just punishment!"

In desperation, the young man ripped at his companion's arms, attempting to break the grip holding his prey. It was not easy, as the old warrior was still very strong and his determination forceful. Once Two Claws finally consented to release him, Thunder Eyes fell to the ground in a heap, gasping for air.

The two warriors stood there momentarily, catching their breath, staring at the captive in silence. Almost before either of them was aware of what was happening, Thunder Eyes scrambled to his feet and started running toward the trees. Pursuing the fleeing man, Two Claws dove at his legs. The tackled man went sprawling face down on the ground. His captor was clinging to his legs, as the coward clawed at the dirt with his hands, trying to escape.

Recalling his earlier experience with the deadly viper, Flaming Sky stepped firmly on Thunder Eye's neck, exerting the full pressure of his weight. His prey struggled for a short time; then, completely exhausted, he succumbed to his predator. Flaming Sky felt the hilt of his knife in his hand as he slid it out of his waistband. He knelt down, lowering his head next to Thunder Eyes 'face, sensing the evil of this man who had taunted and terrified him since he was a very small boy. This vile thing was responsible for the sinister death of

The Quest

his wife and son. Before he thought about it, his knife was at the coward's throat, poised to make the final cut.

This time it was Two Claws who had to caution the younger warrior. "Remember the command of Running Fox, and our pledge to him!" he said, grabbing the young warriors arm. Flaming Sky, clenching his teeth and holding his breath, restrained himself and, sobbing, finally nodded in agreement. Deep in his soul, he refused to lose himself to the hatred which plagued his nemesis for so long. Returning the knife to its resting place, he reached into the front of his waistband, removing several pieces of rawhide, which he carefully tossed to the old warrior, who was now straddling the fugitive. Taking the rawhide strips, he pinned the villain's arms behind his back and, one at a time, bound the coward's wrists together He quickly tied his captive's arms firmly in place. Once the prisoner was secured, Flaming Sky removed his foot from Thunder Eyes' neck.

The warriors exchanged a look of satisfaction between them, relaxing as they glanced down at their quarry, safely bound and helpless. After a brief pause, allowing the older warrior to catch his breath, they dragged their spent prisoner to the closest tree. Standing him against the trunk, and using the hemp brought with them for this purpose, Two Claws wrapped a piece of the rope around Thunder Eyes' neck. Tying the rope securely behind the tree and cinching it tightly, he made it impossible for the villain to move his upper body without the rope biting into his throat. Flaming Sky bound the prisoner's legs to the base of the tree, while his companion did the same thing at his captive's waist.

Once Thunder Eyes was completely incapacitated, they went about rebuilding the campfire. Tonight, it would not be a cold camp. Exhausted, yet exhilarated, they were glad the hunt was over and had ended successfully. Despite their desire for sleep, it would take time to cool the flames burning within their veins. The fugitive, as commanded by their chief, had been taken alive. It was extremely difficult for them to obey this order, but they had done so.

In his mind, Flaming Sky heard the words of his father: *"Defying their own emotions, true warriors always do what is best for the people."* How many times had Running Fox said these words to him? He and Two Claws were pleased, having performed their duties as true warriors of the Lakota. In the morning they would take their captive home.

Thunder Eyes was denied the dignity of riding his pony into camp. They slung him belly-down over his horse's back, as they would bring home any other wild animal from the hunt. They tied him securely to his mount, preventing him from falling off during the long, uncomfortable journey awaiting him. With their cargo in place, Flaming Sky led the pony through the trees as they started their homeward trek.

Once they entered the clearing, the older warrior dropped back a few paces so he could keep a wary eye on Thunder Eyes. He did not want his prize accidentally falling off and breaking his neck, after the excruciating effort put into capturing him alive. It would be unforgivable to lose him now, after fighting so intensely against the urge to kill him. Two Claws, who was still struggling with his desire for revenge, consoled himself with the knowledge that a humiliating fate at the hands of the council awaited this traitor to his oath as a warrior. "Yes, Running Fox is right," he admitted to himself. "All of the braves must be involved in his judgment…and his execution."

With their prisoner in tow, they arrived at the base camp just as the sun was halfway past its zenith. Even with a full sun, the wind was chilled by autumn's breath. Upon entering the camp, they were met by the women, the old ones and the children, as a majority of the able-bodied villagers were involved in the hunt, which had been going well. The hunting party was due to return the following day. In the mean time, the camp remained extremely busy, as it always was during the last hunt before the snows of winter. Justice would have to

THE QUEST

wait a few more days, until the preparations for the move to winter quarters were completed.

Bound hand and foot, Thunder Eyes was allowed to sleep near one of the fires with the camp dogs. The women feeding the fires and preparing the fresh buffalo meat kept an eye on him at all times. They all loved Morning Star, and were not about to let her murderer out of their sight... not even for an instant.

Retribution arrived a few days later, after the meat and the fruits of the harvest were preserved and stored for the move to winter camp. At midday, the council solemnly gathered to determine the fate of Thunder Eyes. Running Fox sat at the head of the council, White Wolf at his right, and Flaming Sky next to the old shaman. All of the witnesses stood facing the chiefs. Skipping Bird, Spotted Deer and Snow Bird each gave a detailed accounting of what they had observed.

After the women finished their testimony, another seven villagers stepped forward who had seen Thunder Eyes running from his lodge and escaping. A majority of these same people bore witness to the effects of the brutal beating he inflicted upon Morning Star. Confronted with such overwhelming testimony, the perpetrator was unable to deny the truth of the evidence being presented to the council. He remained silent, staring at the ground. There was no question of his guilt. The only issue remaining was to choose the most appropriate punishment for his transgressions.

Two Claws stood in favor of adopting the southern savages' custom of staking the offender spread eagle between two large trees and slowly, painstakingly, skinning him alive, an extremely agonizing way to die. If done skillfully, the skinning process could easily last for several days before death came to release him; but, until that time, every whisper of air, no matter how slight, would inflict him with everlasting pain. Despite admitting that there was a certain amount of justice in this choice, White Wolf could not allow his people to sink to the depths of such barbarism. Such a death was lacking in honour for the people who carried out the punishment, as well as for the culprit. No. As tempting as it might be, the old man could not allow his people to start down that path. He was responsible for safeguarding their spirit.

It did not take the Wicasa long to make his point to the council. Two Claw's angry choice was rejected by the chiefs, who agreed with the old man that this was not the way of the Lakota. The discussion went on. Flaming Sky, at White Wolf's guidance, maintained his own counsel. Someday he would be guiding his people and safeguarding them from degrading behavior. It was not easy for him to stay objective while the others talked, but he managed, somehow, to listen in silence.

Yellow Coyote, who for countless seasons was forced to stand by and tolerate Thunder Eyes' abuse of his daughter, wanted revenge, not only for Morning Star, but for the mistreatment of Snow Bird. The council listened as he suggested, "He should be taken to a high place, where he is bound hand and foot and tossed over a cliff to his death. This will give him time, as he is plunging helplessly to his death, to experience the terror of being completely helpless and totally abandoned." This idea contained a certain degree of appeal to the council.

Finally, no longer able to refrain, Flaming Sky spoke. "No! That is too impersonal, too clean, too neat and…just too easy! No. I want Thunder Eyes to suffer the way Morning Star suffered…the way Two Claws, Spotted Deer and I are suffering. Your chief has lost a daughter and a grandson. Thunder Eyes must feel the full extent of our agony." The council, understanding his desire for this sense of justice, continued evaluating a variety of punishments.

Finally, Running Fox, remembering the perfect solution to the dilemma, shouted. "The gauntlet!" It had been so long since it was last used, most of the younger braves were unsure as to what it was. "The gauntlet," Running Fox instructed them, "is the ancient method of punishing those who have not only dishonoured themselves and their

THE QUEST

people, but have dishonoured the Grand Father. All of the warriors form two lines, facing each other, armed only with sticks and clubs. The accused, barefooted, stripped to the waist and emptyhanded, takes his place at the head of the gauntlet. When the signal is given, the guilty one runs as fast as he can between the two rows of braves, until he comes out the other end," he paused, continuing, "that is… if…he comes out the other end.

"The armed warriors will strike him with their weapons," he explained. "As long as he is running the gauntlet, he may be struck. Even if he falls, he is not exempt from being beaten. If he survives, the debt is paid, and all is as it was before. If he fails to survive the gauntlet, his death cancels out the offense."

Pausing briefly, he added, "Very, very few ever survive. If he is killed in the process, his body is to be stripped of all honour and taken away from the camp to be dumped in the wilderness for the wolves and coyotes to feed upon." This last statement found favor with Two Claws, who immediately gave his approval to the proposal. The other chiefs agreed. It was to be the gauntlet. This solution was satisfactory to Flaming Sky. It was just.

The ceremony was to take place that same day, prior to the setting of the sun. Running Fox gave the command for the braves to prepare for the running of the gauntlet. They fashioned clubs out of tree branches. The perfect weapon was approximately one pace long and fitted firmly into one hand so, when wielded, the fingers and the thumb almost touched. Of course, the straighter the branch, the more dependable the club. If it happened to be a little thicker at the opposite end, it was all the better. In a short while, the men procured enough wood to produce the needed weapons.

For this ceremony, the warriors donned their war paint. This was customary whenever they were about to confront an enemy of the tribe, even if this enemy was one of their own. The gauntlet was set up to run from east to west, so Thunder Eyes will be running into the blinding light from the setting sun. It is a disadvantage for him but, decidedly, an asset to the warriors, whose responsibility is to inflict the most severe damage possible…unto death.

White wolf chose to abstain from taking part in the actual executing of the gauntlet. As a respected member of the council, he sat in judgment of Thunder Eyes, supporting the chosen penalty. It was a duty he owed to the tribe. However, as a servant of the Great Spirit, he chose not to take an active part in the coward's punishment and possible death. It is a difficult thing to kill one of your own. Furthermore, a Holy Man cannot shed the blood of a member of his tribe and remain a Wicasa. He can no longer be caretaker of the Sacred Bundle. To him, the path was clear. The concern in the old man's mind was, "What decision will Flaming Sky make?"

Under tribal law, it was Flaming Sky's right to take his revenge. After all, he lost his wife and son due to Thunder Eyes' violence. His heart was every bit as angry as those of Running Fox and Two Claws, who each lost a daughter and a grandson. White Wolf said nothing to him, leaving the young man to ponder his choices alone. It was a decision only he could make, and it was not an easy one. He reflected upon it the entire day before reaching his conclusion.

"If I engage in his punishment, I will spill the blood of my own people," he thought somberly. "If I do, White Wolf will, no doubt, disapprove. He is wishing for a new Holy One, and is mindful that I may be the one for whom he waits. But, then …" His thoughts gave way to memories of Morning Star and their life together. "If I am truly a Lakota brave, my duty is clear. He must die," he thought firmly, "and, as her husband, it must be by my hand."

The two thoughts raged war for dominance of his spirit. He could kill an enemy without dishonouring himself, that was a given. "But, to kill one of my own," he pondered, "These are the same people who will look to me as their pathfinder, expecting me to heal their bodies, and maybe, someday, guide their spirits. No. To take a life this way holds no honour." Although White Wolf never said anything directly

The Quest

to him, Flaming Sky was aware of the Wicasa's hopes for the well being of his people after he is gone. One of the old man's most fervent prayers was that it will be Flaming Sky who the Great Spirit chooses.

Comprehending full well that whatever resolution he reaches will remain a part of him forever added fuel to his struggling spirit, as he fought with himself throughout the day. In the future, which action would grieve him the most: exacting justice upon Thunder Eyes, or refusing to strike a blow in vengeance for his beloved wife and unborn child?

White Wolf understood, even more clearly than Flaming Sky how important the young man's decision truly was to be. The old man contemplated the problem facing his apprentice. Smoking his pipe, he offered up his prayers requesting clarity and guidance. In the quietness of his mind, he visualized the path of Flaming Sky unfolding right in front of his eyes.

There he was, the little boy beginning his life's journey. Moving forward, the image of the child shifted into that of the young boy in training. With him were his three friends and their fathers. Watching, he saw the young warrior choosing a different path to travel than the one chosen by his friends. The young shaman in the vision was approaching a fork in the road. There Flaming Sky stood, confused and indecisive. First he took one step toward the left path, but immediately retreated. His efforts to move down the right lane were just as futile.

After several failed attempts, he sat down on the dirt road, puzzled and frustrated. While Flaming Sky remained sitting there, White Wolf was allowed a glimpse of what lay at the end of each of the trails. Now he had a clear view of the two possible consequences of Flaming Sky's choice. His cousin's son was to determine his own destiny, based upon the outcome of the decision he was about to make.

On occasion the Great Spirit gives His servants a clear and concise insight. Sometimes, but not always. This was one of those rare times. "Flaming Sky will continue along his present course as a shaman, no matter which choice he makes. Of this, I am now certain beyond any doubt," the old man thought. "I am positive it all hinges upon which the young brave selects. Will he make the decision from his feelings of grief and anger or from his higher spirit?"

Even more important than his insights was the fact that White Wolf was forbidden to share this knowledge with the young man. "He can only walk the brighter path if he proves to be worthy. It is a road he must find by himself and walk alone." he mused. "Therefore, only he can decide the ultimate path of his destiny." As was so often dictated by the circumstances of his position, the old Wicasa was once more burdened with a secret he could not divulge to anyone, especially not to Flaming Sky The old man could do nothing except pray, and await the ramifications of his apprentice's decision.

When Running Fox signaled the braves to form two lines facing each other with their clubs in hand, they all did so, with the exception of White Wolf and Flaming Sky. The old man was extremely pleased with the young shaman's choice not to participate in the gauntlet. "He has made a difficult choice," the old man thought. "But, in making that choice, he opens up the possibility of becoming a Holy One. He has refused to shed the blood of a Lakota, even one like Thunder Eyes, who deserves to die."

Two braves were forcibly dragging Thunder Eyes to the head of the two columns, where they untied him. Four archers were stationed, two on either side of the gauntlet, in case Thunder Eyes decided to try escaping, rather than facing the punishment he deserved. Running Fox stood at the head of one of the lines. Two Claws and Yellow Coyote took up their positions, facing each other at the end of the lines. They knew full well, if Thunder Eyes managed to reach them alive, he would be a slow-moving, easy target, and justice would be served.

It was White Wolf, the symbol of the tribe's spiritual unity, who gave the command. At the shaman's signal, Thunder Eyes started

The Quest

running between the two rows of braves, instinctively putting his arms and hands up in protection of his head and face. This is exactly what Running Fox anticipated. Swinging his club with all of his strength, he landed a blow shattering Thunder Eyes' right knee, causing him to momentarily collapse to the ground. Struggling to his feet while still trying to protect himself, he proceeded down the gauntlet, stumbling and dragging his right leg. The braves beat him severely about his head, chest and shoulders. He was staggering, becoming disoriented by the blood streaming down into his eyes. In addition to several cracked ribs, he could feel at least one broken bone in his shoulder. Still, the clubs of judgment rained down upon him like a mighty thunderstorm.

Thunder Eyes, under the force of the relentless flogging, collapsed to the ground, crawling, as the braves continued beating him. Exhausted, he desperately struggled to his feet. Although in agony, with his strength depleted, he was too terrified to stop. With only ten or twelve paces remaining for him to complete his run to safety, he felt his skin ripping away, hearing the shattering sounds of his own bones breaking.

He lunged forward toward the waiting weapons of Two Claws and Yellow Coyote. Vainly, he tried to run past the last two braves, but lacked the ability to avoid the force of their blows. Yellow Coyote struck him on his hands, which were protecting his eyes. The bones in his hands shattered as his head snapped back with the force of the blow, causing him to lose his balance. Before he could regain his footing, he was devastated by the force of the deathblow delivered by Two Claws. The vicious blow to the base of Thunder Eyes' skull sent him reeling headlong to the ground. Sprawled on his chest and face, he did not move. Shuttering for a few seconds, he released his final breath. There he lay, motionless, never to move again.

It was over. Justice had triumphed. Two Claws and Yellow Coyote had satisfied their need for vengeance upon the coward. All that remained was the disposing of the body. Spotted Deer and Snow

Bird stripped the body as instructed, and his bloodied clothes were added to a campfire as extra fuel. The two older warriors threw the battered body onto the back of a horse. Then, mounting their own ponies, Two Claws took the reins of Thunder Eyes horse as they led the dead rider out of camp.

It was just after dawn when the two men returned to camp leading the rider-less horse. They had been gone all night, having disposed of Thunder Eyes in a wooded area, a half-day's ride east. He was left in a place where he could only be found by the wild animals and no one else…not even the Great Spirit. The two men never spoke of it aloud to anyone. No one ever questioned them about the task they had performed. There was to be no burial ceremony of any kind, nor anything left marking the site where his corpse was dumped. The sooner Thunder Eyes was forgotten, the more quickly the tribe would recover from its losses.

BOOK IV   THE WICASA

Chapter 1

THE FLAMING EAGLE

It was a long, cold, bitterly empty winter for Flaming Sky. Burying himself in his studies, he hoped to divert his mind from his loss. The attempt was only partially successful, at best. With the help of White Wolf, the young shaman practiced directing his energy into developing a stronger trust in his own inner awareness. He understood that healing is an art as well as the practical application of knowledge. It was critical he learn to trust his interpretation of his visions by developing and maintaining complete faith in his own intuitiveness. The sick and wounded are seldom capable of accurately describing their symptoms, or understanding the severity of their illnesses. Therefore, the young man spent long periods in the quietness of his mind, seeking to become more skillfully adept at intuiting the correct treatment for his patients.

White Wolf assigned his two best spirit helpers to tend to the needs of the young medicine man. He sent the oldest, Laughing Water, who was the wisest and the most knowledgeable of the four. For her companion, he chose Gentle Rain, the youngest, and the most energetic and enthusiastic of the group, hoping her zest and love of life might shed a ray of light upon Flaming Sky's dark spirit.

The two women ministered to him the same as they had done for the old man. They gathered the wood; they tended the campfire; they cooked his food. Thus relieved of the mundane aspects of daily living, he was free to work on mastering the proper handling of the herbs and plants. The work was intricate, and he immersed himself in it. Every evening, usually but not always in the company of White Wolf, he smoked his pipe, offering up his prayers to the Grand Father. Afterwards, he patiently waited for signs or visions which might reveal insight or provide guidance along his chosen journey as a shaman.

Thus he passed the cold grey days while awaiting the warm skies of spring. When it was time for the people to move from winter camp, he would not go with them. Rather, he was to travel south with White Wolf, assisting him with the harvesting of a rich supply of herbs and plants growing only in the southern deserts. Flaming Sky's heart was gladdened when finally it was time to prepare for the journey south. He was looking forward to the clear, light blue skies, and the warm breath of the desert wind. As it was time for the tribe to return to their summer quarters, the four women would take care of the moving of White Wolf's and Flaming Sky's tipis, as well as attending to their own. After the medicine men completed their mission and rejoined the main camp, their lodges would be in order and awaiting them.

The young man was anxious for some diversion after six long, lonely moons of greyness. The trip to the southern deserts would take much less time for the two of them to complete than if one of them went alone. With two horses sharing the burden of the harvest, they could still accommodate the weight of riders. By riding rather than walking the horses all the way back to camp, the men could trim eight to ten days off of their journey.

The Quest

There was a heavy chill in the morning air as they started on their sojourn. While the rest of the tribe was occupied with the preparations for moving, the two men headed south with the morning sun, their ponies walking at an unhurried, even gait. It would take at least seven risings of the moon for them to reach the southern prairies leading to the desert. Before the fullness of the next moon, they would be gathering the herbs and plants they were seeking; but, until that time, there was little for them to do except hunt, study and pray.

White Wolf was constantly amazed by the achievements of the younger man. Flaming Sky's knowledge of the specific healing power of each plant and the magic of the ceremonies was almost equal to that of the old shaman himself. He was justly proud of his choice. "Flaming Sky has chosen the bright path, but there is no confirmation that he, or any other brave, is the eagle in my vision."

He had never observed anything remotely resembling an eagle passing unharmed through searing flames. With this uppermost in his mind, he remained vigilant for a sign.

It was on the tenth morning of their journey when it occurred. They were awakened at sunrise by the strong scent of smoke in the air. Only a few days away from their first gathering terrain, they were nearing the territory of the Pawnee. Casting their gaze to the east, the smoke appeared to be emanating from the sun itself. Quickly grabbing their weapons and possessions, they carefully extinguished the campfire and headed toward the black omen. They knew full well the meaning of the smoke. What remained unknown was who was attacking and who was being attacked. That question would be answered soon enough.

It took less time than anticipated to arrive at the smoldering campsite, where many of the tipis were still burning, and the entire area was saturated with thick layers of black smoke. It was immediately apparent from the evidence that the Pawnee had been viciously assaulted by the savages. It was a small winter encampment, with the tipis placed much closer together than they would have been in summer quarters. From the devastation of the camp, it was clear the Pawnee were caught completely off guard. The watch dogs had arrows in their carcasses, most likely slain before being able to warn the braves of the onslaught.

Carefully, they searched through the smoldering debris, looking for survivors, finding only scalped, dead bodies, scattered from one end of the camp to the other. A majority of the dead were warriors, old people, and a few small children. Young women and older children of both sexes were prime booty to the savages; however, it was impossible to determine how many were abducted to be used as slaves or objects of their unbounded lust.

Fighting off the suffocating, heavy soot, they continued searching. Suddenly, single-mindedly, they simultaneously stopped, standing mute, looking at each other, and listening. Several heartbeats passed before they heard it again. From the pitch of the scream, it was obviously coming from a young female. Desperately searching for the source of the sound, they agreed it was emanating from a tangled mass of nearby burning tipis.

Flaming Sky immediately grabbed an unburned blanket and dashing to the nearby stream, he soaked it in the cold water. Then, he quickly ran back to where White Wolf was waiting. Without saying a word, he handed the drenched blanket to the old man and turned around. White Wolf deliberately draped the soaking blanket over his companion's head and outstretched arms. The instant the coverlet was in place, the young warrior went rushing toward the sound of the girl's cries. White Wolf watched his cousin's son with confidence and curiosity, as the young shaman rushed into a nest of flames, with the blanket flapping about him.

Flaming Sky ran directly toward the cries coming from the inferno. He was guided by the girl's continuous pleas for help. Bending down, he tried removing some of the burning debris. At first, his efforts proved to be unsuccessful and, after another

The Quest

unfruitful attempt, he threw down the blanket. Reaching his wet hands and arms inside the fire, he frantically searched for something solid to grab in order to release the girl from her confinement. Eventually, he located an unburned, relatively cool, piece of wood. Taking a firm hold, he struggled, trying to use it to pry up the burning mass of skins and hides. A piece of burning wood fell across the inside of his forearm, searing his skin. His instinct was to release his hold and extract his arm; however, doing so would have thwarted his chance of saving the girl.

Snatching the burning skins in his left hand, and using the stick in his right hand, he slung them away from the pile of half-charred bodies. Tossing the corpses aside, he called to the girl, hoping the sound of his voice would reassure and calm her. Flinging the last carcass out of the way, he exposed the naked child.

More than a girl, she was less than a full-grown women. Terrified and sobbing, her knees were pulled up toward her chest, and her arms were crossed over her stomach. She screamed when she first laid eyes on Flaming Sky. Talking quietly to her, he did his best to reassure her. Exhausted and too tired to care, she stopped yelling at him and lay there, softly sobbing. Reaching down, he gently helped her to her feet. Before she could steady herself, he quickly rewrapped himself in the wet blanket and, lifting her up in his arms, he pulled the front of the blanket around her for protection. Bent over, and only able to see a few steps in front of him, he carried her through the surrounding flames, running for all he was worth.

White Wolf watched the young warrior charging out of the flames with the girl in his arms. The edges of the blanket, now dry, were aflame and flapping in the breeze, like the wings of a fiery eagle, as he stumbled out of the fire. Observing the flames on the bottom of the dried blanket, he shouted a warning to the young man, who immediately spun around. As he did, the fiery blanket flared out like the wings of a soaring, flaming bird of prey. Flaming Sky ran quickly to the stream and sat the girl down safely on the bank to catch her breath and cool her limbs. The young warrior ripped the blanket off his shoulders and threw it to the ground.

White Wolf stood there, stunned and mute. Recovering his senses, he rushed to the young man and examined the wound on his right forearm. "The burn is deep and will scar. It is a perfect match to the scar on the eagle's wing in my vision," White Wolf thought ecstatically. "My cousin's son is the flaming eagle of my vision! The promise has been fulfilled!"

Reaching his arms to the sky, the old Wicasa chanted prayers of thanksgiving to the Grand Father. Finishing, he proclaimed to Flaming Sky, "From this time forward, you will be known as Flaming Eagle. Not only are you the tribe's new medicine man, but your actions have set you upon the path of a Holy Man, as well."

Not questioning the erratic behavior of his Wicasa, Flaming Eagle accepted his new name with grace. However, his attention was still on the girl he pulled from the fire. Now focusing upon the injured girl, White Wolf scooped a cup of water out of the stream and handed it to her. While she sipped at the water, he wrapped her naked body in a clean dry blanket. In the time it took for her to catch her breath, she was able to calm herself. Regaining her composure, she hesitantly began speaking.

"I am Meadow Lark. I am Pawnee," she murmured in a voice stressed from screaming. Softly sobbing, she stated, "I watched the savages kill my family and my people." Finding her voice, and encouraged by White Wolf, she tearfully recounted the scene.

"The entire tribe was sleeping. Just before dawn, the savages fell on us like a nest of crazed hornets. Half awake, I saw my naked parents running out of the tipi. Springing out of bed, I scrambled after them. Once outside, we stood there, dazed and disorientated, watching the slaughter. I was hoping to awaken from this bad dream, but it became more real. Before my father could gather his wits about him, one of the savages impaled him on a lance. Picking up

THE QUEST

my father's knife, my mother lunged at the savage, while shouting at me, 'Run! Run! Run!'…and I did.

"I hid myself under some skins that once had been part of a tipi," she sobbed. "From this hiding place, I saw the whole camp being destroyed. I watched my mother struggling with the savage, stabbing at him over and over again, without success. On her final thrust, he seized her by the wrist and twisted her arm behind her back, forcing her to drop the knife. Grabbing her long hair and pulling her head back, he slit her throat in one swift swipe of his knife." She paused, hardly able to speak. "… but not deeply enough for her to die. As she was struggling for air, he savagely thrust the blade into her bare stomach, just below her naval. Then," she sobbed, "he gutted her with great deliberateness, like…like she was a game animal," she said weeping, hardly able to speak. "After slinging her dead body to the ground, he turned his attention to finding me."

At this point in her story, the girl was crying so hard she could not speak. In between her bouts of sobbing, she felt compelled to complete her story. "It did not take long for the savage to find me. I tried fending him off; but, like my mother, I was not successful. I hit him with my fists, and tried scratching his eyes out; but, in the end, I lost. He hit me on the left cheek, sending me sprawling to the ground on my back. Like a mountain lion, he leaped on top of me, pinning me to the ground, hitting me over and over again. Even though I could no longer move, two of his companions held me down while he…he violated me! When he finished raping me, the other two took their turns as well!"

Having told all of this, she wept uncontrollably. Finally, when she was able to control herself, she went on with her story. She was unsure what occurred next; but for some unknown reason, the three of them abandoned her. Lying there, numb and barely conscious, she was fearful as to what her ultimate fate would be. Having been warned by her mother, she was well aware of the possibilities. Relating her imaginings, she had asked herself, "Are they going to come back and rape me again, maybe even beat me to death? Do they intend to return and carry me off to their camp to be their slave where they will abuse me until I am too old to be of any further use to them?" she shuddered.

"Whatever their intentions, I did not want to find out. Stumbling, half crawling, I made my way to the pile of debris where you found me. Pulling the smoldering pieces of wood and skins over the dead bodies, I burrowed underneath them, hiding from my captors.

As she finished her story, she began choking, trying to catch her breath. They led her farther away from the smoke and fire. Meadow Lark was now calm enough to allow White Wolf to examine her injuries, and to administer some calming herbs. Although she was covered with bruises and lacerations, White Wolf knew it was not her body suffering the major damage.

After attending to her, he turned his attention to his cousin's son's burnt arm. It was a deep burn. He instructed Flaming Eagle to soak his arm in the cool water of the stream. White Wolf dried the wound, and gently spread a light layer of salve over the burnt area. He bandaged the young brave's arm to keep the burn clean, wrapping it lightly enough so the injury could breathe while healing. Once his patients were properly attended, he encouraged Meadow Lark to divulge more of her ordeal, so as to release her terror.

The girl was wary of her rescuers, but she was not afraid of the Holy Man, as she had been raised to respect all Holy Ones, even the Wicasa of their enemies. Still dazed, but breathing more easily, she eventually composed herself well enough to give an objective accounting of the attack on her village, retelling her story. She was wise for one so young, and seemed to observe the attack from a higher awareness.

"The initial attack took place sometime just before dawn. A large war party of savages quietly sneaked up on our village. We were a small winter camp, which had not yet returned to the summer

The Quest

campsite." She estimated, counting the women and children, they numbered less than two hundred.

"The savages slipped up on foot in the dark," she said with no emotion." First, they quickly and silently killed the dogs and the night guard. Surrounding the camp, three of them made their way to the horses. Releasing the animals from their tethers, each mounted a pony. At a prearranged signal, the savages stampeded the horses through the camp, ripping apart as many of the lodges as possible along the way.

"The village was awakened by the sound of war whoops and panicky horses," she continued with her narrative. "Initially, we were disoriented and confused, unsure of what was actually happening. Once the horses were clear of the village, the savages surrounding the camp let loose a rain of arrows, falling down upon us through the grey morning sky. Firing four volleys, they killed a third of the people. In their confusion, our warriors tried desperately to organize a counter attack. However, the savages rushing in from the periphery, forced them to bunch up in the center of the camp, where they were more easily butchered." She paused as she remembered seeing several of the invaders grabbing the women and riding off with them. "It was then I was attacked and raped." The rest of her story they already knew. Exhausted, she stopped talking.

While Meadow Lark was resting, the two men evaluated their present situation, discussing their options. White Wolf spoke softly, "Although the Pawnee are our sworn enemy, we cannot leave her here alone and unprotected. She is not much more than a child." Pausing to ponder for an instant, he continued, "Nor can we take the risk of looking for any of her people. We are far from being friends, and contact between us has always meant 'shoot on sight,'" he said with an ever so slight smile. "She cannot accompany us on the rest of our journey, as she is much too fragile for such an arduous trek."

After careful consideration, they were left with only one reasonable course of action. "We will have to split up," offered Flaming Eagle.

"One of us will take her to our camp, while the other continues gathering the sacred herbs and plants."

"Yes," agreed White Wolf. "The girl is weak from her ordeal, and will have to travel slowly, riding most of the way. Once she is safely at camp, the spirit helpers can then tend to her needs."

It was White Wolf's decision that the one whom the Grand Father renamed Flaming Eagle would escort Meadow Lark to her new home. "Since she will be riding, her companion will have to walk all of the way," he reasoned. "A young man's legs are stronger and more resilient than mine." Flaming Eagle accepted the wisdom of White Wolf and agreed to the duty.

Pitching camp farther upstream, they settled in for the balance of the day. The girl needed rest and time before feeling safe with them. While Flaming Eagle gathered fuel for the fire, White Wolf produced some dried meat and fruit for their morning meal. None of them had eaten, and the two men were famished. Hesitantly, Meadow Lark accepted the food offered by her host. Although she was leery, she was also hungry. She ate in silence, while keeping a vigilant eye on her companions. Even though they had not harmed her in any way, they are still Sioux. "They are the enemy," she thought.. "They cannot be trusted."

Despite her suspicions and fears, tiredness overcame her, eventually, forcing her to sleep. It was a restless, fitful sleep, filled with dark and morbid dreams. White Wolf took this opportunity to go hunting for fresh meat. Due to the wound on his arm, Flaming Eagle remained behind in camp, resting, watching over the girl and pondering the day's events.

It was well past midday when Meadow Lark finally awakened, feeling less skeptical of her new companion. With encouragement from Flaming Eagle, she told him about her family, and the boy she was promised to in marriage. "I saw him fall under a barrage of arrows during the massacre. I am thirteen winters, and was to be

THE QUEST

married after the autumn hunt. Now, I will not be married at all. My entire family, as well as all my friends, were killed in the slaughter."

She felt totally alone, forsaken, abandoned, and terrified. She had never even imagined such an experience, and it left a hollow feeling deep inside of her. It was as though she no longer knew who she was. Flaming Eagle listened attentively and talked gently to her, quelling the fears of her predicament.

By the time White Wolf returned, shortly before sundown, she was much more comfortable, and less guarded. He had a small buck slung across his pony's back, which he eased off the horse and onto the ground. Meadow Lark instinctively went about the business of dressing and preparing the deer for cooking, as she was trained to do. She conducted her work in silence. While the meat was cooking, the two men gathered more wood for the fire as, momentarily, life returned to normal.

White Wolf checked the wounds of his patients. Most of Meadow Lark's injuries were bruises, including a large one on her left cheek., along with few cuts, scratches and, of course, some very painful swelling and bleeding. He carefully applied the appropriate herbs to her sensitive and battered body. Considering her present situation, she was doing quite well. The bandage on Flaming Eagle's arm was in need of changing. Removing the dressing, the old man carefully reapplied a light layer of soothing salve to the burn, and rewrapped it with a clean covering, once again ensuring the wound could breathe. By the time the old man finished, the food was ready. They were all grateful to be eating fresh, hot meat.

After the evening meal, the two men smoked their pipes and prayed. The girl sat back, silently watching. When the men completed the ritual, they added wood to the fire as they prepared for sleep. The night was extraordinarily peaceful and serene. Even though the stars were shining more brightly than they had for many moons, the night air retained a touch of winter's chill. Bundling up and lying a safe distance from the fire, the three travelers settled down for the night.

It was obvious that, if any one of them intended harm to the others, it would have occurred long before now. No. They will all sleep safely tonight. The savages were long gone and there was nothing to fear. In the morning, White Wolf was to continue his journey south while Flaming Eagle escorted Meadow Lark to the Lakota summer camp.

The exhausted child fell asleep very quickly and, at last, was resting peacefully. White Wolf decided to take advantage of this opportunity to inform Flaming Eagle of the light which had illuminated his true path this day. He described the original vision of the flaming eagle he experienced long ago. White Wolf told the new shaman how his fiery metamorphosis was the manifestation of the Grand Father's promise.

"Wakan Tanka gave me the vision of the flaming eagle long before your training to become a shaman," explained White Wolf. "In His wisdom, He made it known to me that I was to choose the medicine man; but, He, in His own time, would choose a new Holy One…or not. I puzzled over this image until I could no longer think."

The young man trusted White Wolf more than all others, save his father, Running Fox. As always, when it was the proper time and place, the old man unraveled the mystery. To be truthful, Flaming Eagle accepted his new name immediately. It was as if he were finally being addressed correctly. He listened intently to every word the old man spoke.

"This morning, when you carried Meadow Lark out of the smoldering rubble, you looked like a giant eagle with blazing wings. You became Flaming Eagle!" exclaimed White Wolf. "You have been given the opportunity to walk the path for which only a few are chosen, and even fewer succeed. But the choice is there for you," he assured him.

"My recent vision in this quest clarified that your own choice was to be involved in the process. Your decision was to be an important step in determining your destiny," he continued. Flaming Eagle looked at his Wicasa with a puzzled expression. White Wolf smiled, thinking to himself, "He did not realize he was being tested."

The Quest

Explaining the vision further, he continued, "I was shown that you had two paths to follow...more accurately, one path which split. Either trail would take you to your destiny as a shaman, but only one could also take you on your journey of discovery as a Holy One. You passed this test when you overcame your rage and desire for revenge, and did not take part in the gauntlet. You took the correct road when you chose not shed the blood of Thunder Eyes, a Lakota.

It has been passed down from the Ancients that the Grand Father disfavors anyone who spills the blood of his own people.

Before the young man fully comprehended the old man's words, White Wolf was continuing with his story. "The vision I was given of you and the two potential paths was in answer to my many prayers, requesting one who will replace me as Wicasa. I have no doubt your own choice opened the door, allowing the sign to be shown to me. The manifestation of the flaming eagle which occurred this morning was the confirmation that the Grand Father finally made His selection. The image of you, Flaming Eagle, emerging from the fire was the validation of the vision I have puzzled over for so long." He was clearly relieved and extremely grateful.

Flaming Eagle had indeed chosen the brighter path. "But," White Wolf cautioned him, "it takes a very long time to evolve into a Holy Man, if you ever do. There is no guarantee for your success. Even knowing the path is open, it is you who will have to walk it, and you will have to walk it the only way it can be walked: carefully...and always alone."

Meadow Lark had been asleep for a good part of the night when she was awakened rather abruptly. She knew she had just conceived. She could tell by the reaction within her body, the small energy charge occurring the instant the egg was impregnated. Although she was not a fully-grown woman, she was certainly old enough to know what was happening inside her body. This was what her mother and the other women had spoken of so many times. The irony sickened her. "The Grand Father must surely be punishing me for something, for I, a Pawnee, am to become the mother of a child fathered by one of the savages who raped me." Suddenly, a new stream of tears trickled from her dark brown eyes.

"How can I endure carrying a child of the evil ones who slaughtered my entire village?" she wondered, agonized. Despite her wishes to the contrary, the fact could not be denied. She was indeed pregnant, and in ten moons would give birth to a child of her most dreaded enemy: a desert devil.

Chapter 2

MEADOW LARK

Initially, it was an uneasy truce between Flaming Eagle and Meadow Lark. Having been enemies their entire lives, the relationship remained very tenuous, at best. They traveled from sunup to sunset. A majority of the time he walked. Occasionally they rode double on Pawnee, trying to cover as much ground as possible. During daylight, they only stopped long enough to eat, rest the pony, and tend to their wounds. Once having made their way into safe territory, they allowed themselves the luxury of a comfortable campfire, enabling them to enjoy hot food for the first time since leaving White Wolf.

After several days, Meadow Lark was feeling more trusting of her traveling companion. She had been delivered from the hands of one enemy into the hands of another. However, unlike the savages, this brave treated her with kindness, respect and patience. Feeling safer with the young shaman, she revealed more about herself and her life prior to their meeting. As a gifted listener, he easily wove the pieces together.

Her father was a Pawnee chief, one of the first to be killed in the massacre. The group separated from the larger village when they headed to winter camp. Consisting of slightly over one-hundred-fifty, counting the braves, women, children and elders, the villagers were making preparations to move to summer camp to join the rest of the tribe when they were attacked. Their plans were set. Once they settled at the summer site, she was to marry a young warrior named Shadow Hawk. They were promised to each other when they were not much more than young saplings and, as they grew up, somewhere along the way, they fell in love. Being the daughter of a chief, the price he paid for her was very high, and Shadow Hawk was more than willing to pay it.

When Shadow Hawk was slain in the raid, all of their plans and dreams ended in the consuming flames which ravaged their peaceful encampment. She was completely alone in the world, and desperately in need of a friend. Although they could not be thought of as close friends by the time they arrived at Flaming Eagle's village, at least they were no longer fearsome enemies. Sometime during their journey, they learned to trust each other enough to allow themselves to sleep with both eyes closed.

Flaming Eagle quickly developed an appreciation of her wildly untamed spirit. On the other hand, she gained a deep respect for the gentle wisdom of the young shaman. In addition to getting to know each other, they used their time to contemplate Meadow Lark's fate. She was yet to reveal the secret of her pregnancy, remaining unsure as to how this might affect her future. However, she did not have long to wait before receiving an answer to her unspoken question.

Upon entering the village, Flaming Eagle rode directly to the lodge of his father. Stepping out of his lodge, Running Fox greeted his son and his new companion, as the young warrior, dismounting, assisted Meadow Lark. When his father greeted the young man by his old name, his son corrected him, informing his chief, "Our Wicasa has renamed me Flaming Eagle." Smiling at the puzzled look on

The Quest

his father's face, the young man promised, "I will explain the entire situation later. For now, we have a more important issue needing to be addressed." Smiling, the chief nodded his head approvingly, motioning them to sit.

He listened intently to his son's story of how he and White Wolf originally came upon Meadow Lark. It did not take long for Flaming Eagle to bring his father up to the present. Observing carefully, and perceiving she was safe with these people, Meadow Lark chose this moment to be forthright and honourable, as was her way. She divulged the fact she was pregnant with the child of a savage. Upon hearing this, Running Fox held up his hand, saying, "It is in everyone's best interest to immediately convene a council meeting."

Runners were sent throughout the camp, announcing an emergency assembly was to be held at sunset. With this accomplished, they instructed the spirit helpers to see to Meadow Lark's comfort. Her burdens were many, and she was desperately in need of nourishment and rest. The women prepared her a bed and, after the young girl had eaten, she curled up next to the fire and drifted into sleep. Flaming Eagle and his father now had some quiet time in which they could talk. Uppermost on Running Fox's mind was White Wolf's sudden renaming of his son from Flaming Sky to Flaming Eagle.

The young man quickly recapped the early part of his journey with the old man. Beginning with the events leading up to their discovery of the smoldering village, he described their search for survivors before hearing Meadow Lark's cries for help. "White Wolf draped me with a water soaked blanket before I started digging through the fiery rubble that once had been tipis. Eventually I found her; but, as I was carrying her from the blaze, the dried-out ends of the blanket caught fire. As I turned with the flaring blanket afire, in White Wolf's eyes, I was transforming into the flaming eagle of his vision. Confident that I had been chosen by the Grand Father as the new Wicasa for whom he had been waiting, he immediately renamed me Flaming Eagle."

Running Fox was pleased with his son's telling of the events. It was an honour to be named by the medicine man, but to be renamed by the Wicasa placed the young man in a very rare and extremely small group of individuals. Such an event had not occurred since the old Holy One had renamed White Wolf. It was a proud day for him and a great day for his son, Flaming Eagle.

Upon completing their evening meal, the chiefs and elders proceeded to the council fire, quickly assuming their proper place within the circle. In the absence of White Wolf, the ritual ceremony of the pipe became the responsibility of Flaming Eagle. Running Fox looked at his son with pride, as the young shaman took the first draw of the pipe before passing it to his father. Once the pipe completed its rounds and returned safely into the hands of the young medicine man, Running Fox spoke. Summarizing the story told to him by his son, he ended with Meadow Lark's revelation concerning her pregnancy.

At this point, the girl was asked to stand and corroborate the truth of what Running Fox said. She was extremely nervous and unsure of herself; eventually, she calmed herself enough to validate the story as told. Skipping Bird and Spotted Deer, who had spent time questioning the girl, were called upon to address the council. Based upon her answers, the women concluded that she is, indeed, with child.

The council members murmured among themselves for several moments until called back to order by their chief. A multitude of suggestions ensued as to how they should deal with the girl and her situation. It was clear they were focusing on how one would deal with an enemy. One member of the council recommended she be driven out of camp and left on her own to survive or not, thus leaving her fate to the Great Spirit. Other suggestions included auctioning her off as a slave, or giving her to one of the young, unwed braves to use as he would. The suggestion of trying to return her to her tribe

The Quest

was rejected as being risky, and much too dangerous under their present circumstances.

Finally, after several other unacceptable suggestions had been voiced, Two Claws stood and addressed the chiefs. His words were gentle, thoughtful and sincere. "Since I first heard the rumors of her tale, I have thought long and hard about this," he said. "I have talked at great length with my woman. I have listened to her words, as well. If Meadow Lark is willing, we will take her…not as a slave, but as our daughter." There was a murmuring of surprise and some objections among the council. Two Claws continued, "Through her, my family will continue to live. We will be her father and her mother. We will be the grandparents of her unborn child." Having made his statement, Two Claws resumed his seat within the circle, his words casting a completely new perspective on a lifetime of tribal hatred.

Running Fox glanced at Spotted Deer, who was nodding her head in agreement. He looked at the faces gathered around the council fire. After a few moments of reflection, the initially confused council members were now signaling their approval of Two Claws' proposal. They were inspired by this great warrior, overburdened with grief by the loss of his daughter and grandson. Intuitively, they understood and respected his wish to fill the emptiness in his life.

The chief motioned for Meadow Lark to rise and give her answer. Standing in awe of what was occurring, the girl took a moment to collect her thoughts. Having spent much of the day with the older woman, she knew Spotted Deer was a good person. The words of Two Claws had touched her heart. She was humbled by his generous spirit, and could hardly believe what was now unfolding. The thought of becoming part of a family again nearly overwhelmed her. This loving invitation brought a glimmer of hope that she might find a renewed sense of identity.

"Oh, yes," she said breathlessly.

When Meadow Lark voiced her acceptance of the offer, the final seal of approval was pronounced by the tribe's young shaman,

Flaming Eagle. It was done. The girl was to be fully accepted as a member of the tribe. In one swift motion by the council, she was now as much a Lakota as any other member of the village. Tearfully, the grateful girl walked with her adopted parents across the campsite to a new home, and her new family.

Flaming Eagle was pleased with the change of perspective influenced by Two Claws and Spotted Deer, as well as the speed and peacefulness with which his people reached a solution. With his mission completed, and time available, he related his adventures, including the story of his renaming, to his mother. His father proudly sat by in silence.

"To White Wolf, watching me combating the burning skins covering Meadow Lark, it appeared I was being consumed by smoke and fire. As I emerged from the flames carrying Meadow Lark in my arms, he acknowledged me as the answer to his quest for confirmation of his vision of the flaming eagle. The old man was convinced his prayers were being answered, and our people were being given their new Holy Man." Flaming Eagle went on to explain he accepted his new name in deference to White Wolf's wisdom and power. Running Fox had been familiar with his cousin's magic for much too long to ever doubt the truth and wisdom of the old man's visions. The young man who had been offered the path of the Wicasa would forevermore be called Flaming Eagle.

Having seen to the disposition of his charge, Flaming Eagle was now free to rejoin White Wolf in the southern plains. His wound was rapidly healing. "I am sure it will take no more than seven or eight sunrises to catch up to the old man," he conjectured. "With only one passenger and no other cargo, Pawnee can cover the distance swiftly. The days are continuing to grow longer, and he is reaching the time in his harvesting when he will no longer be riding. With White Wolf on foot and leading his pony, it will be easy for me to quickly catch up with him."

The Quest

Taking a generous supply of preserved meat and fresh water, Flaming Eagle began his return trip to the south, stopping long enough to pay his respects to his parents. "Since the old man has not had time to hunt game, the freshly smoked meat will, no doubt, be greatly appreciated," he thought. If they were successful in their quest, he and White Wolf would remain gone at least another moon. If they were not, they would remain even longer.

The passage of the moon went by very quickly for Meadow Lark. A trust and love was slowly growing between her and her new parents. They were warm, caring people, and very much in need of someone to fill the void left by the death of their daughter and grandson. Although she did not yet show any outward signs of being with child, Meadow Lark's body was going through many radical changes in preparation for giving birth. She felt life growing inside of her, just as strongly as the beating of her heart. She and Spotted Deer spent most of their free time making clothes and blankets for her unborn.

Much to her surprise, Meadow Lark discovered she and her new family had more in common than she initially believed. The men hunted, fought wars, bragged and exaggerated the stories of their glorious deeds of valour. Women cultivated the domestic arts of sewing, cooking and gossiping. Children cried when they were hurt, and laughed when they were happy. They all believed in the Great Spirit. Only one unspoken disagreement existed in their hearts... who did He most favor and protect? Their rites of marriage were similar. A ruling council of chiefs guides the actions of both tribes. A shaman is respected and revered as a wise man and healer. In truth, the more she examined their differences, the more similarities she found. It did not take her long to adjust to her new environment and living circumstances. By the time White Wolf and Flaming Eagle returned, she was truly the daughter of Spotted Deer and Two Claws.

The old man remained aware his time was growing closer with the passage of each day. He was content and greatly relieved, having a worthy replacement to protect the spirit of his people. As the long, warm days passed, White Wolf watched approvingly as Flaming Eagle gradually took over more of the responsibilities as shaman. Thus freed of obligation, White Wolf spent a majority of his time in prayer and meditation. It was during one of these peaceful times that the Grand Father sent him the vision.

The image came in as a thick, heavily swirling mist. Gradually forming within the haze was a picture of Meadow Lark. Watching, he saw a second figure materializing next to her. It was the image of a young girl, whom he took to be Meadow Lark's daughter. He watched the two females slowly growing older in front of his eyes. The young girl evolved into a woman, with a young boy standing at her side. He believed this to mean the boy was her child and the grandson of Meadow Lark, who appeared to be a woman in midlife.

Standing in the background behind the boy was the likeness of Flaming Eagle, whose appearance was that of a much older man, wearing a white buffalo skullcap headdress of a Wicasa. White Wolf watched the images of Flaming Eagle and the boy merging into one, as did the images of the two women. The two remaining double images of male and female blended into one, bursting into a brilliant white light within the thick mist. First expanding, the image then imploded upon itself, until it was condensed into a single bright point of shimmering light, which faded into the mist, vanishing into the darkness of night.

Although he was perplexed, and did not yet fully comprehend the meaning of his vision, he was sure it was important, and would have to be shared with Flaming Eagle as soon as possible. White Wolf located his cousin's son in his own lodge. Ever since Morning Star's death, Flaming Eagle chose to remain here rather than return to the tipi of the unmarried men. When the old man finished telling his story, he sat quietly, watching the young shaman contemplating the deeper meaning of the images.

The Quest

"It is obvious Meadow Lark will live a long life," Flaming Eagle stated. "She will give birth to a daughter who, in time, will present her with a grandson. The three of them together, as well as individually, will play an important part in my life. However, exactly what that implies remains a mystery, at least for the moment. It also appears I will become a Wicasa and live long. As you have taught me, it often takes a long time before that which is hidden comes to light. So it is with your vision. Beyond this, the only thing abundantly clear is this unfolding will occur long after you have passed over into the spirit world."

White Wolf was extremely pleased with the insight displayed by the young man. "You have done well," he said with a smile. "The spiritual health of my people is in good hands." Since this was the first time in several days they were together, it presented Flaming Eagle with the opportunity, in turn, to ask for the old man's insight into one of his own visions.

"I saw you wearing your ceremonial robes and head dress, floating on your back above the ground. Your eyes were closed as if you were sleeping. As you lay there, drifting above the earth, a cloud descending from the sky slowly and gracefully encased you in a cocoon of shimmering light. I watched the cloud changing into a white robe, made of the hide of a White Buffalo." Pausing momentarily, he continued slowly.

"Next, the robe, with you wearing it, became vapor. Like smoke rising from the ceremonial prayer pipe, it drifted upward, toward the home of the Great Spirit, and of our ancestors."

Stopping momentarily, he scanned his mind to see if he had left out anything of importance. Confident he had not forgotten any pertinent information, he indicated to White Wolf that he was, in fact, finished.

The old man shook his head softly up and down, smiling. "And how would you interpret this vision?" he asked.

Flaming Eagle thought about it, carefully contemplating before attempting to make his reply. "I would interpret this to mean that, when it comes time for you to join our ancestors in the spirit world, you are to be wrapped in the robe of a White Buffalo. This will, somehow, ensure your safe passage into the next life."

Content he had gleaned the true intent from the image, he sat back, waiting for the old man's response. White Wolf nodded his approval.

"However," the old man added, "the magic of the White Buffalo is strong medicine. Always it has been known among our people that only he who has been visited by the spirit of the White Buffalo would even have an opportunity of finding one. Generation after generation has passed without anyone in the tribe ever seeing such a magnificent creature, let alone slaying one!" he exclaimed. "You are the only one among us, in at least three generations, to have such a visitation. You, and you alone, may be able to successfully locate this extremely rare beast."

The conversation now shifted to the old man's death and his burial. Traditionally, those members of the tribe who die with honour are buried in the sky. That has been the way of it, since the beginning, remaining unaltered by time. On extremely rare occasions, men of great esteem, such as White Wolf, make their journey to the spirit world as an offering of smoke from a funeral pyre. His prized possessions are sent with him, making them available to their owner in his after life. It was during this conversation that Flaming Eagle received the first images of his mentor's burial site. As the vision unfolded, he described it to his Wicasa.

"Although I have never physically been there, the terrain the area appears familiar. The forest... the path... the furiously cascading waterfall... the pool of water... even the faces of the mountains have a look about them that I seem to recognize. The scene lays many long-days' ride north of the summer camp, outside the boundaries of Lakota territory.

The Quest

"I am certain I can lead you to this place when it is your time," said the young man. The old man smiled approvingly as he listened to the new shaman describing the images. It was difficult for the Wicasa to believe he was deserving of the privilege of being buried in sky fire. It was an honour that he was not ready to accept. As White Wolf pondered, Flaming Eagle proceeded with describing his vision of the funeral pyre, itself.

"I see *a large, dry tree, whose thick branches are intertwined into a canopy above the first major notch in the trunk. The lower branches are interwoven into masses of almost completely solid wood, making it the perfect resting place for an old man's body.*" Continuing, Flaming Eagle described the actual image of the fire consuming the tree.

"*I see flames creating a bed of fire beneath your resting place. As the sparks shoot wildly upward toward the interlaced branches, the upper boughs of the tree bursts into bright red and orange incandescent particles. The entire tree is being consumed. The funeral pyre resembles the bud of a large red flower, on the verge of blooming. Small upper branches give way, separating from each other, unfolding petals of flame opening up to the twilight sky. It is a beautiful red flower, not unlike the desert blood I brought back to you from the land of the savages.*"

Watching the vision in his mind, the young shaman paused, waiting quietly for a further unveiling.

"*The higher branches are giving completely away, falling inward upon the body. The only thing visible is the burning tree, and the thin, swirling wisp of bluish-white smoke, twisting its way from the heart of the inferno to the stars.*"

The old man could no longer resist the clarity of Flaming Eagle's vision. It was impossible to dispute the truth of the young shaman's image. Having trained him in his accuracy, he now had to acquiesce and reluctantly agree to a burial by fire in the sky. The strength of Flaming Eagle's vision laid waste to his doubt. They were in complete accord.

"Yes," he thought, "this is the way it is meant to be."

The men remained sitting silently, pondering what they had been seeing and discussing. They were aware White Wolf's time was drawing near…one or two winters, at the most…possibly, even less. Flaming Eagle was comfortable with his intuition, believing he would know when and where to hunt the White Buffalo. Except in his vision, he had never actually seen one. Like many other stories told around the campfire, he often wondered about its authenticity. But he was not about to doubt the truth of his vision.

"No," he said, dismissing other thoughts. "There is a White Buffalo, and it is out there. When the time comes, I will find it. I will slay it. I will eat its flesh for food. I will use the carcass for tools and weapons. Its hide is destined to be the burial robe for our Wicasa." He felt a mixture of pride and humility to be chosen for such a noble duty.

Once again, the autumn hunt was plentiful, and the harvest bountiful. The tribe was well supplied for their seasonal move to winter camp. Meadow Lark was showing her pregnancy, displaying a firm, round belly. Even though her body was adjusting to her condition, her emotions remained erratic. She was constantly pampered by her new parents, but not solely because of her condition. The three of them had grown close, and were bonded as tightly as any parents and daughter. True, they all had a void needing to be filled, but the love between them was real, strong, and growing.

Although she was often uncomfortable, the baby had not yet become a burden, as the unborn tend to do toward the end of pregnancy. As she would deliver during the time of the moonless grey months, her duties at winter camp would be light. To reduce any risk of her losing the child, her mother would attend to the heavy work. The wounds in the hearts of Spotted Deer and Two Claws' from the loss of their first daughter and grandson were not yet healed. It would be impossible for them to survive a second one after so short a time.

The Quest

All precautions were being taken to prevent any harm from befalling the girl and her unborn.

Flaming Eagle and Meadow Lark became close friends at the winter camp. He was very protective of her, feeling a strong sense of responsibility as her rescuer and advocate. By ancient laws and traditions, her life belonged to him. Accepting the responsibility, he guarded her as if she were his younger sister.

They spent the cold winter afternoons in front of a fire, talking and laughing. One night, to pass the time, Flaming Eagle told her of Running Moon. "It is a legend from our almost forgotten past, handed down from storyteller to storyteller, and told to the girls in transition into womanhood. It is the tale of a maiden, often referred to as White Buffalo Woman, who united the warring Sioux tribes into one people. Over the endless seasons of telling and retelling the story, her name is often changed.

"Tired of the perpetual pattern of war and killing, she set out to put an end to it, once and for all. Attempting to capture the attention of the warring chiefs, she walked naked and unarmed through the dangerous wilderness, going from camp to camp, from tribe to tribe, begging for peace and unity among the people. She described her vision of all of the small tribes banding together as one people, increasing their chances of survival against the harsh elements, as well as their enemies. For many seasons she was ignored, at best. On more than one occasion, she was pelted with stones and driven away from the campsites.

"Despite this, she never gave up her dream that, someday, our people would make peace among themselves," he continued. "She remained persistent, returning season after season, until their scorn eventually began giving way to respect as, one by one, the councils listened to her. Over time, the gentleness of her spirit softened the hearts of our leaders, as the chiefs comprehended the wisdom of her words," he concluded. "And so it was the maiden, the White Buffalo

Woman, often known as Running Moon, successfully sowed the seeds of unity among my people."

Meadow Lark had a look of curiosity on her face. "Yes, it is a pleasant story and, yes, even inspiring," she thought. "But, why is he choosing to tell me, and why now?" Before she could ask the question, Flaming Eagle spoke.

"I have told you of the great woman who brought peace to our people. She is one of the few women whose life was important enough to earn a place in our history. She was wise and, more importantly, she was determined and unwavering in her path, eventually forging a lasting peace among the warring tribes. Your daughter has a savage for a father and a Pawnee for a mother; but, she is also Lakota. I was hoping you might be persuaded to name your daughter after this great woman, this peacemaker of the Sioux Nation."

Meadow Lark sat quietly, smiling approvingly at his suggestion. Deeply moved, she appreciated the honour being bestowed upon her and her unborn daughter. Flaming Eagle had told her earlier of White Wolf's vision of her daughter and grandson; therefore, it was accepted she would bear a female child.

Her parents, listening to her and the young shaman from inside their tipi, beamed with pride and happiness at this news. The name, Running Moon, had not been used for countless generations, as the original owner of the name was held in such reverence. Having the name of Running Moon bestowed upon a child by the medicine man was not an honour to be refused. No child had ever bore that name within the collective memory of the tribe.

Flaming Eagle told her he had spoken to the council of chiefs and elders and, by unanimous decision, they gave their approval for the name to be conferred upon Meadow Lark's daughter. It was not often the naming of a child was worthy of submission by the medicine man to the council for its endorsement. Running Moon was due to arrive in approximately two moons.

THE QUEST

When he was not visiting with Meadow Lark and her family, or working on his healing arts with White Wolf, Flaming Eagle meditated upon the image of the Great White Buffalo. After several attempts, he was finally capable of holding the visualization in his mind, effortlessly.

He surveyed the terrain, looking for familiar landmarks… but there were none. What he saw were images of great mountains, capped with humongous layers of snow, and enormous rivers frozen solid with ice thicker than any he had ever seen. Not even during the coldest of winters had he ever witnessed such heavy blankets of snow. From what he could ascertain, the Great Tatanka was in the northern territory, hiding in the land of the frozen wind. Deep within the blackness of the forest, it waited for him. Flaming Eagle saw the Great White Buffalo looking back at him at the exact same moment that he saw it in his vision. He stared deeply into its huge, pink eyes, surrounded by a gigantic head with horns longer than any he had ever laid eyes upon. Snorting, the great beast anxiously pawed at the snow-laden ground. Its hot breath created a steam so thick that it partially obscured its massive head.

So, White Wolf was correct, again. Flaming Eagle was actually seeing the beast in its lair. It was real. It did exist. It was impatiently waiting for him to come for it. Flaming Eagle and the Great White Tatanka were both aware that the time of their encounter was at hand. They awaited the day when they would at last come face-toface in a struggle which could only end in death.

Chapter 3

CYCLES

Meadow Lark gave birth to her daughter during the coldest moon of the snowy nights. The air was chilled by the icy breath of the north wind. The moon was full. The sky was clear. It was a night when, looking into the heavens, one could swear to have caught glimpses of the spirit world. Her labour was short and, happily, it was relatively pain free. She was young, strong and hardy. Although she was exhausted after delivery, she was strangely energized, and overjoyed by the arrival of her daughter, Running Moon.

The child was oval faced, with penetrating dark eyes which looked deeply into things others did not see. Her skin was slightly less brown than average. She possessed strong, healthy lungs, as attested to by her birth cries. Despite the circumstances of her conception, the instant Meadow Lark first looked upon her daughter she felt love stronger than anything she had ever experienced. The love generated by the birth of this child filled Meadow Lark's heart with joy.

The older spirit helpers gently cleaned the baby while the others attended to the needs of the mother. As soon as the child was

THE QUEST

presentable, the grandfather, Two Claws, was invited to enter the tipi. He welcomed the daughter of his daughter into the living circle of the people. The grandparents were the happiest they had been since the birth of the daughter of their blood, Morning Star. After her grandfather completed his prayers of thanksgiving, the child was next presented to Chief Running Fox, and the Wicasa, White Wolf, as well as the new shaman, Flaming Eagle. Needless to say, Running Moon met with their approval.

White Wolf always suspected this child would be important to the people. "If I am aware that she is special, Flaming Eagle must also know it," he mused to himself, as he proceeded to quietly chant the prayers of welcome. He moved gracefully and rhythmically in a circle around the child resting in the arms of Flaming Eagle. This was the last ritualistic act performed by the retiring shaman.

The old man's body was showing signs of steady decline, but there was no lessening of his mental capacities, nor of his perceptual abilities. Each day he grew older, and one step closer to completing his return journey to the Great Spirit. It was time to place the physical care and the spiritual health of the tribe solely into the skillful hands of his cousin's son. They were extremely capable hands. By relinquishing his responsibilities, the old man was free to spend the little time left to him in prayer and meditation.

When the tribe was ready to return to summer camp, Flaming Eagle was comfortably assuming the full responsibilities of his new position. White Wolf remained available to guide him when it was necessary, and they often prayed together in the evenings. One of the older spirit helpers recently passed over to the other side; however, with his duties lessened, he decided not to replace her. No longer responsible for conducting the healings, one helper was all he needed. His people trusted Flaming Eagle without hesitation. Their Wicasa had shown complete faith in him and, therefore, so did they. Flaming

Eagle learned well from the old man, and possessed a natural healing talent of his own, inherited from his mother, Skipping Bird.

His meditation skills were improving steadily and, for short periods, he was able to master the bliss of the silent mind. On occasion, Flaming Eagle absented himself from the camp for days at a time, whenever he needed solitude to strengthen the clarity of his visions. Packing some dried meat and whatever fruit might be in season, he rode to the nearby buttes where he quietly camped on a high bluff, sleeping under a clear, night sky filled with countless stars.

It was customary for him to visit the old man before leaving on one of his spiritual retreats. During his absence, White Wolf was always prepared to resume the role of shaman if and when the situation warranted it. Otherwise, the attending of the sick was left in the capable hands of the spirit helpers. Having the old man available was a luxury for Flaming Eagle, one that could come to an end at any moment; therefore, he made the most of his opportunities with his Wicasa whenever possible.

It was in mid-summer, during one of Flaming Eagle's pilgrimages, when he was again visited by the spirit of the Great White Buffalo. It occurred late on the fourth evening of his retreat, just after he concluded releasing his prayers to the Great Spirit by way of the four winds. He watched the smoke rising upward, spreading itself into a light swirling haze. Gazing into the wisps of smoke, he watched a vision taking shape.

The scene was of the northern mountains and forests. He saw the white beast taking form within the landscape. Against the backdrop of greens and browns from the mountains and valleys, the animal appeared gigantic. The beast was snorting and pawing at the earth, ripping out large chunks of sod. Bright coloured leaves were drifting down into the image, as the trees of the forest shed their foliage. The sunlight reflecting off the rustling, multi-coloured leaves added a mystical rainbow effect to the scene.

The Quest

The young shaman watched, as the gently falling leaves were gradually replaced by a sprinkling of raindrops. In turn, the droplets of rain transformed into lightly drifting snowflakes. As they cooled, the wind violently blew, obscuring the great animal within a blur of pounding snow. Gradually, the snowstorm diminished into a soft breath of descending flakes, floating as they gently encircled the animal. The snow was soon replaced by a cleansing spring rain, which, in its turn, gave way to clear, blue skies and warm, spring breezes. The Great White Buffalo was no longer in the image. The beast was absent from the high, snowy country of the far north. It had vanished with the dissipating snows.

"The Mighty Beast will die within the full cycle of the seasons, before the return of the spring rains." he concluded. Immediately, another image confirmed his interpretation..

There, in the warmth of a summer moon, he saw White Wolf standing by a campfire with a white buffalo robe draped around his shoulders. The vision shifted and changed until displaying the red moon of late summer. The robe, freefalling, landed on a campfire and burst into flame, as heavy, white smoke spewed forth on the breath of the prairie winds.

Then, as suddenly as it appeared, the image faded into the nothingness of the lonely night, which was engulfing him. Even though the visions were gone, their meanings were clear to Flaming Eagle. He was to confront the Great Tatanka during the bleakest of the seasons, and its hide was to be the white buffalo robe in which White Wolf will be offered up to the Great Spirit.

By the end of summer, Meadow Lark's loathing of her attackers softened into a disdainful disrespect for the savages who had misused her. However, she possessed a normal curiosity as to which savage was the seed father of Running Moon, as, at the time, her attention had not been focused upon studying their faces. She saw reflections of herself in her daughter; however, she was mystified when it came to identifying the other features making up the balance of her child's physical characteristics.

There was no denying the little girl was, indeed, very pretty. She had a thick head of straight black hair. In contrast with the lighter tone of her skin, her dark eyes looked even darker. Her smile warmed the hearts of everyone who came within her orbit. Meadow Lark prayed Running Moon would always be a source of happiness and joy to her and her adopted parents. The new mother dreaded the day, which would eventually come to pass, when she would have to tell her daughter the full story of her conception and heritage. When this time came, it would be up to the entire village to prove to Running Moon that she was truly one of them. Despite how she came to the people, she was, and would always be, Lakota.

It took a while after the birth of her child for Meadow Lark to fully accept her new life as one of the people. Since her arrival, she had always been treated with respect, but it was mixed with a certain amount of suspicion and curiosity. As she grew more comfortable in the company of her adopted parents, she gradually became more accepting of her new people, and they of her.

With the passing of days, Meadow Lark was completely accepted as a member of the tribe. She was, after all, the adopted daughter of a great war chief, and was befriended by the tribe's young shaman, whose father was their chief. There was absolutely no doubt as to her place within the unbroken circle of the people. Her daughter's position was also secure. The child was given a name of great power and reverence by Flaming Eagle. The souls of the descendants of Meadow Lark and Running Moon would be forever connected to the spirit of the Lakota.

Upon returning to the encampment, Flaming Eagle went directly to the tipi of White Wolf. Anxious to describe his vision to the old man, he was eager to learn whether or not the old man's interpretation would match his own. After paying his proper respects

The Quest

to the Wicasa, he began telling his story. Starting his tale with the Great White Buffalo's first appearance in its northern habitat, he described everything from the changing of the seasons through the final image of the old Wicasa wearing the robe.

From the description Flaming Eagle was imparting, White Wolf started sketching a map in the earth. The old man had not hunted the northern expanse for many winters, but he remembered the territory. The area pictured in Flaming Eagle's image was very rugged and extremely dangerous. In the winter, there were cutting winds. and a constant threat of avalanches. In the springtime, the lakes and rivers overflowed, flooding the land. As the seasons became drier, rockslides were a common occurrence. If the White Buffalo was truly to be confronted here, then its strength and fury had to be added to the sum of the dangers already awaiting him.

As if the conditions of the terrain, itself, were not enough, the territory of the despised Crow also had to be crossed before even getting there, who, unlike the Cheyenne, were not friendly to his people. Despite White Wolf's words of caution, Flaming Eagle would not be dissuaded from this hunt to which his heart and spirit were honour-bound. They each quietly pondered the challenges awaiting him.

The silence was finally broken when White Wolf spoke. "If your vision is true, as we believe it to be, I will be leaving this world in less than a complete cycle of the seasons, during the moon of the ripening cherries," he said wistfully.

Up until this moment, this part of the prophecy had been consciously ignored by Flaming Eagle. He was so consumed by the challenge of finding the great beast, he had not allowed himself to see the obvious. For the first time, this very sobering thought was seeping into his mind. Observing the concern on the young man's face, White Wolf smiled.

"It is time for me to leave this world, just as it is time for you to be the tribe's only shaman," he said wisely. "The people trust you as their healer, and you must now accept the honour and the responsibility of overseeing their spiritual well being."

Returning their discussion to the challenge at hand, White Wolf continued with his lessons. "The White Buffalo is far more dangerous than any regular bull, not only because of its size, but also because it is far more aggressive. It is half again as large as the largest herd bull. When you hunt it," he said firmly, "you must be extremely careful not to allow yourself to become the hunted."

They discussed strategies as to the most effective ways of stalking and slaying the beast. White Wolf suggested that, due to its size, it should be hunted with the lance rather than with the bow and arrow. Flaming Eagle agreed on the importance of his becoming adept with the lance as the weapon of choice.

The Wicasa took this opportunity to teach Flaming Eagle a special invocation which was to be said over the corpse of the great beast. It was an ancient prayer passed down through countless generations of shaman, yet very seldom, if ever, had it actually been used by any of them.

"I, myself, have never seen a White Buffalo, dead or alive," he confided, "neither in my daily life nor in my visions. Even though I never used the prayer, I know the words you need to speak."

Anticipating Flaming Eagle would have the opportunity to use the prayer, he taught him the rituals and chants to be used in sanctifying the Great White Buffalo robe.

"The prayer and the proper chants will incorporate the spirit of the Grand Father into the hide," explained the Wicasa. "The blending of the sacred words with the power of Tatanka will invest the robe with strong medicine."

"The robe, infused with the Great Spirit, will be worthy to be worn by a Holy Man throughout eternity," mused Flaming Eagle to himself..

The Quest

The men finished their conversation before offering their evening prayers. The Wicasa invited the young shaman to lead them in offering up their nightly thanksgiving for the gift of another day. White Wolf asked the shaman not to use pre-blended herbs for this evening's ceremony, and the young man excused himself so he could retrieve the requested herbs from his lodge. Returning shortly with the pure, unblended herbs, he watched the old man carefully and respectfully unveil the pipe. To Flaming Eagle's surprise, it was not his everyday one. It was the sacred ceremonial pipe.

Taking the pipe, he passed it to Flaming Eagle to fill with the fresh mixture of herbs and tobacco. The young man carefully packed the bowl before passing the pipe back to White Wolf, who declined. Instead, he took a small burning stick from the campfire, passing the flame to the new shaman for use in igniting the mixture. Pleased and proud, Flaming Eagle offered up his prayers for the winds to convey to Wakan Tanka. Finishing, he passed the sacred pipe to White Wolf, who reinforced his prayers with his own. When his prayers were completed, he placed the ceremonial pipe in the young man's hands for safe keeping…from this time forward.

There was a peaceful relief in White Wolf's spirit, comforted by knowing he would soon be released from his earthly shackles. His spirit, liberated from form, will expand, joining the spirits of his ancestors, ultimately merging with the Great Spirit, Himself. He was more than satisfied that his successor would serve the people well, and had no regrets for the life he had lived. No. Actually, he was looking forward to a well-deserved rest. With each passing day, his body was growing more tired as the aches and pains from ancient wounds were constantly growing more distracting. At the same time, the weakness in his hand from his most recent injury was intensifying, and his vision had grown cloudy. Objects held close to his eyes were blurry, often unrecognizable. There was no question his body was wearing down. Not so with his mind, which maintained its clarity.

Flaming Eagle was not nearly as peaceful with the approaching eminence of the old man's demise. The young man looked upon the Wicasa as a source of wisdom and guidance which he was not ready to relinquish. White Wolf was the father of his spirit, just as Running Fox was the father of his mind, body and blood. There was still so much he was hoping to learn from the old man; however, the amount of information available to him was severely limited by White Wolf's time upon the earth.

There was no reason for the young shaman to doubt White Wolf's interpretation of the vision. He will be gone in nine or ten moons. Twelve was the most for which he could hope. Flaming Eagle hungrily increased the time he spent in daily lessons with White Wolf, questioning him mercilessly, hoping to glean every possible grain of information and knowledge. Quite often, because of his quest for knowledge combined with the limited number of seasons remaining to them, the effort seemed futile.

Despite the amount of time he was spending with White Wolf, Flaming Eagle set aside generous portions for Meadow Lark and her daughter. Since the birth of Running Moon, he and the young mother had become even closer. During this period, he became firmly entrenched as the child's surrogate father. Meadow Lark enjoyed having him around, knowing it was important and necessary for her daughter to have the strong guidance and protection of a father. She was grateful for the friendship of the shaman. It pleased her that Running Moon had access to his wisdom and counsel.

To Flaming Eagle, the girl became the child he had been denied. The bond between them was as strong as any between a father and daughter. Throughout their lives, Flaming Eagle's mind was often preoccupied with the memory of White Wolf's vision of Meadow Lark, her daughter, and her grandson. There was no doubt the four of them were bound together, and would always remain so.

The Quest

The days of summer slipped by quickly, and the autumn hunt was drawing near. Deciding it was prudent to follow his father's cousin's suggestion, Flaming Eagle chose to hunt the Great White Buffalo with the lance rather than the bow and arrow. If his visions were accurate, it would take more than one lance to bring down the behemoth. The deathblow will have to be deep, strong, and true. He will have to lethally thrust a lance into the vulnerable hump at the base of the animal's skull, where the hide is thick and difficult to penetrate. Flaming Eagle was looking forward to this autumn hunt, as it allowed him to hone his technique and skill with the lance, providing the training needed for his quest to procure the burial robe for his Wicasa.

Flaming Eagle realized it would be difficult to carry more than one lance when pursuing the beast, especially since he was anticipating the need to put at least two lances into the great bull. Meadow Lark was quick to volunteer her skills by making a large quiver for his lances, just as he had a quiver for his arrows. Her first order of business was to gather the necessary materials. Taking some deer skin, rawhide strips, and a buffalo bone needle, she set about making a holder for his weapons. She constructed the deerskin container wider at the top than at the bottom. A long, wide strap of rawhide was attached to the mouth of the quiver. The design of the strap was such that it encircled the horse's neck, fastening to the opposite side of the quiver, thus assuring it would remain snug around Pawnee's neck. In a like manner, the narrower end of the holder was fastened to the horse's midsection, just above the haunch. His new quiver was capable of holding five lances. These, plus the lance he carried in his hand, would surely provide him with more than enough of an arsenal to bring down the White Tatanka.

By the first day of the hunt, Flaming Eagle was ready to test his new weapons and style of hunting. He made his approach at an angle into the herd, cutting out a large bull. Riding stride-for-stride with the animal, he took out his first lance and, with both hands, drove it deep into the hump of the beast. The animal slowed down slightly, veering to the right, away from the main herd. Reaching down by the pony's neck, he withdrew another lance. In the meantime, Pawnee was running abreast of his prey while Flaming Eagle prepared to strike again. This time, he buried the blade all the way up to the shaft in the animal's soft hump. The buffalo's knees buckled as it toppled forward, skidding to a stop.

Flaming Eagle promptly went racing after another bull at the edge of the herd. Riding straight at the animal, he cut inward, causing the beast to separate from the rest. In doing so, the buffalo exposed the vulnerable spot between its head and its hump. Taking careful aim, Flaming Eagle embedded his lance in the base of its skull. The lance severed the animal's spinal cord, causing it to immediately drop, like a dead bird falling from the endless sky.

After four days of hunting, Flaming Eagle was so proficient with the lance, he was bringing down most of his kills with only one blow. Having sharpened his technique to such a degree, he was certain he would have the White Buffalo's hide before White Wolf's journey to the other side. "The robe's medicine will protect the old man from any mishaps along his journey," Flaming Eagle affirmed. The decision was firm: he would begin his quest as soon as winter camp was established. Then he would find and kill the magical, mystical Great White Tatanka.

Chapter 4

TATANKA

The winter snow came earlier than usual, but not before camp was successfully relocated. White, slow, drifting flakes of frozen water were descending as messengers of the bitter weather soon to follow. Time was approaching for Flaming Eagle's quest. Once the tribe settled into quarters, the young warrior prepared for his hunt. Two of White Wolf's spirit helpers continued serving as healers in his absence under the guidance of the old Wicasa.

Before leaving, the shaman presented the ceremonial pipe to the old man for safekeeping. He selected a fresh supply of pre-blended herbs and tobacco for his nightly prayer offerings. Collecting his weapons, he chose the thickest buffalo hides for warmth and protection against the cold winds that slice a man into pieces, arranging the hides to also provide protection and warmth for Pawnee. Thus covered, they trudged into the frigid winds.

This Tatanka did not migrate with the herds. It was impatiently waiting for its adversary in the frozen mountains of the bitter north. Successfully reaching the terrain of his vision, Flaming Eagle and Pawnee slowly fought their way into the icy, teeth-chattering breath of the northern gales. Relentless, chilling gusts, bouncing off the face of the craggy slopes, surrounded them in a frozen whirlwind. Abruptly, the light, floating snowflakes began cascading down faster and harder, swirling like a multitude of small tornados. As they traveled north, the trail steepened, increasing the difficulty of their journey. The only way he knew for certain they were heading in the correct direction was by the constant, shredding winds ricocheting southward from the bleak mountains.

Struggling deeper into the numbing, unknown, northern territory, each day was taking them closer to the Great White Buffalo. It was waiting for him somewhere in one of the dark valleys within the timberline. "Is it hiding, or is it lying in ambush for me?" Flaming Eagle questioned, knowing the answer would become clear only when he and the beast finally came face-to-face. The farther north he traveled, the closer he came to the inevitable encounter awaiting him. The anticipated inevitable moment of their meeting was drawing near.

Each night, he pitched camp in the thickest grove he could find. Stretching two buffalo hides between small trees and low branches, he secured them as a windbreak for himself and Pawnee, enabling them to sleep more comfortably. He did his best to protect himself and his pony from the harsh winter elements, despite the fact that he was unable to make a campfire. The animal, like all horses, was terrified of flames. Instead, he brought the horse in close to the windbreak, hobbling and covering it with a buffalo hide. Wrapping himself in the remaining skins, he curled up between the windbreak and the pony. This procedure did not take the place of a warm fire, but it was helpful in blocking the constantly blowing sleet carried on the icy winds.

On milder days, when the snow floated gently to the ground, he hunted for food…usually snow rabbits and deer. When his luck was poor, or his aim bad, he relied on the dried buffalo strips to appease his appetite. Thus he survived, always pushing northward. By day,

THE QUEST

he forced his way into the wind. At night, he did his best to hide from it. Whenever the opportunity presented itself, he gathered what burnable wood and buffalo chips he could find, saving them for the time when he could safely make a small fire to warm himself and, hopefully, cook some fresh meat.

The days stretched into two full moon cycles, with still no sign of his prey. Flaming Eagle was on the verge of doubting the truth of his visions, when he received a sign in the snow. Half covered by powdery drifts, he saw the gigantic hoof prints. As in his vision, they were larger than any buffalo prints he ever encountered…and they were leading deep into the woods.

"Odd behavior for a buffalo," he muttered aloud, trailing the beast into the increasing darkness of the forest.

By nightfall, no longer able to follow the animal, he made camp. It was a rare, mild evening, allowing him to hobble Pawnee far enough away to build a small fire and cook the rabbit he shot earlier in the day. Setting up the lean-to as usual, he warmed himself by the fire, taking great pleasure in the first hot meal he had eaten in several days. After he finished eating, he smoked his pipe, offering up his evening prayers to the Great Spirit. Once the fire burned itself down into red coals, he hobbled Pawnee closer to him. Lying down between his pony and the remaining embers, he quickly drifted into a peaceful sleep.

Several days passed before Flaming Eagle again picked up the trail of the great beast. This time, the signs were fresher, and the hoof prints were deeper. They followed the animal into a clearing, where the trail abruptly ended. There was no sign of it having gone any farther in any direction. He was confused as to how these tracks suddenly disappeared.

"Curious," he thought, pondering the situation while fine-tuning his senses.

Soon he heard the sound of the Great Beast, snorting and pawing the ground. Out of nowhere, the White Monster came, attacking from the dark shelter of the trees, its head down, charging directly at him. Its pink eyes were glistening coals of fire. This aggressive behavior caught Flaming Eagle completely off guard. Unlike the docile buffalo of the herds with extremely poor eyesight, this extraordinary buffalo was clearly staring at him, and was most certainly on the assault.

Flaming Eagle turned Pawnee sharply to the left, speeding into the protection of the forest, as the raging Beast shot past him. Coming to a stop on the other side of the clearing, the Great Bull turned around, pawing angrily at the ground, searching for the elusive warrior. Steam came pouring furiously from its flaring nostrils, as the Great White frantically shook its head.

In the meantime, Flaming Eagle was guiding Pawnee swiftly through the trees. Having ridden in a semi-circle, they were quietly sneaking up behind the raging animal. The Beast continued pawing the ground, snapping its head sharply back-and-forth, its red eyes searching for the missing shaman.

"No, this is no common buffalo," he affirmed to himself. "It possesses strong medicine."

Carefully, Flaming Eagle removed a lance from the quiver tied to Pawnee's side. With the lance poised in his hand, he slowly and quietly advanced on the furious Beast. Reaching the edge of the trees, he nudged Pawnee in the flank, commencing his offence against his prey. Suddenly, the Great White Buffalo turned toward him. Startled, the hunter released his lance prematurely, missing the target entirely. His failed assault only intensified Tatanka's wrath, as it now became the hunter pursuing the brave, who fled into the protection of the trees on Pawnee.

The frozen terrain under the snow was shredded under the hooves of the rushing Giant, as it lunged past the escaping warrior. Dodging his way through the trees, Flaming Eagle returned to the clearing, where he retrieved his lance. At this exact moment, the infuriated

The Quest

Bull turned, once more preparing to go on the attack. Saplings were uprooted by the fury of its charge, as the Colossus launched itself at its foe. With its head lowered, it came flying like an arrow from a bow directly toward the young shaman.

Remembering a strategy taught to him by Running Fox many winters ago, Flaming Eagle changed his tactics. Instead of trying to escape the Beast, he turned his pony and rode straight at it. The Great White Buffalo was charging in full attack, head lowered, sharp horns at the ready. With his pony galloping at top speed, the brave held his lance poised to strike. In a lightning quick move, Flaming Eagle cut sharply to the right, half a breath before colliding with his mighty attacker. Quickly turning his pony, he gave chase. Approaching the Bull, he again readied his lance. He released it, driving it deep into the hump of the Beast. Enraged by the pain, Tatanka vigorously shook itself, attempting to dislodge the weapon; however, the lance was much too secure to be easily shaken out. It was in to stay.

Bellowing in rage and pain, the mighty Beast turned, vengefully renewing its combat with the brave. It shook its head vigorously, painfully aware of the lance buried deep within its flesh. Once more,

Flaming Eagle fled into the trees, hoping the enraged Beast would be foolish enough to follow. Dashing into the woods, the warrior headed straight toward a large, snow-covered boulder. Dismounting, he scampered up the huge, slippery rock to the top. There, with his lance grasped firmly in his hand, he awaited the onrushing assault.

His wait was short. The charging Beast churned the snow into billowing clouds of fine, white powder, flying wildly in all directions. Watching his attacker's rapid approach, Flaming Eagle raised the lance high above his head. Just as the Great Beast went rushing past the boulder, the hunter jumped, intending to land astride its back while driving the lance deep into the vulnerable area of its flesh. Sailing through the air, the brave successfully imbedded the lance perfectly into its neck. However, failing to properly accomplish his landing, he ended up sprawled face-down, half buried in a deep snowdrift.

The wounded, charging hulk slowed down, stumbling and gasping. Flaming Eagle's lance had severed its throat, making it impossible to breathe in the frigid, life-giving air. Lunging forward, its front legs collapsed under its weight, as the gigantic Beast slid to a halt at the base of a tree. The Great White Buffalo fell forever silent.

Flaming Eagle, gasping to breathe, pulled himself out of the drift and wiped the snow from his face, only then realizing that, indeed, the Colossus was dead. Stunned, and uneasy on his feet, he brushed off the heavy snow caked on his clothing as he made his way toward his worthy adversary. Standing over the breathless Behemoth, he stared at it in wonder. Even in death, the Great White Buffalo was magnificent.

Once recovering his senses, Flaming Eagle took a moment to feast his eyes upon the splendor of his majestic kill before turning to the task of removing its hide, which was as brilliant as the white robe of his visions. He chanted the prayer White Wolf taught him, thanking the Grand Father for His gift. Due to the bitter cold, the formal ritual of thanksgiving would have to wait until after shelter was located.

Skinning the beast, the immediate task at hand, was not easily accomplished. The hide was extremely thick, and Flaming Eagle's hands were very cold, a difficult combination for the job in front of him. After several attempts, he eventually pierced the hide. Working, he warmed his hands the best he could on the steaming, hot flesh of the animal, as he went about the task of skinning, very slowly and carefully. Removing the hide from the flesh, he took extra care to avoid damaging it. This beautiful hide was destined to be the burial robe of the old Wicasa. The skullcap, on the other hand, was claimed by Flaming Eagle as his new ceremonial headdress, serving as a constant validation of the truth of his story, a story which would be told around the campfire for generations to come.

Flaming Eagle, regrettably, could only take a small portion of the flesh with him. He intended to possess the medicine of the Great Beast, whose essence lay within its heart, as it does with all living

The Quest

things. It was always known by his people that the true power of an animal can only be incorporated into another while the organ is still fresh and warm. To cook it would destroy the energy of the mighty Tatanka. Taking the heart of the animal, he carefully cut it into four equal pieces, praying over each before consuming them.

The liver was laid aside, as he prepared to go about slicing off larger slabs of meat. It was necessary to work quickly, before the flesh became frozen solid in the frigid air. Flaming Eagle threw the precious hide over Pawnee, skin side up. Once the hide was draped over his pony, he laid the large pieces of fresh buffalo meat across it, wedging the liver firmly in between the slabs. Satisfied nothing else remained to be done, he proceeded to clean his knife with snow before retrieving his lance.

He led Pawnee back toward a small cave, which he had spotted earlier, before originally picking up the tracks of the Great Beast. Now that this part of his quest was complete, he decided to take advantage of the protection of the cave, where the hide could be processed in warmth and at his leisure. They headed southward, toward an opening at the base of one of the frozen mountains. The mouth of the cave was high enough and broad enough to easily accommodate a horse and its rider.

To Flaming Eagle's surprise, the shelter was deeper than he originally thought, so he guided the horse inside, out of the freezing twilight. Approximately ten paces inside the entrance was a wall of stone Opposite this wall, the other side jutted out in a curved pattern, approximately five or six paces, creating a small alcove which he could use as his sleeping area. The two protruding walls created an archway leading deeper into the cavern. Once through this narrow passage, the cavity broadened, taking a sweeping turn to the left, where it ended at about fourteen paces. This sheltered area was large enough to hold Pawnee, protecting him from the cold, while sheltering him from the direct view of the fire that would be burning between Flaming Eagle's sleeping area and the mouth of the cave.

Although it appeared to have been unused for a while, there was a large store of dried wood and buffalo chips stacked against the rear wall. With fresh meat, a fire, and a safe place to spend a warm night, an exhausted Flaming Eagle was gratefully content. He hobbled Pawnee around the corner, at the far end of the enclosure, facing the wall, as far away from the fire as possible.

The young shaman found his hunger overwhelming his exhaustion. Once the fire was burning steadily near the mouth of the cave, he sliced off a chunk of meat, skewering it with a small stick, suspending it between two short-forked branches embedded in the ground on each side of the fire pit. While the meat was cooking, he went about cutting the liver into small, thin pieces, laying them, one at a time, on the warm rocks surrounding the fire. Here they were to remain drying slowly throughout the night, completing the first step in their processing. When Flaming Eagle finished eating his fill of roasted buffalo, he unwrapped his pipe and proceeded offering the ceremonial prayers of thanksgiving taught to him by his Wicasa. Before retiring, he sent his nightly prayers, by way of the four winds to Wakan Tanka. Wrapping himself in his robes, he lay down to sleep on the side of the campfire farthest from the mouth of the cave.

By morning a blizzard was on the rampage, howling wildly, blasting its way past the front of the cavern. Fighting the gusting winds, Flaming Eagle fastened hides to the tree roots and protruding rock formations around the entrance. He anchored them near the base of the cave, attempting to cut off the chilling winds while leaving an opening for the escaping smoke. Next, he added a few buffalo chips to the embers. The chips burned hot and slow, providing a longer supply of heat than just the wood alone.

This was the most comfortable he had been since starting his quest. Taking advantage of the present situation, he decided to remain here for a while, at least until the storm blew over, before making his homeward journey. Now was a time for him to rest, an opportunity

The Quest

to scrape the hide clean, and an occasion for meditation and prayer. With the front of his temporary home now protected from the howling winds, the air inside the shelter was quite comfortable. After completing his evening agenda, the young shaman painstakingly filled his pipe with the sacred herbs, in preparation for his evening devotion. As always, his words were carried by the four winds to the waiting ear of the Grand Father, Who hears all.

By afternoon of the second day, the gale had run its course, and the snow was no longer falling. The icy winds were calm, and the sky was filled with large patches of crystal blue. Flaming Eagle used this change in the weather to hunt for more wood and buffalo chips. Fuel was not only needed to replenish his own fire, but to replace the supply he found in the cave. Taking some cold, spent charcoal, he darkened the area around his eyes, to help protect them from the glowing, white light streaming down through the clouds and brightly reflecting off the snowy landscape. Searching the area, he found himself heading in the general direction of the place where the corpse of the slain Beast still lay. Even skinned, the massive carcass, partially covered with snow, was still an impressive sight.

It only took a short while to accomplish his mission. In very little time he was well supplied with ample fuel, and making his way back to the cave. The going was extremely slow, as it was difficult for Pawnee to plow through the heavy drifts of snow, which were often chest high. Before nightfall, however, they were safely back inside the protective shelter. Flaming Eagle decided to enjoy one more night of relative comfort before returning to the sacred Black Hills.

After smoking his pipe and offering up his nightly prayers, the young shaman went into that deep, dark, quiet place within himself. His thoughts drifted away as his consciousness faded, flooding the void with the silvery-blue light which often filled his inner-awareness.

The brightness was simultaneously calming and stimulating, a blue flame, dancing and swirling, like a coy maiden teasing her lover. She was an alluring, wily temptress, enticing the shy vision hiding within the deep recesses of his mind to come forward and expose itself. Initially, the image was blending in-and-out with the floating light, playing hide-and-go-seek within its allusive sanctuary. Soon, the illumination faded into the background, as the manifesting image became clear enough for him to gaze upon.

He was looking at an manifestation of White Wolf. In the vision, the Wicasa appeared very tired and weak. Flaming Eagle sensed the heaviness that was pressing down upon the old man's shoulders. It was the weightiness from a lifetime responsibility of caring for the well being of his people.

Gradually the image changed into a picture of White Wolf lying very still, peacefully wrapped in the White Buffalo robe. His withered face emitted a soft glow, as the Wicasa, closing his eyes for the last time, spoke his final words. Unfortunately, Flaming Eagle was unable to clearly hear them. The old man smiled before drifting into a serene sleep.

He continued watching a miraculous sunset, spreading pink, orange and lavender colours, feathering endlessly in all directions across the blue-green sky. Scanning the horizon and the mountains within the image, he realized this place was hidden deep beyond the Sacred Hills…a land so lost that none of his own people had ever walked upon its soil. It was as if he were the first person to ever view this breathtaking scene.

Eventually, as the image faded, he entered the waking sleep, remaining there until dawn.

Breaking camp early next morning, Flaming Eagle resumed his journey at dawn. Although having been gone for three moons, he estimated his return trip would take approximately a half-cycle of the moon or, possibly, a few days more. As always, the determining factor was the weather. The sky was clear as he started homeward. He had a stiff wind at his back, which was less harsh, but still bitter cold. His main difficulty was dealing with a glaring sun and its blinding reflection off the snow. Even with the area around his eyes blackened, he was squinting while straining to see clearly. Despite the severe glare, he guided Pawnee southward toward the Black Hills of home. The

The Quest

prevailing wind, shifting back and forth through the mountainous terrain, was sharp, biting deeply into his face. His dry lips were already swollen, and cracking. Pulling the hide down over his head and face, he hoped to provide himself with what protection he could while trekking through the icy valleys of the frozen mountains.

Even though the journey itself was uneventful, Flaming Eagle was spurred on by the memory of his vision and his awareness that time was fast running out for the old man. If he was interpreting the vision correctly, White Wolf would join the ancestors before the waning moon in the season of the ripening cherries. His thoughts were inundated with memories of training, and his relationship with the old shaman, remembering when he and his friends first heard stories about the old man. Even at an early age, Flaming Eagle was impressed with the uniqueness White Wolf wore like a royal mantel. The old shaman never corrected him nor the other boys in anger, but was always gentle, yet firm, in his handling of them. This was in great contrast to their fathers, who were often irate and impatient with their sons; especially Thunder Eyes, who never learned to control his emotions, nor to dispense just punishment with an even hand. No. White Wolf had always been special, even in ways that were still incomprehensible to the young shaman.

It was a few days past the half-moon when the returning hunter arrived at his destination. Through a very light flurry of snow, he spotted the winter camp. Approaching the village, he watched the smoke lazily rising from the tipis. The trees were heavily laden with their winter burden, and the terrain was frozen, rock-solid. With the robe of the Great White Buffalo draped across his shoulders and flowing down to the rear haunches of his pony, Flaming Eagle rode leisurely into the camp. He knew his father and chief would understand the appropriateness of his destination, as he immediately proceeded to White Wolf's lodge. There he remained astride Pawnee, in full view of everyone, for several moments before dismounting.

Announcing himself to White Wolf, who was warming himself by a crackling fire, the young man entered the tipi. Despite his tiredness, the old man managed an enormous smile when he laid eyes upon Flaming Eagle and his magnificent gift. Kneeling in front of him, he greeted his teacher. They sat quietly together, taking pleasure in the silence of each other's company. Standing, the young man draped the glorious robe over White Wolf's shoulders, stepping back to admire the vision in front of him. He had never seen his father's cousin so happy, nor so deeply appreciative. It was, indeed, a wondrous gift he had been allowed to bestow upon his Wicasa.

Flaming Eagle recounted the story of his travels, while the men were served food by the spirit helpers, all of whom attended to the old man during the young shaman's absence. Eating their fill, they quietly talked of things to come. White Wolf was imparting his very last lessons to Flaming Eagle, who listened attentively, knowing only a few moons were left to glean his master's wisdom. They talked late into the darkness of night. The young man had more questions than he could ask. The old man possessed a lifetime of information which could never be deliver in the interval allotted him. The best he could hope to do was pass on the most important information within the time remaining.

By the time the moon was high overhead, White Wolf was exhausted, and in need of recuperative sleep. Before dismissing the young man, he smiled and, caressing the robe, imparted unto Flaming Eagle a great, constant and unchanging wisdom: "You must always speak the truth; however, without credibility, it will neither be heard nor accepted."

The young man quietly departed, leaving White Wolf to his nightly rest. They would talk on the morrow, as they would on every tomorrow left to the old man. For now, the old Wicasa slept the peaceful sleep of contentment. The younger man, on the other hand, slept very little, his mind echoing with a torrent of unanswered questions.

Chapter 5

THE LAST COMBAT

The old man was cognitively aware in body and spirit that his time here would soon be finished. He would remain long enough to welcome the full moon at the time of the dance to the sun, but he would not remain to greet the new moon, which was to follow close behind. Intensely aware of the forces old age was exerting upon him, his body was constantly at war with this unseen enemy. Although his steps were strong, he walked more slowly, with a shorter stride, aware of his body's heaviness, as well as his spirit's desire to be free of it. Old wounds, long believed healed, returned like sorrowful echoes of the pain originally accompanying them.

This season, he did not make the annual journey to the southern desert in search of rare ceremonial plants and herbs. The responsibility rested in the hands of the new shaman. Flaming Eagle gathered the harvest alone for the first time, sorrowfully aware he would continue harvesting by himself until given his own replacement. White Wolf's mind spent most of its energy remembering the past, with the present and the future becoming less important as the warm days lazily drifted by.

It was Flaming Eagle's honour and spiritual obligation to escort White Wolf to his final resting place, seen only in his vision. This fact was unimportant to the old man, who maintained complete faith in his student. The old man trusted his cousin's son with his life and, more importantly, with his death. If the truth were known, the Wicasa was very pleased not to have to think about the details of when and where he was to be buried. His only concern was how he would die; the rest was already determined. The how was for him, and him alone, to decide.

Taking advantage of his free time, White Wolf prepared himself by spending his nights in the dreamless sleep. By day, he instructed Flaming Eagle. He offered up prayers of gratitude for his life as a Lakota. Creating his own death chant, he found reciting it added to the lightness of his spirit. After finishing his evening meal, served by his spirit helper, he smoked the pipe of herbs, offering prayers to the Great Spirit on the breath of the wind, as he had always done.

Most tribes respect the sanctity of the burial grounds. Most, that is, but not all. Flaming Eagle was being guided by the Grand Father to a place where no one would ever find White Wolf's body, let alone desecrate it. His father's cousin was truly a Holy One, whose spirit will move forward, achieving new tasks, only if his bodily remains are undisturbed and at peace.

"Your spirit will take the power of the White Buffalo with it into the next world…strong medicine, indeed," Flaming Eagle proclaimed to White Wolf. "Your burial site must be protected from marauders and scavengers. The high place beyond the Sacred Mountains is where your ashes and those of the white robe will remain lying safe throughout eternity. Released from your body by fire, your spirit will freely soar, carried upon the four winds."

On the first night of the new moon, they made preparations for their last journey together. White Wolf was visited at his tipi by the entire tribe, coming a few at a time to bid him farewell. The spirit

The Quest

helpers were not the only ones having difficulty hiding their sorrow. Tears were shed by Meadow Lark, Skipping Bird, Spotted Deer and many other women. The men did their best to control their emotions, speaking to him in a normal tone of voice while maintaining their stoic facade.

After all of the others left, White Wolf, his cousin, Running Fox, and his cousin's son, Flaming Eagle, remained sitting alone, quietly talking. The chief always participated in the most pious ceremonies. The passing of a Wicasa was certainly one of those momentous occasions. Knowing he would never see his cousin again after this night, Running Fox's heart was filled with a sense of loss, and loving memories of their times together. This was a difficult moment for him.

Preparing the ceremonial pipe, Flaming Eagle handed it to the Wicasa, nodding respectfully as White Wolf accepted it. Taking a flaming stick from the campfire, the old man ignited the bowl of herbs, drawing deeply, holding the smoke for a long time. In a whisper, he released his prayers to the waiting winds of the Sacred Mountains, watching the smoke spreading itself into a thin wisp, growing less and less dense, until it finally, completely, and silently vanished into the blackness of the surrounding night.

With first light, Flaming Eagle was outside of White Wolf's tipi, waiting for the old man to emerge. They did not speak; it was unnecessary. All that needed to be said had been said. Quietly eating, they watched the new sun clearing the top of the small range of mountains far to the east. After finishing, they collected their weapons and supplies for the journey.

The nights were not as cold as they had been, allowing them to travel lighter, faster, and unencumbered. Draping the buffalo robes over the backs of the ponies not only freed their hands, it also increased the comfort level of their ride. Flaming Eagle carried his lances in the sheath Meadow Lark made for him. They slung their bows and quivers over their shoulders, resting on their backs. Each carried a knife and a tomahawk in their waistbands, and a second knife tucked into their mukluks. It was a precaution Flaming Eagle learned from his father, Running Fox, who learned it from his older cousin, White Wolf.

Riding at a slow, easy gate, they started on the path leading to the old man's final resting place. The sound of the hoof-beats on the stones along the riverbank was echoing more hollowly than usual in the uncommonly peaceful morning air. It was one of those rare days when the winds were nonexistent, allowing the other sounds of the prairie to be more clearly heard. Flowing over the rocks, the cadence of the water was lyrical. Softly drifting toward them from the opposite bank of the river came the serene song of a meadowlark.. They heard familiar sounds emanating from the village, and the rustling of small animals scurrying through the dry underbrush. Taking their time, they listened to the symphony of life all around them…subtle sounds, usually muffled by the ever-present winds. In the absence of the breeze, the sun felt hotter on their skin. Outside the camp, the stand of trees resembled stone carvings, rather than living things.

Riding past the silent sentinels, they watched beams of light streaming from the sky through the branches of the trees.

Long before sunset of the fourth day, they were moving through the foothills of the northern mountains. Thus far, it was an easy trail for Flaming Eagle to follow. This part of the vision remained crystalline, just as the actual burial stand, itself, was always clearly represented in his mind. What was missing, however, was a concise image of the trail leading from where they were to where they needed to be. This part of the vision remained unseen. Pausing, he scanned the area, signaling White Wolf to stop.

"This is where the vision becomes indistinct," Flaming Eagle told him. "Maybe we should make camp early, and I will search for the trail leading us in the right direction at morning light."

The Quest

The old man nodded his head in agreement. White Wolf proceeded to a stand of nearby trees, a green area with running water and grass for the ponies. Their luck held and there was a plentiful supply of dead wood lying around the gulch, suitable for building an evening fire. Since they had not stopped to hunt, they had been eating only dried meat and whatever edible plants, berries or roots they gathered along the way. Tonight, they decided to take advantage of making an early camp, using this opportunity to hunt.

While Flaming Eagle hunted with a bow and arrows, White Wolf used one of the young man's lances as a fishing spear. The old man was much too tired to be chasing rabbits and deer. Instead, he preferred to hunt the mountain stream for rainbow trout, a less strenuous activity, more to his present liking. Spreading a buffalo hide across a grassy area by the stream, he settled down to the spearing of fish. His luck was good; his aim was true. By sunset, he had speared six hardy rainbow trout for their evening meal. Returning to the camp, he set aside his catch, gathering twigs and small pieces of wood for the campfire. When the young man returned, the old man had a hot fire ready for cooking. Flaming Eagle had also fared well, producing four rabbits in need of skinning. White Wolf went about the business of cooking the fish, while the young man tended to the preparation of the rabbits.

First, White Wolf gutted and cleaned the trout, which were easily and quickly scaled. Pouring a little water on a pile of heavy dirt, he mixed it into a smooth mud-paste. One at a time, he encased each fish in a mud cocoon. Once they were all prepared, he buried them deep within the live coals and flames to bake.

Washing his hands, he prepared to skin one of the two remaining undressed rabbits. Tying the rodent to a low branch by its rear legs, he made the first incision down the length of its body, slitting it from groin to neck. Running the knife up the inside of each of its rear legs to the feet, he encircled each foot with the blade, separating the outer skin between the circular cuts. Making a V-shaped cut into the space between its hind legs, he cut away and removed the outer organs, tossing them aside, along with the tail. Separating the skin on the hind legs, he expertly pulled the fur down to the head and front paws of the small animal. In essence, he turned the rabbit inside out. He amputated the low front paws, and decapitated it. Making an incision at the chest, he cut upward through the stomach, allowing the internal organs and intestines to spill onto the earth.

Meanwhile, Flaming Eagle placed the first two rabbits over the fire to roast. By the time they finished skinning the last rabbit, it was time to turn the ones that were slowly basting over the lightly dancing flames. Flaming Eagle tended to the browning rabbits, while White Wolf poked at the coals, moving them around so the baking fish could receive the fullest benefit of the heat. They worked naturally well together.

They talked quietly while waiting for their food to finish cooking. Well, actually, it was White Wolf who talked and Flaming Eagle who intently listened, asking numerous questions. The old man retained more information than was possible for him to communicate to the young shaman, who was eager to hear it all, desperate to absorb as much knowledge as possible. Flaming Eagle regretted that he only had days left to spend with his Wicasa. By the time White Wolf finished digging the fish out of the coals, the rabbit was also cooked.

"Fresh-caught trout and hot, delicious rabbit! We shall eat well this night," White Wolf smiled.

Later, when White Wolf prepared the pipe, he changed the ratio of the herbs in hopes of clarifying the vision his young companion was seeking. The blend was heavier and more pungent than the standard mixture. They smoked, offering up their prayers to Wakan Tanka. Hanging in the night air, the smoke was like a cloud resting on a mountaintop. Finishing the pipe, they sat in silence, meditating, waiting for the connection to the spirit that overshadows all, hoping for an opening, a gateway into the ever-

The Quest

present now. Their wait was short, as White Wolf's new blend quickly accomplished its task. Visions immediately filled Flaming Eagle's mind, appearing in great detail.

A trail was leading them past a waterfall and into a heavily wooded forest. Although the path ended, he saw a way allowing him to reach White Wolf's burial stand. Within the vision, the old man appeared, peacefully wrapped in the white robe, resting on the lower boughs of a huge, dead tree. It was a secluded, natural burial site, guarded by a tall, circular stand of trees, a perfect funeral pyre waiting to be used.

Shifting back to the waterfall, he saw into the deep pool of clear, choppy water at its base. Behind the waterfall was an opening to a cave, hidden by the cascading water. The image became blurry, finally fading out of focus. Eventually he realized he was looking through fast running water, into an underwater passageway leading from the first cave to a another one, which was hidden twenty paces behind the first. One could only reach the opening in the floor of the second cave by swimming underwater through the dark moving current. There was an underwater entrance, large enough to accommodate two or three people, which was the only way in or out of the enclosure

Without warning, the image shattered into small fragments, like the reflecting sun shimmering in a pool of standing, clear water, which was just disturbed. Slowly, the shifting images settled into shapes of faces covered with war paint…faces of their disdained enemy, the treacherous Pawnee. Appearing were six enemy faces whose eyes were frantically searching, looking for him and White Wolf. The faces settled into whispers of mist, gradually abating into the darkness, disappearing in the surrounding night.

White Wolf's vision, on the other hand, was very peaceful.

His mind's eye filled with images of loved ones who had gone on before him. They were friendly faces, with warmth in their smiles, and love for him in their eyes. Each, in turn, was greeting him. Some paid respects to him as their Wicasa. Others were friends who had been old when he was in his early youth. But, most important and most comforting were the embraces of his family. His parents, brothers, sisters, uncles, aunts and cousins were all there with him. Among them were others he did not recognize, including the elders of his people, most of whom had passed on before he was born. He felt complete, realizing for the first time that this was what his spirit had been longing for his entire life. Now he understood what he was always missing.

Sighing with newfound contentment, he at last drifted into sleep, a deep sleep wherein he dreamed the dreams that only old men may dream.

It was late morning of the following day when they spotted the enemy. The Pawnee were riding along a ridge above them. Although they were out of hearing range, White Wolf knew by their excited pointing and jabbing that his white robe was the source of their excitement. This, in and of itself, was hardly surprising. Taking a Great White Buffalo in the hunt is an extremely rare event, and word of it spreads over the plains like the wind. Such news is sure to lure scavengers looking to steal a valuable prize they are unworthy of possessing. They knew, sooner or later, worthy or not, when the time seemed right, the Pawnee would make their move. Now, obviously having been spotted, sooner appeared much more likely than later. The braves on the ridge shouted out war cries and threats while searching for a path leading to the forest floor, and to the white robe.

Signaling White Wolf to follow him, the young shaman headed for a path leading through the trees. It was the path shown to him in his vision. They were snaking their way quickly through the heavy mass of trees when, all of a sudden, Flaming Eagle stopped. Dismounting, he motioned for White Wolf to grab the robe and do the same. Seizing the white buffalo robe, the old man followed him into the thicket. Once they were safely hidden, the Wicasa took the robe and securely stuffed it under the thick underbrush. Flaming Eagle spread

The Quest

his brown buffalo hide over the top of it, and they proceeded to camouflage the robes with available brush and fallen tree branches.

Immediately upon completion of their task, backtracking, they used small branches as brooms to erase all signs of ever having passed that way. Remounting their ponies, they rode at a hard gallop through the thickly wooded area to the path leading to the waterfall. It was important they stay far enough ahead to keep the Pawnee unaware that the robe was no longer in White Wolf's possession.

Upon reaching the waterfall, they dismounted. White Wolf followed the younger warrior's lead, and also secured his bow and arrows to his pony. In the type of battle they would be waging, these weapons would be of no use to them. Taking two lances from his sheath, Flaming Eagle threw one of them to the old man. With the lance in his hand, the young brave dove into the icy pool, with White Wolf following right behind him. The coldness of the water stunned them breathless, momentarily, before they were able to start swimming toward the waterfall and the mouth of the first cave.

Once behind the sheeting water, they scrambled onto the ledge, preparing themselves for what was predestined. They did not have long to wait. The voices on the other side of the waterfall were very close to where they were hiding. As the voices got closer, the two Lakota warriors backed away from the slippery lip of the ledge. Standing with their lances poised to strike, they waited for the inevitable attack, watching the dark shadow swimming underwater toward them.

Popping his head up out of the water, the Pawnee was shocked as White Wolf drove his lance deep into his enemy's chest. Exploding from his torso, the blood gushed into the surrounding water. In disbelief, choking on his own blood, the wounded brave stared at the Wicasa, distraught with the realization that he was dying at the hands of a very old man. Withdrawing his lance, White Wolf plunged it into the Pawnee's neck with a force that pushed the vanguard brave back into the waterfall. His blood mixed with the churning water flowing into the pool, immediately drawing the attention of the warriors who were scouring the rocky areas around the pool. The blood leaking onto their side of the cascading waterfall ignited their curiosity as to what might be behind it. Now was time for Flaming Eagle and White Wolf to leave, and depart they did.

Sliding into the churning water, they swam under the lip of the cave, away from the falls. The water, which was growing colder and darker, numbed their bodies while making it increasingly difficult to see. On the verge of running out of light and air, they spotted a small, bright, glowing speck beckoning to them from within the center of the darkness. Swimming as fast as they could, they arrived at the mouth of the second cave simultaneously. The instant their heads cleared water, they gasped for breath in unison.

To their surprise and relief, the air was fresh and breathable. Looking around, they spotted a hole in the side of the cave, the source of the sunlight and air filling the cave. Pulling themselves out of the water and onto the cold, rock floor, they lay resting until they could breathe easily. Once recuperated, they did the only thing they could do…wait. By this time, there was no doubt their pursuers had found the first cave. Flaming Eagle was hoping the bloody lance left behind by White Wolf convinced the Pawnee that they had drowned. In silence, they anxiously waited.

Feeling enough time passed, Flaming Eagle decided to carefully return to the waterfall in order to determine if their pursuers were still searching for them. It was agreed that White Wolf would remain waiting in the cave until Flaming Eagle returned for him, once he ascertained it was safe. He checked his weapons, making a quick inventory to ensure he was properly armed. Except for his lance, which he gave to White Wolf, his weaponry was intact.

Taking several quick breaths and one very deep one, he inhaled as much air as he could hold before diving into the frigid water. Once he adjusted to the chill, he looked for the light streaming into the pool from the other side of the falls. He searched the dark under-area

THE QUEST

of the first cave for any sign of the attackers. Seeing none, he swam under the rushing sheet of water, emerging on the outside of the waterfall, blinded by the glaring sun.

Cautiously raising his head above water, he waited for his eyes to readjust to the light. Carefully searching the area, he saw nothing indicating his pursuers were in the vicinity. He continued scanning the shoreline, cautiously swimming to the bank, and then surveyed the surrounding area. Seeing no sign of the enemy, he became suspicious, noticing the two Lakota ponies standing exactly where they were tied earlier.

"There is no way they would go away without taking the ponies." he thought.

Warily, he crawled out of the water, while inspecting the landscape. Although he did not see them, he sensed the Pawnee were nearby, watching him. He was certain they were waiting for him to retrieve the white robe before attacking. "At least one of them will be hiding near the ponies, waiting for us to return," he thought. Silently, making his way to the tree line, he entered at an angle, following a path leading away from the ponies.

Avoiding dry twigs, stepping as lightly as possible, he judiciously located himself into position a safe distance beyond the ponies. He stopped, perusing the terrain for any sign of the hidden enemy. As the area appeared to be safe, he circled through the trees in a pattern taking him closer to the waiting horses and, more importantly, the rest of his weapons. If this was to be to a fight in the open, his bow and arrows were now highly desirable. He made his way toward the ponies, constantly alert for the ones lying in wait to ambush him. Stopping, he pressed his body close to a tree and listened.

"There it is again," he confirmed to himself. It was the soft snapping sound of small twigs shattering under foot, just a few trees to his left. One of his pursuers was working his way closer to the waiting ponies. Flaming Eagle deliberately tiptoed backward, easing his way around the tree, still monitoring the approaching footsteps.

Slipping around to the backside of the trunk, he breathlessly waited. Then, as the Pawnee brave tried sneaking past his position, the Lakota brave attacked.

Wrapping his left arm firmly around the neck of his prey to silence him, the shaman drew his knife from his waistband. Reaching around his enemy's flailing arms, Flaming Eagle drove the knife directly into the Pawnee's chest. He felt resistance from the man's rib cage; but, as the knife forced its way deeper into the cracking ribs, the tension gave way. His plunging knife penetrated a heart that was no longer pumping. The dead warrior went limp in Flaming Eagle's arms, his slumping body making a dull, thudding sound as it crumpled to the ground. "Assuming I was accurate in my original count," he thought, "only four more of them remain out there…somewhere."

"If we are going to get out of this encounter alive, I will need assistance. I must signal the old man in the way I have been trained, using a technique that will reach him immediately." Searching the area until he was convinced he was alone momentarily, he carefully worked his way underneath the low hanging branches of a nearby tree. Safely hidden within the refuge of the pine, he sat on the firm ground. Taking a long, deep breath, he began his meditation. Quieting his thoughts quickly, he allowed his mind to drift into the timeless oneness, gradually raising his awareness to the level of the light which connects all living spirits.

Finding the peace that always resides within, he expanded his mind, reaching out to the consciousness of the Wicasa, where he remained waiting in the secret cave. He intuitively projected an image, a strong vision of the old shaman's presence here with him. He created a picture in his mind of White Wolf standing next to their ponies, with his bow and arrows in his hands, ready to do battle.

Maintaining the discipline of his meditation, he held this image for as long as it was safe for him to do so. Sensing the enemy close

The Quest

by, he knew it would be wise to return his attention to his immediate surroundings, and keep on moving.

White Wolf grew impatient waiting for the return of the young shaman. When Flaming Eagle failed to return within what White Wolf considered a reasonable length of time, he became concerned for his young companion's well being. He was aware of what they had agreed to, and why they had chosen to do so; however, he understood that the situation might have drastically changed. Knowing he was safely hidden in the cave, he set aside his lance. Sitting with his legs intertwined and his arms crossed over his chest, he breathed deeply, slowly quieting his thoughts. Soon, his mind and the light were merging into one. Within a few moments, the first manifestation appeared.

Originally faint and unclear, the image slowly clarified into a discernable picture of Flaming Eagle eliminating the Pawnee who was attempting to sneak up on the ponies.

The vision confirmed the safety of Flaming Eagle, thereby lightening the old man's heart. However, he remained unsure as to what his cousin's son wished him to do. Eagerly he waited for whatever other images might manifest. His time of waiting was short. Very soon, images were solidifying within the mistiness of his mind.

The form of their ponies was taking shape in the swirling light. The image of the horses grew steadily clearer, as he saw himself standing next to them, armed for battle. Despite the fact the old man could not see him, it was obvious Flaming Eagle was nearby, watching over him. Sensing danger all around them, he continued waiting to see if there might be more information within the vision. When he sensed nothing more forthcoming from Flaming Eagle, he comprehended his cousin's son's request.

Gently he guided his mind back into the present time and place. He would have to be extremely cautious, once he left the protection of the cave, cognizant of the danger awaiting him in the woods.

"Flaming Eagle's chances of survival will be greatly enhanced if the two of us can combine our forces against the remaining Pawnee," he affirmed. Securing his hand weapons, he picked up his lance and diving into the icy water, he eagerly hurried toward the awaiting battle…the battle which was destined to be his last combat.

Chapter 6

THE FINAL OFFERING

Flaming Eagle watched the old man stealthily making his way through the scrub brush and into the trees, cautiously approaching the ponies that were bait for the Pawnee trap, which was waiting for the exact right moment to be sprung. The young warrior scanned the area, continuously searching for the hidden enemy. Stopping, he fixed his gaze upon the thick underbrush, only thirty paces away, as the rustling sounds grew steadily louder. Emerging noisily from the thicket was a Pawnee brave, armed with a bow and arrow, taking deadly aim at White Wolf. Flaming Eagle had not yet retrieved his own bow, leaving his tomahawk and knives as the only weapons at his disposal. He was very good with a tomahawk, but he was even better with a knife. Swiftly his hand went to his belt and, as he grabbed the handle of the knife, he let the blade slide up into the palm of his hand. Grasping the blade, in one continuous motion, he raised the weapon to the height of his head to a spot slightly behind the crown. With his arm coming forward, he let it fly, hurling it directly at his enemy. With deadly accuracy, the blade bit into the Pawnee's back, just below his left shoulder blade. The shocked brave stood motionless for a heart beat, then, making a soft grunting sound, he toppled, face-first, into the heavy brush.

White Wolf, turning toward the sound of the fallen warrior, barely avoided an arrow zipping past his head, embedding into the tree trunk next to him. Quickly grabbing both sets of bows and arrows from the backs of the ponies, the old man raced as fast as he could to where Flaming Eagle was waiting for him. He threw a bow and a quiver of arrows to his companion before taking refuge behind a large log, just as another arrow came cutting through the air, slamming into the fallen tree.

Flaming Eagle, slipping the notch of an arrow into the string, pulled the bow halfway back and waited for the enemy to expose himself.

The Lakota warrior watched the Pawnee archer sneaking out from behind a tree, preparing to let loose another shaft. Extending the arch of his bow, Flaming Eagle released the flying death which, sailing true to its course, struck the Pawnee in the chest, just below his neck. Slumping to his knees, the dead warrior sprawled lifelessly to the ground.

Through the branches of a tree behind them, a silent arrow came winging its way toward them, finding its home in White Wolf's left shoulder. The biting tip cut deeply into his brown, bare flesh. Hearing the sound of his collarbone snapping, he felt the pain of his ripping flesh as the arrowhead emerged from his back. Whether the Pawnee had not seen Flaming Eagle or momentarily forgot about him made little difference. In either case, the enemy brave came rushing at the Wicasa, his lance poised, preparing to skewer the old man. The young Lakota warrior let loose another arrow which lodged in the charging brave's right thigh, causing him to plummet to the ground. Scrambling to his feet, trying desperately to regain his footing, the Pawnee raised his weapon, resuming his attack on White Wolf.

Grabbing the old man's lance, Flaming Eagle launched it at the assassin. He watched it sailing twenty paces through the air, embedding itself in the Pawnee's mid-section, piercing his lower

The Quest

abdomen and slashing through his intestines. A large gush of blood spurted out of the wound, as the head of the lance, carrying pieces of his intestines, protruded from his back. The dying man automatically clutched the shaft of the weapon, as if to dislodge it. Stopping suddenly, he stood motionless, as his eyes glazed over, gazing into the nothingness stretching endlessly in front of him. Releasing his hands from the shaft of the lance, the Pawnee fell lifelessly to the ground.

Turning toward the old man, Flaming Eagle saw White Wolf signaling he was all right. As if of one mind, the men searched the area, anxiously seeking the one remaining brave. Hearing a noise at the edge of the clearing, they turned in time to observe the last of their enemies running toward safety and away from the battle. Flaming Eagle let loose two more arrows, even though moving targets were never his strength as an archer. The Pawnee was last seen running on foot into the woods on the far side of the lake, never looking back to see if he was being pursued. Lowering his head, he ran as if his life depended upon it, which it most certainly did. Escaping unscathed, the coward disappeared.

With their final enemy fleeing, the young warrior turned his attention to his injured teacher. The wound was serious, much more so than the old man had led Flaming Eagle to believe. Kneeling next to White Wolf, he closely inspected the damage. It was obvious the arrow had cut through several veins, causing internal bleeding. His attempt to remove the arrow was stopped by the old warrior. Shaking his head slowly, the old man smiled, aware of the severity of his condition. "There is nothing either of us can do to alter the natural flow of events about to unfold," he said to his solemn companion. "I will continue bleeding internally, growing progressively weaker, until I can no longer cling to life. It is the way of things," he smiled.

Flaming Eagle broke off the protruding piece of the arrow, leaving the remaining shaft in the wound, allowing it to slow down the old man's loss of blood. The young shaman bound White Wolf's wound tightly before gently helping him to his feet. Carefully, they made their way back to where the ponies were waiting. Mounting his horse was exceedingly painful; however, with Flaming Eagle's assistance, the wounded man eventually accomplished it. Once mounted, they rode slowly northward. Fortunately, they did not have far to go, and were confident of reaching their destination prior to nightfall.

The tree where they had hidden the robe was easily located. Dismounting, Flaming Eagle made his way to the stashed White Buffalo robe. He brushed away leaves and debris, and removed the brown buffalo pelt, exposing the hidden burial robe, which he retrieved and proudly returned to the old man. Returning for the second hide, slinging it over his shoulder and smiling victoriously, he leisurely strolled back to where White Wolf was waiting.

When Flaming Eagle arrived, he observed the old man unfolding the white hide. Carefully removing the Sacred Bundle, White Wolf smiled with relief, confirming that it was still safe and secure. Beaming gratefully, he glanced at his young companion, and, with no further explanation, he simply stated, "We can go now." Flaming Eagle was silent, only nodding in agreement.

For the first time, Flaming Eagle realized how exhausted he was.

Remounting his paint with a great deal of effort, he encouraged Pawnee to work through the thickening trees. The fatigued warriors rode until coming upon an open expanse of land, which, though not large, was sufficient for a campsite. Possessing an ample supply of smoked, dried meat and fresh water, all they needed was fuel, and the area was plentifully supplied with usable firewood. He called a halt to their journey, as the burial stand was within easy walking distance. The site was safe and secluded, and it would be a comfortable camp during the long night that lay ahead of them.

After helping the old man dismount, Flaming Eagle spread a robe on the grass, making a place for White Wolf to recline. Checking the older warrior's shoulder, he carefully removed the bloody bandage, replacing it with a clean cloth, using torn strips to tightly bind the wound. Having attended to his companion, the young medicine

The Quest

man turned his attention to gathering wood and chips for a fire. The task was accomplished quickly, and within a short time, he had the makings of a respectable campfire.

Hobbling the horses for the night, he then made a place for himself near the old man next to the fire. Serving the food and water for their evening meal, they ate in silence, each remaining within his own contemplations. Their thoughts, however, concerned the same thing: White Wolf's death. After all, he had come to this place to die. His enemy, the Pawnee, lent a helping hand, thus ensuring a successful achievement of his goal. The travelers knew the old Wicasa would not survive another full day.

After eating, Flaming Eagle took the pouches of herbs, crushing and blending them for use in their evening devotion. Meticulously, he filled the bowl with the fresh mixture. Lighting the prayer pipe, his heart was heavy, knowing this was the last time they would smoke together. It was his final night to be in the company of his Wicasa. He did his best to hide his sorrow, but the old man was not at all deceived by his student's pretense. White Wolf quietly watched the young shaman ceremoniously take the first draw of the herbs, holding the smoke for a long time before releasing it with his prayers to the four winds, for conveyance to Wakan Tanka. Once he completed his invocation to the Great Spirit, he placed the pipe into the hands of White Wolf, who inhaled deeply of the smoke, releasing it as homage to the Grand Father. The silence hung in the air until broken by the spoken word of White Wolf.

"I have taught you all of the secrets of the herbs and plants, except for this one thing. It is time for you to learn the mystery of the rare Desert Blood, the red flowers, which, as you know, grow sparsely only in the southern desert." Flaming Eagle scooted closer to the fire. Crossing his legs, he leaned forward, intently listening to White Wolf's words. "The five petals of the blossom are to be gently removed, one at a time. They are to be dried slowly, safely out of the direct rays of the desert sun." Reverently, he recited the prayers to be used when crushing the dried petals, pulverizing them by rubbing them between the palms of the hands.

"By this process, the potency of the flower immediately blends with the essence of the one who is to use them. The flowers have the power to send one far into the land of the spirits. It is a dangerous journey, even for one who is familiar with the deceptions and hazards along the path leading in and out of the spirit realm. The flowers are to be used sparingly, and only when the need of the people is great or during extremely important ceremonies.

"Desert Blood is not generally blended with other herbs; however, when it is added to the ritual blend, it is to be layered between the pomatote and the sage. The smoke is held as long as possible before releasing it to the prairie breezes. The pipe is to be smoked until the petals are completely consumed. This practice is to be performed only at a time when your mind is clear, your emotions are at rest, and your spirit is pure and at peace. You have seen the results of the misuse of their power in the downfall of Thunder Eyes."

They conversed long into the night, even after White Wolf completed his instructions on the proper preparation and the prudent use of the potent petals of Desert Blood. Remaining awake, they reminisced about Flaming Eagle's early days of training with his three friends. The death of Short Bear was spoken of with great sorrow. "But he died the death of a Lakota," said White Wolf. The young shaman slowly shook his head in agreement. They reexamined the possible meanings of each of the visions the boys had seen.

Following a long pause, they spoke of the link established between them earlier in the day. Talking, eventually fitting the pieces of the incident into a discernable pattern of sequences, they managed to patch together a decipherable, coherent meaning of their experience. Each had known for a long time that they shared a special connection, but neither of them had ever experienced a bonding as strong or clear as the one occurring today. Such a contact, having once been

The Quest

established, would continue on, with only a slightly lesser degree of intensity.

They talked until their bodies surrendered to the tiredness overtaking them, eventually drifting into a very light sleep. White Wolf was suffering the effects of his wounds. Flaming Eagle was dreading the arrival of the morning sun. The old Wicasa grew weaker during the course of his short night's sleep, the shoulder wound throbbing with searing pain, growing more intense with each pulsation of his heart. No longer able to accompany the young warrior any farther, he decided to stay behind in the morning, waiting at the campsite, while Flaming Eagle prepared the burial stand to receive the old man's physical remains.

White Wolf stationed himself by the comforting fire, resting up for his final journey. Refusing food, he replenished himself with a few sips of cool water. He was comfortable with the fact that, very soon, he would have no further need for food or water. Reclining there, he accepted as inevitable the aching in his knees and the fire in his hip sockets. The fogginess in his head was a cloud, keeping his mind from synchronizing with his body and his environment. His stomach felt as though it were being stomped upon by a raging buffalo, and his skin was fiery to the touch. Breathing became more laboured with each breath he inhaled. Hoping Flaming Eagle would complete his task soon and return, the old man was acutely aware that he was rapidly running out of time.

After finishing his morning meal, Flaming Eagle trudged into the thickening grove on foot. Instinctively following an invisible path, he arrived at the tree he had been shown in his image. There was the burial location, the tree, the branches, the abundance of dried wood… all of it, exactly as he had seen in his vision. It was as if the Great Spirit, Himself, had built it, patiently awaiting the arrival of His old friend. The two large lower branches, almost an equal distance from the ground, were separated by the length of two paces…a perfect size for the old man's bed. The site was almost complete, making it easy to finish the needed preparations quickly. After securing together four fist-sized thick branches, providing a surface on which to lay the old man, he went about gathering the fuel necessary for the funeral pyre.

Above the death cradle was a hanging branch, draping all the way to the ground. Flaming Eagle viewed the work of man and nature, thinking with satisfaction, "Soon, the branch will be a flaming canopy, covering the stand, and White Wolf's physical remains will be veiled from the eyes of men for all time. Resting safely, his ashes will never be disturbed. His body will return to the four elements from which it came, forever nourishing the earth. My father's cousin's spirit will henceforth be free to safely dream its eternal dream."

Completing his work, the young shaman made his way back to the camp where the old Wicasa awaited him. He described in great detail the natural burial stand within the protection of nature, which was the manifestation of his vision. Pausing for a moment, touching the old man's face, Flaming Eagle determined the fever was no better than it was before he left. In fact, White Wolf's face was feeling even hotter to the touch now. He offered water to the wounded man, who took a few small sips. Meanwhile, Flaming Eagle poured water onto a piece of cloth and cooled the old shaman's face.

Picking up the brown robe and throwing it over his shoulder, Flaming Eagle returned to the stand. He spread the robe on the bed of thick branches he had laid out earlier. Once finished, he returned quickly to his Wicasa.

White Wolf was sitting, chanting, as he painstakingly unfolded the white robe. Drawing the Sacred Bundle from its resting place, he lifted it above his head as far as his arms would allow. He motioned for Flaming to join him.

"My last official act as your Wicasa is to pass on the Sacred Bundle. From this time forward, it is your honour, blessing and sacred responsibility to safeguard it unto death. In time, if the Grand

The Quest

Father so wills it, you, in turn, will give it into the keeping of your own successor."

Flaming Eagle hesitated, reluctant to receive the Bundle.

"Why do you not accept? Why do you resist?" White wolf inquired.

"I do not feel worthy to become its guardian," he replied.

"Good!" the old man sagely smiled. "That is how I know you are worthy. In time, you will come to terms with yourself and acknowledge that you are deserving of the task."

Accepting the Sacred Bundle, Flaming Eagle pondered aloud, "What if, when my time comes to join the ancestors, I have no successor? What should I do? How will I know the best way to safeguard it?"

"You will not," replied the old man "The Grand Father will. He, as always, will guide your actions."

Content that he received all the information forthcoming, he assisted White Wolf in achieving an upright stance, and collected the old man's weapons. Draping the bow and quiver of arrows over the wounded man's good shoulder, he helped the old warrior tuck his tomahawk and favorite knife into his waistband. He handed the ancient warrior his lance, which he used as a cane on his walk to the stand of trees and the funeral pyre. Flaming Eagle wrapped White Wolf in the white robe, and, placing his arm around him, slowly guided the Wicasa to his final resting place.

Even though it was not far, the trip was difficult for White Wolf. Supporting himself by holding onto the younger man while leaning on the lance, he made his way as best he could. The internal bleeding was causing his body to bloat, and walking was becoming more painful with each advancing step. Struggling for his very breath, his body was weighted down by a lifetime of service to the people. His feet were numb and lifeless, and he was experiencing a tingling sensation in the tips of his fingers.

Mentally, White Wolf was inundated with floating visions from his past. Most of the images were of deceased relatives and old friends, making it extremely difficult to maintain his thoughts in present time. He was remembering his parents, along with fleeting flashes of his early childhood. There were the faces of boys that grew up with him. Among the faces, he remembered the men with whom he had gone hunting, and the warriors with whom he had ridden into battle. White Wolf was greatly relieved when they finally arrived at the clearing in front of the funeral tree. Here he could rest for a while.

Standing on a large, exposed root of the gigantic tree gave Flaming Eagle easy access to White Wolf's death cradle. He placed the old man's lance, bow, and the quiver of arrows on the hide covering the dried fir branches, which he had spread earlier. "White Wolf's tomahawk and knife will remain on his person," he thought. "He will enter into the spirit world wearing his ceremonial headdress. His every day pipe, filled with freshly blended herbs, will be placed in his hands, which will be crossed over his abdomen." The old man had long since surrendered the ceremonial pipe to Flaming Eagle for safekeeping.

The sun was high by the time the final preparations were nearing completion, and soon they would chant the burial prayers together. Although time was of the essence, they did not allow this to interfere with conducting the ceremony properly. Finishing their prayer to the Grand Father, they continued the preparations for White Wolf's passage into the spirit world of his ancestors.

With Flaming Eagle's help, the old man struggled to his feet as they made their way toward the tree. Upon reaching the burial site, they stopped, allowing White Wolf a moment to rest. His breathing was growing increasingly more shallow and erratic. With every breath, he felt the pain in his lungs more intensely, and he was releasing large amounts of moisture through his perspiration. Although. his skin was saturated with sweat, he felt winter cold, shivering in the warmth of the midday sun. Blinding shafts of light streamed down

The Quest

onto the shadowy earth below, reflecting off the softly turning leaves. The entire tree was ablaze with a glowing, mystical haze.

Flaming Eagle led the Wicasa to the protruding tree root. Gently holding White Wolf's legs and pressing his shoulder into the old man's buttocks, he boosted him onto the covered stand. Once White Wolf was safely within the branches, the young brave went around to the side of the trunk and, using a low branch as a stepping-stone, ascended into the boughs of the great tree. Quickly, he made his way to White Wolf and eased the old man onto the prepared pallet. Taking his time, he was careful to ensure that everything needed for the Wicasa's journey was in his possession.

Once satisfied that all was in readiness, he carefully covered the old man with the magnificent robe of the Great White Buffalo. It was at this moment that Flaming Eagle finally understood the reason for this splendid covering. "The purpose of the sacred robe is not to cover White Wolf so as to make him presentable and worthy of being received by the Great Spirit. No. The Grand Father always welcomes his Holy Ones home, His arms wide open to them. Indeed, the old man is already a gift, deserving of acceptance. In truth, it is imperative that the covering be as noble as the gift, itself." Pulling the white robe up, even with White Wolf's neck, he tucked it tightly around the old Wicasa's shoulders, ensuring his warmth throughout eternity. They remained in silence until the sun began descending toward the horizon.

Taking a dried red petal of the Desert Blood from his pouch, Flaming Eagle slipped it into the dying man's mouth. The petal was still dissolving on his tongue when White Wolf first heard her howling at the rising full moon, which was making its presence known in the approaching twilight. After yipping a few times, she wailed her fullthroated night cry to the silvery sphere. Struggling, the old man turned his face in her direction. The she-wolf stood out like a white shadow of reflecting light against a sky no longer playing host to the sun.

"My old friend," he murmured. "After all of this time, you have returned to say 'goodbye' to your name sake, White Wolf. I have missed you. I hope the Grand Father has been kind to you."

"Grand Father," the old man prayed, "long have I tread the path that You set me upon in my youth. I am tired, and at long last have come to the end of my journey. Now that You have chosen a new Holy One, my final prayer is that You guide him along his way, as You have always guided me. Watch over him, as You have watched over me. Guide his feet along the way and keep him strong, that he may successfully safeguard the spirit of Your people and serve Your will."

Motioning for Flaming Eagle to lean closer, the old man whispered quietly to him. Finishing his words, he laid his head down on the brown robe lining the bed of his final resting place. Looking up at the young man, White Wolf smiled broadly. The light in his eyes flared up momentarily, then faded into eternity as he closed them forever.

Flaming Eagle turned his attention toward the white she-wolf, remembering the story of how his father's cousin was renamed White Wolf when he was a small child. Deeds earning a warrior a new name are usually achieved in early manhood. Not so with White Wolf. The animal sought him out for a healing when he was very young. Such a visitation from a wounded wolf had been unheard of prior to her seeking out the boy. Looking at the full moon, now free of the horizon, the young man listened as the she-wolf continued her lamentation for the passing of the old man.

"Has she returned to bid White Wolf farewell," Flaming Eagle wondered, "or has she come to welcome him home?"

The young shaman sat in the tree with the old man's body late into the night. When the full moon reached the center of the sky, he slowly walked to the small, smoldering fire in the clearing. Lighting a torch from the coals, he returned to the funeral tree. He touched the glowing stick to the stack of dried wood, quickly igniting the pyre, which immediately encased the old man's remains in flames.

The Quest

Even while chanting the prayers, Flaming Eagle was certain White Wolf was remaining faithful in his duties to his people. As his body was being consumed by the blazing tree, White Wolf's spirit, carried by the smoke, was the old man's last offering to Wakan Tanka. It was his final prayer, which he was delivering in person. Continuing to chant the prayers taught to him by his companion and friend, the young shaman remained with the old man until the flames were diminishing embers. Content that he had properly performed his soulful duty, Flaming Eagle retraced his footsteps to the campsite they had shared just the night before.

Upon returning to the camp, Flaming Eagle rebuilt the fire and attended to the needs of the ponies. Once they had been cared for, he sat quietly adding wood to his fire, a few twigs at a time. He would sorely miss the old man and his wisdom. Over the passing seasons, White Wolf had become as important in Flaming Eagle's life as his own father. It was Running Fox who taught him the skills necessary to become a formidable warrior, including the art of using the bow and arrow and the proficient use of the lance with deadly accuracy. Both his stealth and cunning as a hunter and a warrior were the results of Running Fox's instruction. Although Flaming Eagle and his friends studied with White Wolf since they were very young, the old man's influence on their lives was minor…minor that is, until the time of preparing for their rite of passage.

What Flaming Eagle learned from White Wolf during the many winters since then was to face life's challenges, and to walk in any dark forest alone, without fear. Inheriting the secrets of the herbs and the art of healing, he was taught how to serve his people, not only as a warrior, but as their medicine man. The old man often maneuvered him into situations where he was forced into making extremely difficult decisions. White Wolf never uttered a word to him as to what he should or should not do when Thunder Eyes ran the gauntlet. However, Flaming Eagle was confident he had seen confirmation in his Wicasa's eyes that he had chosen correctly. There were many occasions when he found it easy to make the right decisions by simply following the old man's example.

Recalling the trips they had shared gave him a feeling of great pleasure. Smiling to himself, he remembered the close calls they experienced, both independently and together, on their journeys. The gift of the pipe, their nightly prayers to the Grand Father, the many discussions when White Wolf imparted his wisdom…there were so many memories remaining forever on his mind and in his heart. He was struck with a sobering fact. "Tonight, and henceforth, I will smoke the pipe alone!"

Rebuilding the fire, he retrieved the blankets from the ponies' backs. Despite being the moon of the sun dance, the nights this far north carried a chill when the northern winds were blowing. He proceeded preparing his offering to the Great Spirit. Drawing more deeply and slowly of the mixture, he held the smoke in his lungs for as long as he could before releasing it. The camp area was well protected from the wind by the shelter of the surrounding trees, allowing the smoke to remain thick as it gently drifted on the soft air currents. The smoke swirling upward from his pipe merged with the smoke from the campfire. It was a good omen. The effortless intermingling of the two into one was seen by Flaming Eagle as a message of acceptance by the Great Spirit.

Finishing his pipe, he packed it safely with the rest of his belongings. Sitting with his back resting against an old tree trunk, he reviewed the events of the day, being especially drawn to the peaceful image of White Wolf at the time of his death., his skin bathed in radiant light. "I remember how he smiled, looking deep into my eyes as his spirit departed, returning home at the end of his life's journey." Flaming Eagle listened again to the last words of wisdom whispered to him by White Wolf, offering comfort and cheer to the young man's grieving heart, as he struggled with his overwhelming sense of loss: "It is a good day to die."

Epilogue

The old man carefully unwrapped his prayer pipe. It was not the highly decorated ceremonial one passed down through countless generations of medicine men. No. This one was quite different from the revered ritual pipe left in his beloved sacred Black Hills for safekeeping, in the care of Meadow Lark and the other spirit helpers. No. This was the one his teacher, White Wolf, made for him many long winters ago.

Holding it in his hands, Flaming Eagle pondered, "Soon, it will it be my turn to make an everyday pipe for Crowfoot, whom I have chosen to follow me as shaman. Even though he is of mixed blood, he is Lakota, being the son of Running Moon. His spirit is strong and, like his mother and grandmother, his mind is quick. He is a good choice, and one of whom my people can be proud" The choice of Crowfoot was timely, as the boy had recently begun his training in earnest to become a Sioux warrior.

His decision of choosing a new medicine man provided him with some relief. However, the question of whether or not his people would be given a new Holy One preyed on his mind. Daily, he searched for a sign. Nightly, he prayed, "Where is the one who is to replace me after I am gone? There are so many things I need to teach him in preparation for his long, arduous journey as a Wicasa."

Returning his attention to the matter at hand, Flaming Eagle chanted, passing the pipe meticulously over the flames four times, purifying it for use. Extracting the four pouches of sacred herbs from his waistband, he carefully opened them, reverently blending them in a wooden bowl, as he had been doing for over thirty winters. Taking the mixture, one pinch at a time, he firmly packed it into the bowl. Using a small, burning stick from the campfire, he lit the pipe as he had throughout his adult life. He offered up his words on the smoke, which would be conveyed by the four winds to the Great Spirit in thanksgiving for His plentiful bounties.

The passage of time was deeply etched into his brown skin. Although his face and his body were showing the signs of aging, the spirit in his eyes was burning as brightly as ever. Drawing deeply of the mixture in the bowl, he held the smoke, focusing his prayers within the quietness of his mind. The gentle evening breeze carried his invocation on the smoke to Wakan Tanka, the Great Spirit, Protector of his people. He watched the smoke filling the empty spaces between the distant stars, at peace within himself and in harmony with his environment. Sighing deeply, he continued his nightly devotion.

"Grandfather, the trail of the Holy One You placed me upon has been long and hard. I have done my best to guide my people, as You have guided me. I thank You for giving me the strength and wisdom to watch over Your people, and to serve them." The old Wicasa released the smoke and waited in silence.

In the far distance, Flaming Eagle heard the mournful, echoing calls of wolves wandering freely in the southern plains. Sitting crosslegged, smoking his pipe, he prayed for the one who was to follow in his footsteps, as he had followed in the footsteps of White Wolf. Like his teacher before him, he was born to the responsibility, an extremely difficult trail to navigate. "It will take a special brave,

The Quest

one with the rare courage to walk this less traveled road," he thought. Taking another long, deep draw of the herbs, and releasing the smoke on the soft breeze, he sat in silence, awaiting a sign from the Grand Father. "Who is to be my replacement?" he repeated while drifting into the waking sleep.

Fading in and out, his thoughts were like the smoke from his pipe. He retreated to the safety of the cave within, here hoping to be touched by the Great Spirit. Soon his mind filled with the bright, clear blueness, as his spirit was drawn into the illuminating clarity, merging into oneness with it, like the blending of smoke and air. Soaring freely within the light, he awaited an answer.

Slowly, a faint vision took shape within the mistiness, at first appearing as little more than a white haze. Watching intently, he saw the blurriness shifting into a landscape of snow. Through the drifting flurries, he saw a cavern nestled in the south side of the hills.

Lumbering out of the thicket of spruce came two large, furry bears, like shadows moving slowly, advancing on the cave. They stopped, looking briefly in his direction; then, turning their backs, headed for the shelter. The interior was more than large enough to accommodate them. Curling up close to each other for extra warmth, they settled down for their long sleep of winter. The bears peeked at Flaming Eagle through half-opened eyes and then, with a slight shrug of their massive shoulders, dismissed him completely. Closing their eyes, they quickly descended into a warm slumber.

The soft flakes drifting down from the sky decreased as the winds dissipated. Slowly the image of winter melted, transforming into the picture of a bright, early-spring day. The bears remained peacefully slumbering as a small boy wandered onto the lush, green, prairie grass at the mouth of their cave. From the way the child walked, it was apparent he had seen no more than two winters. Coming into clearer focus, Flaming Eagle recognized the toddler as Running Moon's son, Crowfoot.

The little boy, struggling to maintain his balance, went staggering head-first into the cave, where he paused, staring at the large, living, bearskin rugs. Without hesitation, Crowfoot wedged himself comfortably in between the snoring bears, who did not seem to mind their new sleeping companion. If the truth be told, they barely acknowledged his presence. The three of them lay there, with the youngster in the middle, warm, safe and content.

The scene was once more decimated with harsh winds and driving snow, completely obscuring the three sleeping companions. As before, the vision changed seasons, this time repeatedly, until at last the image settled into a clear, bright morning. To his surprise, stepping out of the cave was not the toddler he had watched going in, but the figure of a young warrior. Looking long and hard, the old man eventually recognized Crowfoot as a brave, carrying the scars on his chest from the Sun Dance. At his feet was the headdress of the Wicasa, Flaming Eagle's own white buffalo skull.

The young man looked down, studying the headdress, unwilling to claim the sacred object. Bending down, almost touching it, he immediately withdrew. Repeating his effort, he attempted to retrieve it two more times. After an extremely long pause, Crowfoot tried again for the fourth and final time. Overcoming his internal struggle, he respectfully lifted the skull slowly from the ground, exposing the Sacred Bundle as he did. Holding the Bundle in one hand, he placed the headdress of the Wicasa on his head. There he stood silently, slowly growing older, until he evolved into a man of over fifty winters.

The old man watched the image spinning faster and faster, gradually accelerating until it exploded into nothingness. "Wakan Tanka has clearly shown me who is to be the heir to my wisdom and guardian of my people's spirit," he thought with gratitude and relief. "Tomorrow I will begin training the grandson of Meadow Lark, Crowfoot, who is to be renamed Two Bears Sleeping. Two Bears Sleeping will follow in my footsteps, just as I followed in those of White Wolf." Content and at peace, Flaming Eagle descended into a tranquil sleep, dreaming of his youth, childhood friends, and his carefree days of play. Once more, he was flying like his namesake, the eagle.

The Quest

As it had always been, even after all the long, lonely winters that aged him, he dreamed of Sleeping Possum. Together, they wandered happily through his memories of that comforting time. Even in sleep, he smiled, recalling their very first encounter at the stream. Remembering her gentle smile, and the softness of their first kiss, he clearly recalled the day they made a silent pledge, sealing it with the blood from their cut wrists. All these things, and more, he retained; but, what was no longer available was the sound of her voice and the cadence of her laughter. Willingly, he would have given everything he possessed to hear her speak just once more. Holding her image close to his heart, his mind made the passage from dreaming to the void, where the paintings are no more. The old man drifted into the dark, quiet forgetfulness.

Flaming Eagle awakened just as the sun's first rays were making their way over the distant mountains. Adding wood to the fire and warming himself, he settled down to cook a rabbit, which he had caught in a snare the previous day. Washing the food down with sips of clear water, he concluded his meal by consuming small pieces of the dried fruit he brought with him. He doused the campfire with dirt mixed with water, then replenished his container from the fresh stream before repacking his horse. By the time the sun cleared the mountaintops, he was on his homeward journey.

Leading the horse, he traveled at a leisurely, even pace. It would take a while to reach the camp of his people; but, having received the answer to his prayers, time now seemed abundant. Walking allowed the old man's mind to drift.

So many of the people were gone. His teacher, White Wolf, his parents, Running Fox and Skipping Bird, and most of the others he cared about, had been gone for many winters. Standing Elk, who was now a war chief, and his brother, Lone Feather, were also showing their age. The grey in Meadow Lark's hair was another sign of the ravages of time. White Wolf's spirit helpers had long since been replaced by four younger women, serving Flaming Eagle. Chief among them was Meadow Lark, who became a spirit helper after her daughter, Running Moon, married the brave who came to be known as He Who Sees Afar.

Several more days of weary travel found Flaming Eagle coming to one of his old campsites on the plateau overlooking the valley. The sky above him spread out in all directions, as far as he could see, and beyond. From this vantage point, he possessed a clear view of the winding river and the tipis of his people alongside its banks. He sat watching, as hundreds of campfires sent light wisps of swirling smoke into the endless dark blue, now changing into an enveloping black. This was the final campsite along his journey home. Tomorrow he would return to his village with a new supply of freshly harvested plants and herbs. He took his time unpacking his pony before feeding, watering and hobbling it for the night. This was his fourth pony since Pawnee died in battle.

As was his nightly custom, he prepared the pipe and lit it, drawing slowly and deeply from the mixture in the bowl. Tonight he sent up special words of thanksgiving to the Great Spirit. At last, his prayers were answered, and his quest to find a Wicasa was at an end. The old man approved of the Great Spirit's choice. "Soon, Two Bears Sleeping, in addition to receiving the ceremonial pipe as the tribal shaman, will be given the opportunity to walk the path of a Holy One, and I will be free of my responsibilities," he sighed with great relief.

Flaming Eagle was now at peace. His path was clear, and he would conclude his mission, as usual, with the aid of the Great Spirit. "There is more than enough time to complete the training of Two Bears Sleeping," he thought. "I will teach him all he needs to know to become a medicine man. This I can do," he affirmed. "His guidance along the path of a Holy One is in the hands of the Grand Father, and soon I will finally be allowed to join my ancestors." He looked forward to being with his old teacher in the bliss of the afterlife awaiting him. Here he would enjoy eternity, knowing he had faithfully served and safeguarded his people's spirit to the end.

The Quest

"If he is to follow me and White Wolf on the path of a Wicasa, he must find it and walk it alone, as it always has been, and always shall be. I have but one request, Grand Father," he asked humbly. "When it is my time, I wish to know, as White Wolf before me knew, that 'it is a good day to die.'"

"*...AND SO IT SHALL BE.*"

About The Author

Mr. Latona has over forty years of experience dealing with human nature through its many ranges. He graduated from San Jose State with a BA in English literature and acting. His experience as an amateur and professional actor gave him an opportunity to play a variety of diverse roles, increasing his understanding of the human heart and the idiosyncrasies created by the human spirit. His literary education revealed that honor and perseverance are among our greatest assets in our quests for fulfillment in life. He began writing poetry and short stories in high school, receiving his first rejection slip at the age of twenty-two. While on tour as a professional actor, he was introduced to the beauty and majesty of Montana, Wyoming, and the Sacred Black Hills of the Dakotas. These memories and images strongly influenced him and are clearly reflected in his stories of the indigenous people of the region. With a masters degree in social work from the University of California at Sacramento and licensed as a clinical social worker, he gained further experience and insight working for welfare, probation, institutions for

Charles Richard Latona

juvenile delinquents and prisons. He spent twenty years in private practice, working with relationships, families, societal issues, and addictions. Married with two children and four grandchildren, he cherishes his time as an involved father and grandfather.

www.ingramcontent.com/pod-product-compliance
Lightning Source LLC
Chambersburg PA
CBHW060350080526
44583CB00012B/242